KEY CONCEPTS IN MANAGEMENT

Palgrave Key Concepts

Palgrave Key Concepts provide an accessible and comprehensive range of subject glossaries at undergraduate level. They are the ideal companion to a standard textbook, making them invaluable reading for students throughout their course of study, and especially useful as a revision aid.

The key concepts are arranged alphabetically so you can quickly find terms or entries of immediate interest. All major theories, concepts, terms and theorists are incorporated and cross-referenced. Additional reading or website research opportunities are included. With hundreds of key terms defined, **Palgrave Key Concepts** represent a comprehensive must-have reference for undergraduates.

Published

Key Concepts in Accounting and Finance
Key Concepts in Business Practice
Key Concepts in Human Resource Management
Key Concepts in International Business
Key Concepts in Management
Key Concepts in Marketing
Key Concepts in Operations Management
Key Concepts in Politics
Key Concepts in Strategic Management
Linguistic Terms and Concepts
Literary Terms and Criticism (*third edition*)

Further titles are in preparation

www.palgravekeyconcepts.com

Palgrave Key Concepts
Series Standing Order ISBN 1–4039–3210–7
(*outside North America only*)

You can receive future titles in this series as they are published by placing a standing order. Please contact your bookseller or, in case of difficulty, write to us at the address below with your name and address, the title of the series, and the ISBN quoted above.

Customer Services Department, Macmillan Distribution Ltd,
Houndmills, Basingstoke, Hampshire RG21 6XS, England

Key Concepts in Management

Jonathan Sutherland and Diane Canwell

First published 2004 by
PALGRAVE MACMILLAN
Houndmills, Basingstoke, Hampshire RG21 6XS and
175 Fifth Avenue, New York, N.Y. 10010
Companies and representatives throughout the world

PALGRAVE MACMILLAN is the global academic imprint of the Palgrave
Macmillan division of St. Martin's Press, LLC and of Palgrave Macmillan Ltd.
Macmillan® is a registered trademark in the United States, United Kingdom
and other countries. Palgrave is a registered trademark in the European
Union and other countries.

ISBN 1–4039–1533–4

This book is printed on paper suitable for recycling and made from fully
managed and sustained forest sources.

A catalogue record for this book is available from the British Library.

Library of Congress Cataloging-in-Publication Data
Sutherland, Jonathan.
   Key concepts in management / Jonathan Sutherland and
Diane Canwell.
      p. cm. – (Palgrave key concepts)
   Includes bibliographical references and index.
   ISBN 1–4039–1533–4 (pbk.)
      1. Industrial management—Dictionaries. I. Canwell, Diane. II. Title.
III. Series.

   HD30.15.S95 2004
   658'.003–dc22   2003070292

10 9 8 7 6 5 4 3 2 1
13 12 11 10 09 08 07 06 05 04

Printed and bound in Great Britain by
Creative Print & Design (Wales), Ebbw Vale

Contents

Introduction

The art of management is not simply restricted to the organization of processes and operations. Neither is management restricted to problem solving and decision making. Management is an all-encompassing discipline, which requires an expansive range of skills and abilities, about which millions of words have been written and millions more will be written. Every year several hundred management 'bibles' are produced, expounding new theories of management, as consultants and theorists vie to become the new leaders in management thought.

Management has been a discipline and a fact of life for centuries, but it is only in recent years that it has been described as both a profession and a science. The development of management theory can be traced back over hundreds of years and has been influenced by key thinkers such as Karl Marx, Max Weber, Henri Fayol, Frederick Winslow Taylor, Elton Mayo, Dale Carnegie, Igor Ansoff and Henry Mintzberg, to name but a few.

Successive waves of theorists have dissected the nature of management, the environment in which it operates, the inter-relationships between managers and employees, the nature of change, communication, teams and groups. Successive theorists have examined the differences between leadership and management, coming to many radically different conclusions about their nature and their dependence upon one another. Other theorists have focused on motivation, or the management of conflict, and, in latter years, attention has been drawn to performance management.

No study of management or leadership can ever be complete; neither can it hope to be the last word on the subject. The discipline continues to develop, spawning new sub-disciplines. Whilst skilled workers, with defined tasks, duties and roles, may have a blueprint to work from, there is no such blueprint for management; there are no precise plans, there is no ideal way in which to manage. Management depends upon circumstance, personal style, the environment, the organizational structure and its processes. Management is a continually moving field and few attain sufficient proficiency in the art to do much more than cope with situations as they present themselves.

The structure of the glossary

Every attempt has been made to include all of the key concepts in this discipline, taking into account currently used terminology, ratios and jargon common throughout management in organizations everywhere. There are notable differences in legislation and procedure when we compare approaches in the United Kingdom, Europe, the United States and Japan. However, the majority of these key management concepts are standard and in widespread use throughout organizations around the world, and the majority of the underlying concepts of management and leadership are universally recognized, regardless of their origin.

Each of the key concepts has been placed alphabetically in order to ensure that the reader can quickly find the term or entry of immediate interest. It is normally the case that a brief description of the term is presented, followed by a more expansive explanation.

The majority of the key concepts have the following in common:

- They may have a reference, within the text, to another key concept identified by a word or phrase that is in **bold** print – this should enable readers to investigate a directly related key concept should they require clarification of the definition at that point.
- They may have a series of related key concepts, which are featured at the end of the definition – this allows readers to continue their research and to investigate subsidiary or allied key concepts.
- They may include book or journal references – a vital feature for the reader to undertake follow-up research for more expansive explanations, often written by the originator or by a leading writer in that particular field of study.
- They may include website references – it is notoriously difficult to ensure that websites are still running at the time of going to print, let alone several months beyond that time, but in the majority of cases long-established websites have been selected, or governmental websites that are unlikely to be closed or to have a major address change.

Glossary terms – a guide

Whilst the majority of the key concepts have an international flavour, readers are cautioned to access the legislation, in particular, which refers to their native country or the country in which they are working.

It is also often the case that there are terms which have no currency in a particular country, as they may be allied to specific legislation of another country. Readers should check whether the description does include a specific reference to such law and should not assume that every key concept is a generic one that can be applied universally to the understanding of management and leadership.

In all cases, references to other books, journals and websites are based on the latest available information. It was not always possible to ensure that the key text or printed reference is in print, but most well-stocked college or university libraries should have access to the original materials. In the majority of cases, when generic management books have been referenced, these are, in the view of the writers, the best and most available additional reading texts.

In *Key Concepts in Management*, the focus of the key concepts has been on the more generic concepts, applicable to most areas of management. Clearly, it has not been possible to include all management-related areas specific to particular management disciplines. We would, therefore, recommend the following *Key Concepts* glossaries for further information in specific specialisms:

- *Key Concepts in Human Resource Management* – which covers management techniques and disciplines regarding the practice of employee management and development.
- *Key Concepts in Accounting and Finance* – which addresses the issues of financial measurement, budgeting and control.
- *Key Concepts in International Business* – which specifically addresses the management function in an international or global context.
- *Key Concepts in Marketing* – which covers management of the marketing function, including brand management.
- *Key Concepts in Business Practice* – which addresses the daily procedural functions related to management.
- *Key Concepts in Strategic Management* – which takes the next logical management step to incorporate broader issues related to the management function.

Abell, Derek F.

British-born Derek F. Abell was a professor at the Harvard Business School in Boston from 1969 to 1981. He is a published author in the fields of marketing, strategic planning and general management. He has worked as a consultant for both US and European multinational corporations.

Abell is, perhaps, best known for his identification of competitors. He identified three dimensions, which were:

- customer functions;
- customer groups;
- alternative technologies.

Abell, Derek F., *Defining the Business: Starting Point of Strategic Planning*. Englewood Cliffs, NJ: Prentice-Hall, 1980.
Abell, Derek F., *Managing with Dual Strategies: Mastering the Present, Pre-empting the Future*. New York: Free Press, 1993.

www.imd.ch/faculty/vitae/index

Absolute cost advantage

The term 'absolute cost advantage' is largely associated with one of the many **barriers to entry** which prevent businesses from entering new markets. Absolute cost advantages are the advantages which a larger, more established business can benefit from as a result of **economies of scale**, or an innovation which has allowed them to reduce costs. Typically, a new competitor entering the market may face a price war, which often causes new entrants to fail, whilst the incumbent, having the absolute cost advantage, manages to survive.

The incumbent, having taken account of relevant opportunity costs, will expend resources and secure a **first-mover advantage** in a new market or with a new innovation, and will be able to enjoy, relatively speaking, monopoly profits. Any potential entrant into the market must devise a profitable entry plan. The scale of these costs is often referred to as the 'height' of an entry barrier.

Absorptive capacity

The absorptive capacity of a business represents its abilities to identify, and to value, assimilate and then utilize any new knowledge. In other words, it is the ability of the business to recognize the value of new, often external, information, then assimilate it and apply it to its own commercial advantage. Businesses have increasingly realized that outside sources of knowledge are important if not crucial in continuing to innovate.

It is believed that there is a negative relationship between a business's absorptive capacity and the practice of **outsourcing**. Businesses which carry out their own **research and development** are more likely to achieve absorptive capacity as a by-product of this activity.

Cohen, W. M. and Levinthal, D. A., 'Absorptive Capacity: A New Perspective on Learning and Innovation', *Administrative and Science Quarterly*, 35(1) (1990).

www.ifs.org.uk/workingpapers/wp0103.pdf

Accountability matrix

The accountability and responsibility matrix (Figure 1) is a concept designed by David Brin. Brin contends that individuals see the top two boxes of the matrix as being good and the bottom two boxes as being bad. Businesses or society require boxes 1 and 3, since these create accountability. Businesses and society are averse to boxes 2 and 4 since they pit employees against one another.

Brin, David, *The Transparent Society: Will Technology Force us to Choose Between Privacy and Freedom?* New York: Perseus Books Group, 1999.

Acquisition and restructuring

The term 'acquisition and restructuring', in referring to a **business strategy**, is formulated on the presumption that a business which has a superior internal governance system can create value simply by acquiring less efficient, or poorly managed, businesses and improving their efficiency.

An acquisition can be differentiated from either a merger or a take-over in as much as it is a transaction where one business buys another with the primary purpose of using that business's **core competence** by making it a subsidiary.

There are a number of reasons why businesses choose to acquire another business, these include:

Accountability Matrix

1 Tools that help me see what others are up to	2 Tools that prvent others from seeing what I am up to
3 Tools that help others see what I am up to	4 Tools that prevent me from seeing what others are up to

Brin argues:

- Where it says 'others' insert some person or group, such as 'government' or 'corporations' or whoever you perceive as a dangerous power centre.
- People are likely to call 'good' any device, law or technical advance that enhances the effectiveness of 1 or 2. In contrast, whatever comes along that increases the effectiveness of 3 or 4 may raise your discomfort, if not ire.
- If our aim is to live in a society that is fair and free, the tools needed by our commons will be those favouring 1 and 3.
- The most dangerous trends, laws, and technologies are those promoting 2 and 4, pitting citizens against one another in an arms race of masks, secrets, and indignation.

Figure 1 Accountability matrix

- Increased speed to market – which is a term closely related to **barriers to entry** as it allows market entry more easily.
- Diversification – which allows the business to move quickly towards gaining experience and depth.
- Reshaping competitive scope – which relates to acquisitions as a primary means by which a business reduces its dependence on a few products or markets

Effective acquisitions can be achieved by addressing the following issues:

- Complementary assets and resources – buying businesses with assets that meet current needs and help build competitiveness.
- A well-considered selection process – which incorporates an evaluation as to the ease of integration and whether **synergies** will be built.
- Maintaining a financial reserve – so as not to forgo any other profitable projects as a result of spending all reserves and available cash on the acquisition.

Normally there are three different forms of restructuring, which can be best summarized as in Table 1.

Table 1 Forms of restructuring

Restructuring alternative	Short term	Long term
Downsizing	Reduced labour costs	Loss of human capital
Down-scoping	Reduced debt costs	Potentially lower or higher performance
Leveraged buy-out	High debt costs	Higher performance but higher risk

Action planning

Action planning is an integral part of both goal-setting and problem solving, yet in many business contexts it is a neglected area. Action planning can assist a business in planning for the future, ensuring that as future situations change, they can be controlled. At its most basic, action planning is, in effect, the conversion of goals or objectives into a series of steps, in order to ascertain what has to be done, by whom, and by when. This is variously known as either an action planning process or an event track. The process of formulating the event track follows a set series of procedures:

1 Decide a goal or objective.
2 Identify the sequence of actions required to achieve this.
3 Refine the initial plan by identifying where it may go wrong.
4 Having identified what may go wrong, formulate plans or actions to deal with these problems.

The action plan should explain how the business is to get from where it is now to where it wishes to be, describing in detail how the business proposes to do this. There needs to be a secondary process running alongside the action plan, which checks to see whether the action plan is working.

Effective action planning requires the participation of all relevant **stakeholders**, who should be aware of their role in the process. A full action-plan event track is likely to incorporate the following aspects:

1 Development of a rough action plan, which should combine individual work from the participants, listing the activities they propose in order to reach the goal. Once this has been completed, all of the activities are discussed and, perhaps using a voting technique, the most appropriate ones are chosen. These then need to be arranged in the correct sequence.

2 The action plan now needs to be refined. Above all, the action plan needs to be robust; each event needs to be detailed in terms of what, when and who.

3 Assumptions – checks need to be made of any assumptions made in the creation of the action plan. This may include assumptions regarding skills, time, finance and materials. There may also be assumptions regarding coordination. Above all, the participants need to consider how to deal with any unexpected problems that arise.

4 Contingency plan – no matter how complex the creation of the action plan may have been, it is imperative that a contingency plan is created, which may need to be instituted in the event of the action planning going off track. This means that a monitoring process needs to be put in place, together with a clear idea of how to solve potential problems as they arise, if they require immediate action in order to ensure that the goal is finally reached.

Kaplan, Robert S. and Norton, David P., *The Balanced Scorecard: Translating Strategy into Action*. Boston, MA: Harvard Business School Press, 1996.

Active listening

The purpose of active listening is to improve mutual understanding. This involves a radically different approach to the process of listening and responding. The assumption is that when individuals talk to one another they do not necessarily listen. There may be other issues which distract them. There is a particular problem in situations where the two individuals are in conflict with one another, as they are more concerned with formulating a response than with what is actually being said.

The concept of active listening requires listeners to carefully absorb what the speaker has said and then to repeat it back in their own words. In this way the original speaker can be apprised of whether the listener actually understood, and whether there is any conflict in the intent of what was said. It is a question of interpretation and this is often the root cause of misunderstandings between individuals during a conversation. By repeating what has been said, the two individuals can hope to move towards a consensus through confirming understanding. The process also avoids the two individuals contradicting one another by claiming that the other said something which they did not. Providing the two individuals are attuned to one another in this way, they are likely to explain in detail precisely what they mean, and conflict can be avoided.

Figure 2 illustrates the external factors that prevent an individual from being able to listen actively.

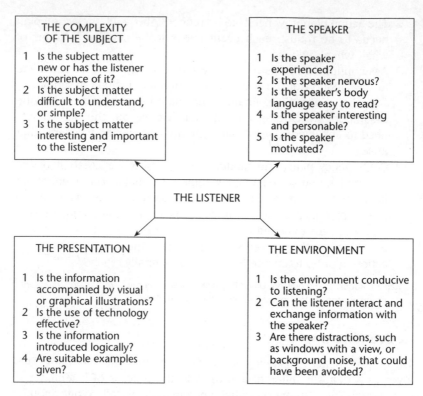

THE COMPLEXITY
OF THE SUBJECT

1 Is the subject matter new or has the listener experience of it?
2 Is the subject matter difficult to understand, or simple?
3 Is the subject matter interesting and important to the listener?

THE SPEAKER

1 Is the speaker experienced?
2 Is the speaker nervous?
3 Is the speaker's body language easy to read?
4 Is the speaker interesting and personable?
5 Is the speaker motivated?

THE LISTENER

THE PRESENTATION

1 Is the information accompanied by visual or graphical illustrations?
2 Is the use of technology effective?
3 Is the information introduced logically?
4 Are suitable examples given?

THE ENVIRONMENT

1 Is the environment conducive to listening?
2 Can the listener interact and exchange information with the speaker?
3 Are there distractions, such as windows with a view, or background noise, that could have been avoided?

Figure 2 Factors that prevent active listening

In order to listen actively, listeners should attempt to ensure that they:

- focus their attention on the subject by stopping all non-relevant activities beforehand, to orient themselves with the speaker or the topic;
- review mentally what they already know about the subject, and organize relevant material in advance, to develop it further;
- avoid distractions by sitting appropriately close to the speaker and avoiding a window or talkative colleague;
- set aside any prejudices or opinions, and be prepared to listen to what the speaker has to say;
- focus on the speaker;
- let the presentation run its course before agreeing or disagreeing;
- actively respond to questions and directions.

Westra, Matthew, *Active Communication*. Florence, KY: Wadsworth Publishing, 1995.

Activity ratio

Activity ratios are a means by which an assessment can be made as to how well a business is managing its assets. Typically, the activity ratios would include the following:

- **Inventory turnover** – which shows whether a business is holding excessive stocks of inventory.
- **Fixed assets turnover** – which shows whether the assets are being used close to capacity.
- **Total assets turnover** – which indicates whether a sufficient volume of business is being generated for the size of the asset investment.
- **Working capital** turnover – which indicates whether funds are being efficiently used.

The activity ratios combine information which can be found on a business's balance sheets or income statements, and are considered to be useful analytical tools in understanding the financial statements. Effectively, the ratios revolve around turnover, or may perhaps include calculations regarding issues such as the **average collection period**.

Temple, Peter, *Magic Numbers: The 33 Key Ratios that Every Investor should Know*. New York: John Wiley & Sons, 2001.

Adaptive culture

Edgar Schein originally proposed the notion that organizational culture is framed by what a business assumes to be true about its organization and the environment in which it operates. He also suggested that culture is unconscious, but can be learned and reinforced when problems can be solved repeatedly using the same approach.

An adaptive culture is an organization which recognizes that it is not the strength of its culture which matters the most, but its adaptability. An adaptable culture is one which allows the adoption of strategies or practices that are able to respond continually to changing markets and new competitive situations. These organizations are forward-looking and tend to be guided by positive change. Research has shown that organizations which do not have adaptive cultures can be short-term successes, but as markets change they are unable to change quickly enough to adapt to new business conditions. The main differences between organizations with high-performance adaptive cultures and those without high-performance adaptive cultures are outlined in Table 2.

A

Table 2 Organizations with and without adaptive cultures

Organizations with high-performance adaptive cultures	Organizations without high-performance adaptive cultures
Ability to maintain a fit between the culture and the business context	Short-termism
Active support within the organization to identify problems	Emphasis on structure and systems
Active support within the organization to identify problems and find workable solutions	Inability to focus on multiple stakeholders
Feeling of confidence amongst employees	Biased perception of the competition
Trust	Inability to deal with negative suggestions or observations
Risk-taking	Feeling of invulnerability
Proactivity	Alternative strategies ignored

Kotter, John and Heskett, J. L., *Corporate Culture and Performance*. New York: Free Press, 1992.

Added value

Value added, or added value, is an increase in the market value of products, parts or components which excludes the cost of materials and services used. In other words, this is a cost-plus-profit concept, defining 'value added' as either the difference between the cost of producing a product and the price obtained for it (the selling price), or an additional benefit offered to purchasers in order to convince them to buy. Added value is the key concept in both the internal and the external accounting systems of an organization and is a useful means of identifying the relative efficiency of a business. It should be noted that the value-added concept looks at the internal input costs in such a way that they are not confused with the external output costs, which may be beyond the control of the organization.

The value of the goods or services supplied may depend on a number of different variables. Obviously, if the organization is processing raw materials into finished products and is responsible for all stages of the production process, then it has a relatively high degree of control over the level of added value involved. Organizations which buy in components or partly finished products do not have this depth and length of control. They purchase products which have had value added to them already. The supplier will have gone through a similar set of calculations prior to selling the components or part-finished products on to the organization, which in turn will continue their processing. In the end, the level of value added to the goods or services supplied is directly related to the price the customer is willing to pay. An organization may decide to add value which would raise the price beyond what the average customer is willing to accept. In such a case, the supplier would have either to accept that it cannot receive the price which it expected, or to drastically reduce its costs, which have contributed to the end-user price.

The most common definition of 'value added' is profit. Before the profit is realized, however, it is necessary to be able to cover the directly applied or overhead costs of the organization. If the organization is able to cover the various costs, then it has gone a considerable distance towards being able to break even. It is only when the added value exceeds the **breakeven point** that the organization moves into real profit. It is, perhaps, this part of the value-added concept that is most important. Profit means a number of things to an organization: for example, additional investment potential, expansion, reorganization or acquisition. It is in the nature of the value added, to have a tendency to push up the end-user price from the moment the raw materials are extracted. In stages, some more dramatic than others, added value will be heaped upon the product. Each layer of the supply chain will demand its rightful profit in handling the product or service. Consequently, if an organization is not involved in the total extraction, processing and sale of a product or service, then it may not be able to curb unnecessary levels of added value elsewhere in the trading cycle.

Sherrington, Mark, *Added Value: The Alchemy of Brand-led Growth*. Basingstoke: Palgrave Macmillan, 2003.

See also **Porter, Michael** *and* **value chain**.

Albrecht, Karl

Karl Albrecht is a management consultant who is essentially concerned with organizational and individual effectiveness. He has written widely on creative thinking, negotiation, service management, **added value**, and humans as assets, as well as customer care.

Karl Albrecht's service triangle addresses the interconnectivity of people, systems and strategy and their impact on service management (see Figure 3).

Figure 3 Albrecht's service triangle

Albrecht, Karl, *Delivering Customer Value: It's Everyone's Job.* Cambridge, MA: Productivity Press, 1995.

www.karlalbrecht.com

Alderfer, Clayton P.

In the 1970s Alderfer identified three categories of human needs which influenced an employee's behaviour (see Figure 4). In essence his theory aimed to address some of the limitations of **Abraham Maslow**'s hierarchy of needs.

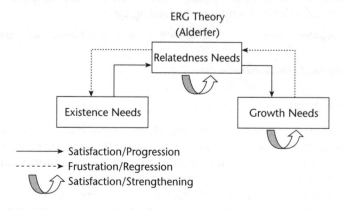

Figure 4 Three categories of human needs

Alderfer's three criteria were:

- *Existence needs* – which incorporate Maslow's first and second levels and include physiological and safety needs.
- *Relatedness needs* – which accord with Maslow's third and fourth needs and include social and external esteem.
- *Growth needs* – which are also in line with Maslow's fourth and fifth levels and include internal esteem needs and self-actualization.

Alderfer did not consider these three criteria to be stepped in any way, unlike Maslow's idea that access to the higher-level needs required satisfaction in the lower-level needs.

In effect, the ERG (Existence, Relatedness, Growth) theory recognizes that the order of importance of the three areas may be different for different individuals. He does, however, recognize that if a particular need remains unfulfilled, then an individual will suffer dissatisfactions, regressions and frustrations. ERG theory is very flexible, as it can explain why individuals may be perfectly prepared to work under poor circumstances, for limited pay, in employment from which they gain a great deal of personal satisfaction, and why others receive recognition for their work, and high pay, yet are frustrated by limitations and boredom.

Alderfer, Clayton P., *Existence, Relatedness and Growth: Human Needs in Organizational Settings*. New York: Free Press, 1973.

Ansoff, Igor H.

The Ansoff matrix (see Figure 5), one of a number of classic marketing concepts, encapsulates the future vision of the business.

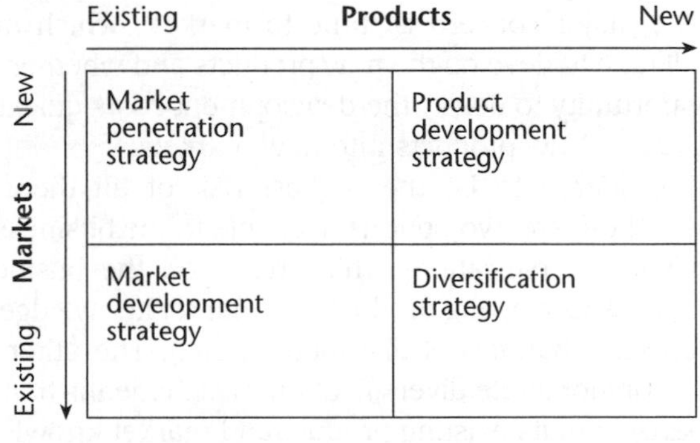

Figure 5 The Ansoff matrix

Igor Ansoff has made major contributions to the concepts surrounding corporate strategy (*A Practical System of Objectives* in *Corporate Strategy*). However, it is for the growth vector matrix that he is best known. The matrix examines the potential strategies available to a business in four areas, cross-referenced as new or existing markets and new or existing products. The matrix suggests the marketing strategies available to the business in each of these areas:

- *Market penetration* – Existing products into existing markets.
  Management seeks to increase its market share with the current product range. This is considered to be the least risky strategy of all of the options available. Existing customers are encouraged to buy more products and services, those at present buying a competing brand are persuaded to switch, and non-buyers are convinced to begin to make purchases. Any readily recognizable weaknesses in the portfolio of the business need to be addressed and strengthened.
- *Market development* – Existing products into new markets.
  Systematic market research should reveal new potential markets for the existing products. Clearly stated segments are then targeted individually, either through existing marketing and distribution channels or by setting up new ones to service the new segments. As the business is moving into new markets, it needs to be aware of the potential differences in reactions, expectations and other factors.
- *Product development* – New products into existing markets.
  Assuming the business has sufficient resources, then new products, or developments in the existing products, can be brought into the market. Provided the business has closely matched the new products with the requirements of its existing markets risks are minimized. The major concern is 'time to market', which means the time it will take to develop the new products and whether there will be the opportunity to defray the development costs quickly.
- *Diversification* – New products into new markets.
  This is considered to be the highest risk of all the strategies. Essentially, there are two options available to the business: the first is synergistic diversification, which relies on the business being able to harness its existing product and market knowledge (production processes, channels of distribution, etc.). The other option is known as conglomerate diversification, which means that the business departs from its existing product and market knowledge. This form of diversification is often achieved by merging with, or taking over, a business operating in another unrelated area (which in fact

converts conglomerate diversification into synergistic diversification).

Ansoff, Igor, *Corporate Strategy* (The Library of Management Classics). London: Sidgwick & Jackson, 1986.

Architecture

Organizational architecture is taken to mean the totality of an international business's organization, including its formal structure, **organizational culture**, processes, incentives and human resources. It is believed that in order for an international business to be profitable, three conditions related to its organizational architecture need to be in place. These are:

- The various elements of the business's organizational architecture must be consistent from an internal standpoint.
- The organizational architecture must match the strategy of the business.
- Both the organizational architecture and strategy must be consistent with the prevailing competitive conditions in the markets in which the organization operates.

www.sixsigma.com/context/C010128a.asp

Argyris, Chris

Argyris has contributed much to the understanding of the relationship between people and organizations, as well as organizational learning itself. Argyris wrote that bureaucratic organizations lead to mistrustful relationships, and that the creation of an environment which incorporates trust leads to greater personal confidence, cooperation and flexibility. Employees desire to be treated like human beings and their complex needs must be recognized by an organization. Businesses should provide opportunities for employees to influence the way in which they work and the way in which the business is structured (see Table 3).

Pyramidal or bureaucratic organizational structures still dominate the majority of businesses and these structures have an impact upon the way in which individuals within an organization behave, and their personal growth characteristics. Argyris created the immaturity/maturity continuum, which sought to identify the ways in which healthy personalities can be developed within an organization that allows career and personal development. This is best summed up as in the diagram in Figure 6.

A

Table 3 Organizational structure

Bureaucratic/pyramidal	Humanistic/democratic
The crucial human relationships are those which relate to the meeting of the business's objectives.	The crucial human relationships are not only those related to meeting the objectives of the business but also those that maintain the business's internal systems and adapt to the environmental issues.
Effectiveness in relationships increases as behaviour becomes more rational, logical, and clearly communicated.	Human relationships increase in effectiveness as all the relevant behaviour becomes conscious, discussed and controlled.
Effectiveness decreases as behaviour becomes more emotional.	
Human relationships are effectively motivated by defined direction, authority, and control. This is in addition to appropriate rewards and penalties that emphasize rational behaviour and the achievement of objectives.	In addition to direction, human relationships are most effectively influenced through control, rewards and penalties, authentic working relationships, internal commitment, psychological success and the use of the process of confirmation.

A

Immaturity	⟶	Maturity
Passive		Active
Dependence		Independence
Limited behaviour range		Capable of behaving in many ways
Erratic shallow interests		Deeper and stronger interests
Short time perspective		Long time perspective (past and future)
Subordinate position		Equal or superordinate position
Lack of awareness of self		Awareness and control over self

Figure 6 The immaturity/maturity continuum

The theory postulates that an organization's culture either inhibits or allows an expression of the growth of an individual who works within that organization. Argyris argued that, at the time of writing, very few organizations had reached maturity in their approach.

Argyris, Chris, *Personality and Organization*. New York: HarperCollins, 1957.

Argyris, Chris, *Knowledge for Action: A Guide to Overcoming Barriers to Organizational Change*. San Francisco, CA: Jossey-Bass, 1993.

See also **double loop learning.**

Asset reduction

An asset-reduction strategy is also known as a 'harvest strategy'. It is a means by which an organization seeks to limit or decrease its investment in its business by extracting as much cash out of the operation as it can. Typically, an asset-reduction strategy would be employed in a declining market or industry, allowing the business to optimize its **cash flow** levels.

Attractiveness–strength matrix

In the early 1970s the General Electric Company (GEC) began to restructure its business, with the assistance of McKinsey Consulting. The GE/McKinsey approach assesses both environmental and business-level situations. In effect, the approach looks at the firm's attractiveness, or carries out an environmental analysis, on the basis of a number of criteria, including:

- market share;
- market growth rate;
- **barriers to entry**;
- inflation;
- industry profitability;
- manpower availability;
- technology;
- social issues;
- environmental issues;
- competitive structure;
- regulation;
- political issues;
- legal issues.

A

The business would also address those of its internal strengths which it considers to be **critical success factors**. These would include:

- market share growth;
- sales force;
- marketing;
- distribution;
- research and development;
- financial resources;
- breadth of product line;
- quality and reliability;
- customer service;
- managerial competence;
- image;
- manufacturing ability.

In order to use the GE/McKinsey approach, five steps are involved:

1 An identification of the external and internal critical success factors.
2 An identification of the external industry factors. This involves attaching a weighted score to the attractiveness of each industry, with the weighted score attempting to capture two dimensions of each factor. An estimate is made of the industry importance of each factor, with the total of the weights adding to 1.00. Each of the factors is then graded between 1 and 5 and then the weight is multiplied by the rating to give the final weighted score.
3 The internal factors are now assessed using precisely the same procedure. The weighted score captures the two dimensions: the weight used to evaluate how far a factor affects the competitive

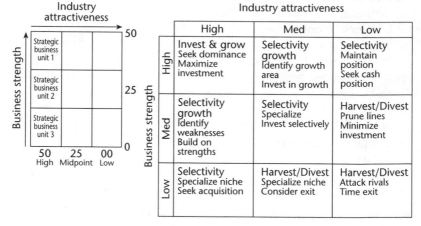

Figure 7 The attractiveness–strength matrix

position, and a weighting which grades the business on each of the factors.

4 Having replicated the task for each business unit within the organization, it is now possible to create an attractiveness–strength matrix (see Figure 7), which notes the difference between any rating scores, or weighting, for each of the business units.

5 A formal strategy is now adopted which determines the position of the business as a whole in the matrix.

Authority

As far as a manager is concerned, authority may come from several different sources, which can broadly be described as either legitimate or illegitimate. The sources of authority, however, can be typified as in Table 4.

Table 4   Sources of authority

Authority	Description
Charisma	More often than not this relates to one individual having the ability to influence another by using the strength of his or her personality.
Coercion	This relates to an individual's ability to threaten others or bribe them into taking action they would not otherwise have taken.
Conformity	Some managers, and also some organizations as a whole, set standards or behaviour values which those wishing to progress within the organization have no alternative but to accept and adopt.
Divine right	This kind of authority could be said to 'come with the position' in that those who consider themselves to be important give an air of expecting others to recognize their authority immediately.
Expertise	This type of authority relates to an individual, or to a group, exercising power because of their knowledge and experience. Used positively it can be beneficial, but when it is used negatively, others may consider this type of authority to be a block on their own progress.
Legality/ rationality	This type of authority relates to an organization which, possibly on setting up, has laid down strict rules and norms which must be complied with. Although this may have been adopted in the initial stages of an organization, other types of authority often develop during the organization's life.

$\Rightarrow$

A

Table 4 Sources of authority (*continued*)

Authority	Description
Physicality	This relates to an individual's body shape, size and strength in relation to those of his or her colleagues. It can also be related to organizations that are large and powerful enough to exert their strength over others.
Punishment	This implies an individual's power to punish, or threaten to punish, others who carry out certain activities or behave in a certain way.
Resource command	This type of authority relates to an individual's power to command certain resources within an organization and thereby influence the actions of others.
Reward	This relates to an individual's ability to influence the behaviour of others through the power to reward them if they comply.
Tradition	Accepted customs and norms dictate this form of authority, which is based on a position that has been handed down over the years.

Autocratic leader

Various theorists have proposed a range of ideas of leadership style, and at one end of the spectrum is a form of leadership known as 'autocratic'. It is exemplified by individuals who prefer to solve problems themselves, make all decisions, supervise subordinates closely and tend to treat their subordinates with little interest and no regard for their views. **Victor Vroom** and Philip Yetton identified two different forms of autocratic leader in 1973. They typified the first as Autocratic I, which were managers who solved problems themselves and made all the decisions themselves whilst using any information that became available to them. A more extreme example was their Autocratic II, which described individuals who collected information from subordinates and then decided on solutions themselves. They saw subordinates primarily as information providers and felt that they did not need to know what the information was for, or how it could be used to solve a problem. Indeed, in the majority of cases, the subordinates were unaware that a problem needed to be solved at all.

John Adair developed his theories on leadership between 1968 and 1998 and exemplified his forms of autocratic leader as having either a benevolent or a tyrannical leadership style. He identified some seven characteristics of autocratic leaders:

- They were the ones who made the final decision.
- They closely supervised their subordinates.
- They believed that an individual's interests were subordinate to that of the organization.
- The views of subordinates were not sought.
- They placed high demands on their subordinates.
- They discouraged questioning from their subordinates.
- They thrived in a coercive or conformist environment.

Adair, John, *Action-Centred Leadership*. Aldershot: Gower, 1979.
Adair, John, *Leadership in Action*. London: Penguin, 1998.
Vroom, Victor H. and Yetton, Philip W., *Leadership and Decision-Making*. Pittsburgh, PA: University of Pittsburgh Press, 1973.

Average collection period

The average collection period is also known as the collection ratio. It is the average length of time for which receivables are outstanding, and is equal to the accounts receivable divided by the average daily sales.

A

Backward integration

Backward integration occurs when a business integrates in some way with another business further back from it in the distribution chain. In other words, it involves perhaps a manufacturer taking over a supplier, or a retailer acquiring a manufacturer. This is largely as a result of the business wishing to guarantee its supplies. The primary concern of the business is to develop into areas which provide the inputs into its current operations.

Balanced scorecard

Robert Kaplan and David Norton developed the balanced scorecard system in the 1990s. The balanced scorecard seeks to assist businesses in clarifying their visions and strategies and provide them with a means by which they can be translated into action.

The balanced scorecard consists of four separate perspectives which aim to allow the business to develop measurement systems, data collection mechanisms and means by which information can be analysed. The four perspectives (see Figure 8) are:

- *Financial* – which includes metrics such as **cost–benefit analysis** and financial **risk assessment**.
- *Internal business processes* – which aim to identify how well the business is performing and whether products and services offered meet customer expectations.
- *Learning and growth* – which seek to identify where employee training budgets can be best deployed with the objective of ensuring continued individual and corporate improvement.
- *Customers* – which focuses on the analysis of different types of customers, their degrees of satisfaction and the mechanisms or processes which are used by the business to deliver products and services to customers.

Figure 8   A balanced scorecard

Kaplan, Robert S., Lowes, Arthur and Norton, David P., *Balanced Scorecard: Translating Strategy into Action*. Watertown, MA: Harvard Business School Press, 1996.

Barriers to entry

'Barriers to entry' is a term used to describe the way in which a business, or group of businesses, seek to keep competition out of markets in which they are currently operating. There are four main ways in which this is achieved:

- A business may have control over a specific resource, such as oil, or an exclusive licence to operate, such as a broadcast agreement.
- A large business which has significant **economies of scale** will have a **competitive advantage** because it can produce products and services at lower costs than other rivals.
- A business may protect its market by investing considerable sums in advertising and marketing, making it very difficult for competitors to make any impression in the marketplace.
- Large and powerful businesses can make a competitor's venture into their market far more risky by raising the exit costs. In this respect they may have established specific ways of hiring employees, perhaps on long-term contracts which have become the industry norm. It will therefore be expensive for a newcomer to the market to try and then fail, as dispensing with staff would be prohibitively expensive.

See also **Porter, Michael.**

B

Barriers to imitation

It would be reasonable to assume that technological innovations and new ideas, which can be brought to the market much more swiftly than was hitherto thought imaginable, would offer little opportunity for competitors to copy them. None the less, businesses are increasingly aware that competitors are not only able to imitate their products, but can also take significant advantage of the ways in which successful businesses operate.

Creating barriers to imitation involves attempts to sustain a **competitive advantage**. This can be done in a number of ways, including:

- legal restrictions, including patents, copyrights and trademarks;
- superior access to inputs or to customers, either by having cost or quality advantages in inputs that make it difficult for competitors to imitate, or in the case of customers, by having access to the best distribution channels or the most productive retail locations.

Behavioural theory

The concept of behavioural theory is derived from the field of psychology and is often referred to as 'behaviourism'. In essence, there are two forms of behaviourism, the first of which is known as 'classical conditioning', which suggests that individuals' behaviour is based on reflex learning. They are conditioned by repetition to continue to behave in a particular way in similar circumstances. A slightly more sophisticated version, known as 'operant conditioning', states that when individuals exhibit a particular behaviour and understand the consequences of what they have done, this is reinforced, making it more likely that they will do it again.

In management terms, particular behaviours can indeed be reinforced in order to ensure that the correct response in certain circumstances is largely guaranteed. Equally, if individuals are not given encouragement and praise for particular behaviour, then it is likely that this form of behaviour will cease. This form of management theory is concerned with behaviour modification, by using praise and discipline, and perhaps rewards, in order to reinforce the desired behaviour. It is suggested that praise is a far more potent form of reinforcement than criticism or punishment, and that feedback is of prime importance in order to ensure behaviour modification.

Belbin, Dr Meredith

Belbin suggested that the most effective teams include between five and seven individuals who have a specific blend of team roles. He identified

Table 5   Building an effective team

Team-role type	Characteristics and contribution
Completer/finisher	An individual who attempts to finish tasks on time whilst seeking out any errors or omissions. Tends to take a conscientious approach to work. They prefer to carry out the work themselves rather than delegate.
Coordinator	A promoter of joint decision making with the ability to clarify goals. Keen to delegate but is often seen as manipulative and willing to pass work on to others.
Implementer	A disciplined and reliable individual who has the ability to transform ideas into practical solutions. Implementers are often seen as slow to adopt new ways of working because of their inflexibility.
Monitor/evaluator	Has the ability to take a wider view and assess all available options. Not considered to be a great motivator and often appears to lack essential drive.
Planter	Essentially a problem solver who is both imaginative and creative. Is more preoccupied with communication than the detail of a task.
Resource investigator	Highly communicative and usually able to identify and deploy useful resources and contacts. Since their contribution is based on their enthusiasm for progress, they can be over optimistic and lose interest if little progress is being made.
Shaper	Able to deal with pressure and to overcome obstacles. They tend to be rather abrasive individuals who can often offend.
Specialist	Has access to specialist information and is often single-minded. They tend to be able to contribute only to certain aspects of a task and are quite technically focused.
Team worker	Cooperative and diplomatic listeners who wish to avoid conflict. They tend to be indecisive and lack the ability to contribute under pressure.

B

nine team-role types (see Table 5), which suggests that an individual has the capacity to perform more then one role in the team.

Belbin also created four categories to identify the different types of teams:

- *Stable extroverts*, who excel in roles with a focus on liaison and cooperation. These are ideal human resource managers.
- *Anxious extroverts*, who tend to work at a higher pace than others and exert pressure on other people. They are typified by a sales manager.
- *Stable introverts*, who work well with a small, stable team, where relationships are a high priority. They are ideal local government officials.
- *Anxious introverts*, who rely on self-direction and persistence and are often committed to the longer term. The majority of creative individuals fall into this category.

Belbin, R. Meredith, *Team Roles at Work*. Oxford: Butterworth-Heinemann, 1995.

Belbin, R. Meredith, *Management Teams: Why they Succeed or Fail*. Oxford: Butterworth-Heinemann, 1996.

Belbin, R. Meredith, *Beyond the Team*. Oxford: Butterworth-Heinemann, 2000.

www.belbin.com/meredith.html

Benchmarking

A benchmark is a predetermined set of standards against which future performance or activities are measured. Usually, benchmarking involves the discovery of the best practice for an activity, either within or outside the business, in an effort to identify the ideal processes and prosecution of that activity.

The purpose of benchmarking is to ensure that future performance and activities conform with the benchmarked ideal in order to improve overall performance. Increased efficiency is a key to the benchmarking process, as in human resource management, improved efficiency, reliability of data and effectiveness of activities will lead to a more competitive edge and ultimately greater profitability.

Damelio, Robert, *The Basics of Benchmarking*. Portland, OR: Productivity Press, 1995.

B

Bennis, Warren

Warren Bennis has written a number of books, primarily on leadership. He discovered that there was no one correct way to lead, but there were some common characteristics or competences. These were:

- the management of attention – which refers to the need for a vision to focus minds;
- the management of meaning – which implies the ability to communicate a vision;

- the management of trust – which requires the leader to be consistent and honest;
- the management of self – which requires the leaders to be aware of their own weaknesses.

In his book *Organizing Genius: The Secrets of Creative Collaboration*, which was published in the 1990s, Bennis turned his attention to groups and concluded that each group required the following:

- a shared vision;
- the willingness to sacrifice personal goals;
- young members of the group prepared to work longer hours;
- protection from management.

Bennis has been an advisor to four Presidents of the US and has written over 20 books on leadership and leadership-related matters.

Bennis, Warren, *Organizing Genius: The Secrets of Creative Collaboration*. Harlow, Essex: Addison-Wesley, 1998.

Bennis, Warren, *On Becoming a Leader: The Leadership Classic – Updated and Expanded*. Cambridge, MA: Perseus Book, 2003.

www.behavior.net/column/bennis/bio.html

Blake, Robert and Jane Mouton

Robert Blake and Jane Mouton developed a grid strongly reminiscent of **Rensis Likert**'s systems 1 to 4. The grid provides an opportunity to identify styles adopted by managers in specific situations. By completing a questionnaire, individuals tally their people- or task-related scores and then cross-reference them to discover to what degree they accord with the four broad types of manager identified on the grid (see Figure 9).

The Country Club manager is typified by an individual who tries to avoid problems and considers productivity to be subservient to staff contentment. Anything that disturbs the balance is avoided.

A Team Leader or Team Manager manages to maintain a high level of simultaneous concern for both productivity and employees. The focus is upon providing the employees with the means by which they can achieve organizational objectives. Employees are encouraged to participate, to state their opinions, not to avoid conflict (as this is seen as a means by which problems can be resolved), and to approach all working relationships with honesty.

An Impoverished Manager is interested in neither productivity nor employee relations. The manager does not encourage creativity or initiative, seeks to avoid conflict and does not seem to wish to contribute. This is an individual who is concerned only with survival.

B

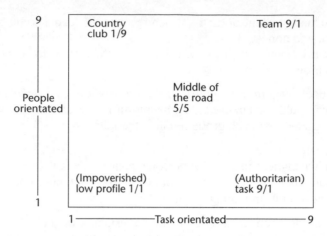

Figure 9 The management-style grid

An Authoritarian is, essentially, a task-orientated autocrat who shows little concern for employees. All issues are subservient to productivity, conflict is suppressed, and social aspects of work are discouraged.

At the very centre of the grid is a midpoint which illustrates that managers could, at various times, adopt the characteristics of any of the four categories. Typically, this point describes the manager as being 'middle of the road', where there is equal concern for productivity and for employees. Conflicts usually end in compromise, and creativity is encouraged, provided it is not too revolutionary.

Blake and Mouton consider the management's leadership qualities within the context of the type of organization in which the manager operates (clearly there would be differences, depending on whether the business was a bureaucracy or some other organizational structure). The theory also takes into account the manager's own values and personal history, which tend to colour the way in which a manager operates, as they will invariably refer to similar situations in the past.

Blake, Robert R. and Mouton, Jane S., *The Managerial Grid*. Burlington, MA: Gulf Publishing, 1994.

Blake, Robert R. and McCanse, Anne Adams, *Leadership Dilemmas: Grid Solutions* (The Blake/Mouton Grid Management and Organization Development Series). Burlington, MA: Gulf Publishing, 1991.

www.nwlink.com/~donclark/leader/bm_model.html

Blanchard, Ken

Originally developed in the 1960s, by Paul Hersey and Kenneth

	S3 Participating	S2 Selling
High	Leader and follower decisions	Leader makes decisions with dialogue

	Components:
	  Encouraging
	  Collaborating
	  Committing
		Components:
		  Explaining
		  Clarification
		  Persuading

Relationship behaviour	Followers able, but unwilling	Followers unable, but willing
	S4 Delegating	S1 Telling
	Follower makes decisions	Leader makes decisions

	Components:
	  Observing
	  Monitoring
	  Fulfilling
		Components:
		  Guiding
		  Directing
		  Establishing

Low	Followers able, and willing	Followers unable, and unwilling

Low   Task Behaviour   High

Figure 10   Situational Leadership model

Source: Adapted from Hersey, Blanchard and Johnson, 1996.

Blanchard, the Situational Leadership model identifies employees as followers, who are measured in terms of their readiness to perform a specific job. This is based on their ability and willingness. As can be seen in Figure 10, the relationship between the followers and the leaders is an important one, as leaders are required to adopt a different approach for specific mixes of followers.

Followers in the R4 category need little direct supervision or encouragement and in most cases jobs can be delegated to them (S4). Followers in the R3 category need to be encouraged to participate (S3), whilst those in the R2 category have to be effectively sold the idea by having it explained or clarified to them (S2). The R1 category, given their unwillingness or insecurity, need to be directed and told what it is that is expected of them (S1).

The model itself has been called into question but it is still widely used, particularly in management training programmes, as it is simple to understand and appears to have a degree of validity. Providing the Situational Leadership model can be dovetailed into a model which looks at goals, then a manager will be able to work using the most effective method of behaviour to deal with a variety of different situations and employees.

Blanchard, Kenneth H. and Hersey, Paul, *Management of Organizational Behavior: Utilizing Human Resources*. Englewood Cliffs, NJ: Prentice-Hall, 1969.

B

Hersey, Paul, Blanchard, Kenneth H. and Johnson, Dewey, *Management of Organizational Behavior: Utilizing Human Resources*. Englewood Cliffs, NJ: Prentice-Hall, 1996.

www.blanchardtraining.com

Block, Peter

Peter Block, a graduate of the University of Kansas and Yale University, has written several books on leadership, accountability, empowerment and stewardship. His contributions tend to focus on empowerment, service and accountability and he has published a number of articles on organizational change.

Block emphasizes an openness and honesty in relationships within business organizations. It is possible to create a matrix of the two axes of agreement and trust, which he considers to be the key political skills in support building (see Figure 11).

	Low trust	High trust
High agreement	Bedfellows	Allies
	Fence sitters	
Low agreement	Adversaries	Opponents

Figure 11 Agreement–trust matrix

Block, Peter, *The Empowered Manager: Positive Political Skills at Work*. New York: Jossey-Bass Wiley, 1991.
Block, Peter and Markowitz, Andrea, *The Flawless Consulting Field Book and Companion: A Guide to Understanding your Expertise*. New York: Jossey-Bass Wiley, 2000.

www.peterblock.com

Board of directors

Many businesses are governed or controlled by an administrative or 'hands-on' board, or policy-governing board. Sometimes the board of directors can also be referred to as the 'board of governors' or the 'board of trustees'.

The major function of the board is to provide leadership and direction to the organization – to govern its affairs on behalf of the shareholders (in the case of profit-driven organizations) or its members (in the case of not-for-profit organizations).

Directors tend to be either elected or appointed to the board and in some cases may be officers of the organization, in which case they fulfil certain corporate responsibilities in roles such as 'president', 'treasurer' or 'secretary'. Directors have three basic duties in relation to their role, as listed in Table 6.

Table 6 Duties of directors

Duty	Explanation
Diligence	To act responsibly, prudently, in good faith, with a view to promoting the best interests of the shareholders or members.
Loyalty	To place the interests of the organization first and not to use their position to further their own interests.
Obedience	To act within the scope of the rules which govern the policies of the organization, taking note of laws, rules and regulations which apply to the organization.

Broadly speaking, directors who fail to fulfil their duties may be liable in several different respects. The term 'liability' refers to their responsibility for the consequences of their conduct if it fails to meet legally required standards. In this case 'consequences' refers to damage or loss suffered by a third party as a result. The rules differ from country to country in respect of liability, but Table 7 summarizes the main implications.

Bonus plan

There are a wide variety of different bonus schemes, which are in operation in various businesses. Bonuses usually relate to additional payments made on either a monthly or an annual basis, as a reward for good work, as compensation for dangerous work, or as a share of the profits.

Other businesses will offer bonuses in relation to referrals. This is an integral part of the way human resource departments tackle difficulties in finding new employees for hard-to-fill jobs, specifically those with special skill requirements. Many businesses will offer a referral bonus

Table 7 Directors' legal liabilities

Liability arising from:	Description
Statute	When laws are actually broken the consequences usually involve the payment of a fine, perhaps imprisonment, and restrictions being placed on the director's rights or privileges.
Contract	Following the breaking or violation of a contract, which is a legally enforceable promise between two or more parties, the breach is corrected through the performance of a service, or through financial compensation.
Tort	An act or a failure to act, whether this is done intentionally or unintentionally, which causes damage to a third party, is usually remedied by the payment of a form of financial compensation.
Wrongful act	Errors or omissions, actions or decisions which harm others, not by damaging their property or selves, but by interfering with their rights, privileges or opportunities, usually require financial compensation.

payment to existing employees for recommending qualified candidates who are subsequently employed by the business. Clearly there are strict regulations in respect of the suitability of the candidate and the length of service that the referred candidate actually completes (usually part of the payment is held back until the referred candidate has been working for the business for six months).

There are difficulties in using this system in particular, as there may be conflicts of interest. Some human resource departments come under intense pressure from existing employees to shortlist candidates that they have referred. In many cases there is also a system set up to ensure that improper promises or assurances of employment to prospective candidates are not made by existing employees.

Keenan, William, *Commissions, Bonuses and Beyond: The Sales and Marketing Management Guide to Sales Compensation Planning.* New York: McGraw-Hill Education, 1994.

Booms and Bitner

Booms and Bitner are credited with the extension of the **marketing mix** which is now familiarly known as the **Seven Ps**.

It had been the case that the original four Ps of the marketing mix referred primarily to tangible products rather than services. It was, therefore, difficult to apply the marketing mix to non-product situations.

In 1981, Booms and Bitner expanded the framework, adding two explicit factors and a third implicit one. The two explicit additions were People and Processes, the third being Physical evidence. Their view on the three new Ps was:

- People make up a vital part of the marketing mix, meaning by this that the employees and the management, collectively, add value to the product or service offering. They are the key elements in attaining, retaining and improving a competitive advantage in meeting the needs of the customer.
- Processes in traditional manufacturing organizations revolve around the production process, which is somewhat separated and of little concern to the customers. In more service-based organizations, the point of contact between the organization and the customers is far more important and is at the core of the activities. In service-based organizations, there is a clear distinction between the operations management and the customer management processes (an essential element of marketing itself).
- Physical evidence is an intangible element of the marketing mix in as much as it refers to the organization's ability to prove to potential customers that can supply the promised levels of service. While well-produced brochures and marketing materials can offer quality and service levels, the proof is in the experience of existing customers and the ability of the business to relay that customer satisfaction to potential customers.

Booms and Bitner's expanded marketing mix also suggests that Place, in a service sense, refers to the accessibility of the services. They also suggest that the Promotion aspect refers to the input of the front-line service personnel and that Price is a key indicator of the quality of the service offered.

Booms, B. H. and Bitner, M. J., 'Marketing Strategies and Organizational Structures for Service Firms', in J. H. Donnelly, and W. R. George (eds), *Marketing of Services*. Chicago, IL: American Marketing Association, 1981.

See also **marketing mix** *and* **Seven Ps.**

Boston growth matrix

The Boston Consulting Group (BCG) was founded in 1963 by Bruce D.

Henderson as the Management and Consulting Division of the Boston Safe Deposit and Trust Company (the Boston Company).

The theory underlying the Boston matrix is the product life cycle concept, which states that business opportunities move through life cycle phases of introduction, growth, maturity and decline. Boston classification, or the BCG matrix, is a classification developed by the Boston Consulting Group to analyse products and businesses by market share and market growth. In this, **cash cow** refers to a business product with a high market share and low market growth, **dog** refers to one with a low market share and low growth, a **problem child** (or 'question mark' or 'wild cat') has a low market share and high growth, and a **star** has high growth and a high market share.

These phases are typically represented by an anti-clockwise movement around the Boston matrix quadrants (see Figure 12), in the following order:

- *From a market entry position as a question mark product.* Products are usually launched into high-growth markets, but suffer from a low market share.
- *To a star position, as sales and market share are increased.* If the investment necessary to build sales and market share is successfully made, then the product's position will move towards the star position of high growth/high market share.
- *To a cash cow position as the market growth rate slows and market leadership is achieved.* As the impact of the product life cycle takes effect and the market growth rate slows, the product will move from the star position of high growth to the cash cow position of low growth/high share.
- *Finally, to a dog position as investment is minimized, as the product ages and loses market share.*

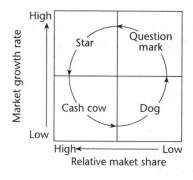

Figure 12　The anti-clockwise movement around the Boston matrix

At each position within the matrix there are a number of opportunities open to the business. For example, at the cash cow stage the options are either to invest to maintain market share, or to minimize investment in the product, maximize the cash returns and grow market dominance with other products.

www.bcg.com

Bottleneck efficiency

'Bottleneck' and 'non-bottleneck' are terms associated with the management of the production process. A bottleneck is effectively a system which cannot, for a variety of reasons, reach the levels of capacity which are demanded. A bottleneck can, therefore, seriously limit the total amount of production on a given production line because production is limited to the total capacity that the bottleneck is able to achieve.

A non-bottleneck is part of a production process that does not appear to have an inherent limit on its ability to produce. In other words, its capacity is considerably higher than the demands placed upon it. Normally an organization would choose to block a non-bottleneck process in order to ensure that it only produces the level of output required. There are a number of reasons for this, the most important of which is that part-finished products produced by a non-bottleneck process consume items from the inventory, and therefore increase the amount of work in progress. A non-bottlenecked process will normally be limited to a defined level of output, usually controlled by a specified storage area. Once this storage area is full, production in the non-bottlenecked process is temporarily terminated.

Clearly, organizations seek to avoid blocking a bottleneck process because the bottleneck is already unable to reach the desired capacity levels and this would simply restrict the ability to produce even more.

B

Bottom–up change

Bottom–up planning is a form of consultative management style. The planning system encourages employee participation in both problem solving and decision making. In effect it is a form of empowerment, which aims to encourage flexibility and creativity across the organization. Bottom–up planning is also closely associated with organizations which have a **flat structure**: in other words, the hierarchy of the organization has few tiers of management, allowing employees far greater access on a day-to-day basis with key decision-makers within the organization. Bottom–up planning is the opposite of what is known as a **top–down** approach.

Bounded rationality

'Bounded rationality' describes the approach of managers who signal that they are competent and that their decisions are the result of intelligent and rational deliberation. Bounded rationality suggests the following:

- Management theory is constructed on the basis that individuals act in a rational manner.
- The essence of managerial roles involves rational decision making, despite the fact that few individuals actually behave rationally.
- The theorist Herbert Simon believed that most managers do act rationally.
- Because most humans find it impossible to process the vast amount of information they are presented with, they construct simplified models which extract the essentials of the problem.
- As a result, bounded rationality managers operate within the limits of the simplified or bounded model.
- The result is that there is a satisficing decision and that solutions are considered adequate.

Simon, Herbert, *Administrative Behaviour: A Study of Decision-Making Processes in Administrative Organizations*. New York: Simon & Schuster, 1997.

Brand loyalty

Brand loyalty reflects a consumer's preference to buy a particular brand in a product category; it is also the ultimate goal a business sets for a branded product.

Customers tend to become brand loyal when they perceive that the brand concerned offers them the right mix of product features and images. Of equal importance is an appropriate level of quality at the right price. Having established this link, the customers are then more likely to use this as the foundation of their buying habits.

Typically, customers would make a trial purchase of a brand, and assuming that they are fully satisfied, they will continue to buy the brand, in the knowledge that this is a safe and reliable purchase. Loyal brand purchasers will be prepared to pay higher prices and they will actively recommend the brand to other potential purchasers.

Brand loyalty is an important concept, and reality, for businesses for the following reasons:

B

- It has been estimated that in the US, for example, an average business loses 50 per cent of its customers every five years (around 13 per cent annually). In any attempt to make a modest increase in growth of 1 or 2 per cent, the business has to add the annual loss to the equation. The reduction of customer losses can dramatically affect business growth, and brand loyalty is seen as a major tool in achieving this goal.
- As brand loyalty increases, customers become less sensitive to price increases, making it possible for the business to charge premium prices for its products and services. Those loyal to the brand recognize that it offers them some unique values that they could not enjoy from a competing brand. Increased purchasing rates may be encouraged by the introduction of promotions, but money-off deals only tend to subsidize purchases that were already being planned by the loyal customers.
- Brand loyalists are willing to search for their favourite brand and are less sensitive to promotions offered by the competitors. The business offering the products or services which enjoy brand loyalty also reap the benefits of lower costs in advertising, marketing and distribution.

Given the fact that it has been estimated that it costs some six times as much to attract a new customer as to retain an existing one, businesses constantly seek means by which they can foster brand loyalty. Typical approaches incorporate the folowing ideas:

- Consumers must like the product in order to develop loyalty to it, therefore positive brand attitudes are important.
- To convert occasional purchasers into brand loyalists, habits must be reinforced.
- Consumers must be reminded of the value of their purchase and encouraged to continue purchasing the product in the future.
- To encourage repeat purchases, advertisements before and after the sale are critical.
- The business needs to become a customer service champion.
- Advertising shapes and reinforces consumer attitudes; these attitudes mature into beliefs, which need to be reinforced until they develop into loyalty.
- The business needs to make sure that customers get what they want from their product.
- To give customers an incentive to repeat their purchase, offer them the chance to win a prize or gift (with proofs of purchase), or in-pack discounts.

● Tie up the distribution so that it is easier for the customers to buy the brand than competing brands.

Freeland, John G. (ed.), *The Ultimate CRM Handbook: Strategies and Concepts for Building Enduring Customer Loyalty and Profitability.* New York: McGraw-Hill, 2002.

Branding

Branding is the creation of an association between the name of a product and various values, images, awareness, recognition, qualities, features and benefits. Branding, in effect, represents the intangible values created by a badge of reassurance, which simultaneously differentiates the product from the competition.

Businesses will brand their products primarily for differentiation, but branding is a hook upon which to hang the advertising and promotion of the product. Coupled with this, branding also encourages customers to recognize and accept the product, helping them with their buying decisions. Above all, branding reduces the need for the business to compete with other businesses purely on the basis of price.

There are several different types of brand, or branding solutions:

● individual brands (e.g. Kit-Kat, Clio);
● a blanket family brand name for all products (e.g. Dyson, Heinz);
● separate family names for different product divisions (e.g. Nescafé and Rowntree);
● the company trade name combined with an individual product name (e.g. Ford Focus, Microsoft Age of Empires).

Branding is relevant only to those products that can achieve mass sales, because of the high cost of branding and the subsequent advertising; or to those whose attributes can be evaluated by consumers.

The advantages of branding include the following:

● It facilitates memory recall, which encourages self-selection and customer loyalty.
● It is a means of obtaining legal protection for product features.
● It assists with market segmentation.
● It builds a strong and positive image (particularly if the brand name is the business name).
● It makes it easier to link advertising to other marketing communications.
● Display space and point-of-sale promotions are more easily obtained.
● Associated products can be added, launched under the brand name.

- Personal selling is no longer a key requirement to obtain sales.

Guilding and Moorehouse developed the concept that there were five factors which contributed to brand valuation:

- Authorization, which involves justifying marketing expenditures.
- Forecasting and planning, which require the setting of budgets and objectives.
- Communication and coordination, which stress the internal marketing benefits.
- Motivation on the part of the business, in order to see the benefits.
- Performance evaluation, which recognizes the lessons to be learned from the processes.

Keller, Kevin Lane, *Strategic Brand Management: Building, Measuring, and Managing Brand Equity* (1st edition). Englewood Cliffs, NJ: Prentice-Hall, 1997.

Braverman, Harry

See **deskilling** *and* **labour process approach**.

Breakeven point

In order to identify an organization's breakeven point, it is necessary to consider the relationships between the various costs and sales in an integrated manner. The breakeven point is defined as being the point at which the level of sales is not great enough for the business to make a profit and yet not low enough for the business to make a loss. In other words, earnings from sales are just sufficient for the business to cover its total costs. This occurs when the total revenue from sales exactly equals the total cost of production.

Breakeven point occurs when total cost = total revenue

From this it can be assumed that if the total revenue from sales is greater than the total costs, then the organization concerned makes a profit. Conversely, if the opposite is true, and the total revenue is less than the total costs, then the organization will make a loss. It is essential that organizations take this very important factor into account. The organization will find that it is essential to determine how many units of output it must produce and sell before it can reach its breakeven point. The total cost of the unit of production is made up of two factors, the fixed and the variable costs, where:

Total cost = fixed costs + variable costs

And the total revenue is given by the number of products sold, multiplied by the selling price:

Total revenue = price × quantity

The drawing up and labelling of a breakeven chart makes the calculation of the breakeven point easier. The breakeven chart requires a considerable amount of labelling in order to enable an exact identification of what the chart is describing about the breakeven point.

As can be seen in Figure 13, the breakeven chart will include:

- Units of production – which are considered to be the most completed product and not, importantly, the components which make up that product.
- Fixed costs (FC) – which are the costs that do not alter in relation to changes in demand or output. They have to be paid regardless of the business's trading level.
- Variable costs (VC) – which change in direct proportion to changes in output, such as raw materials, components, labour and energy. Breakeven charts require the assumption that some costs vary in direct proportion to changes in output. In fact, it is unlikely that any

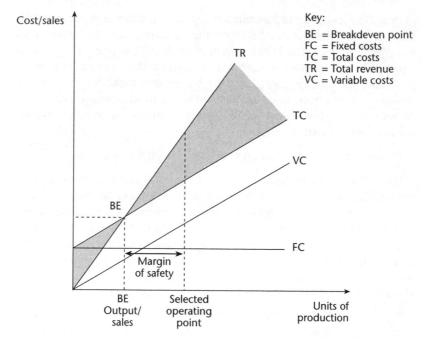

Figure 13 A breakeven chart

costs are totally variable as raw materials, for example, are likely to cost less per unit if the organization buys in bulk. In this instance, it cannot be assumed that the cost of raw materials will double if output doubles.

- Total costs (TC) – these are simply the sum of all the fixed and variable costs.
- Sales and costs – sales are the income (TR) generated from the selling of the units of production to customers. Costs, on the other hand, are expenses incurred by the organization in the purchase of raw materials, other fixed costs, and variable costs.
- Breakeven point (BE) – this is the point at which sales levels are high enough for the organization not to make a loss but not high enough for it to make a profit. In other words, this is the point where total sales equal total costs.
- Profit – in terms of the breakeven chart, and the breakeven point, this is achieved when sales exceed total costs.
- Loss – in terms of the breakeven chart, and the breakeven point, this occurs when revenue from sales has not met the total costs.
- Selected operating point – this is the planned production and sales level, which is assumed to be the same as that in given data.
- Margin of safety – this is the amount by which the selected operating point exceeds the breakeven point. This indicates the amount by which sales could fall from the planned level before the organization ceases to make a profit.

Bricks and clicks/clicks and mortar

'Bricks and clicks', or 'clicks and mortar', refer to the marrying of traditional forms of business using direct, face-to-face customer interaction, with mirrored operations in the form of website customer-interface delivery. In effect, bricks and clicks is a new business model which suggests that both a traditional and a virtual sales channel can be established and maintained successfully by businesses. In essence, the term specifically refers to organizations which have both a traditional and an e-commerce presence.

www.themanager.org/Knowledgebase/E-World/bricks_clicks.htm

B

Broad differentiator

The term 'broad differentiator' refers to businesses which have developed ranges of products or services specifically targeted at particular market segments or niches.

According to P. Ward, D. Bickford and G. Leong (1996), a business can attempt to adopt three different configurations, namely:

- cost leader/differentiator (CD);
- broad differentiator (BD);
- niche differentiator (ND).

The relationships between the three different approaches can be seen in Figure 14.

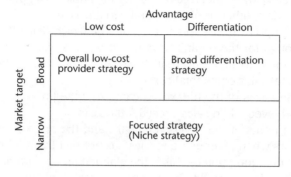

Figure 14   Market segment differentiation

Ward, P., Bickford, D. and Leong, G., 'Configurations of Manufacturing Strategy, Business Strategy, Environment and Structure', *Journal of Management*, 22(4) (1996), pp. 597–626.

See also **Porter, Michael.**

Budgetary control

Budgetary control is related to the establishment and management of budgets by responsible budget holders. Budgetary control tries to ensure that the objectives of any given policy or project are achieved within the confines of a set budget. Budgetary control also includes the analysis of how any relevant finance has been used and whether there has been any variation from the original plans. Budgetary control can be applied to virtually every form of financial commitment and it is imperative that the budget holders understand the inter-relationships between budgeting and budgetary control. There are strong links between each form of budget, as can be seen in Figure 15.

In this particular example we can see that all of the budgets, including the budgets for all other activities, are derived from the sales forecast. In this respect, sales are the limiting factor and the constraints on the budget.

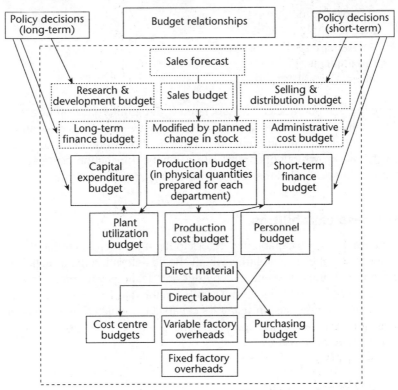

Figure 15 Budget relationships

Bureaucracy

A bureaucracy is a form of **organizational structure** which has highly routine tasks carried out by a workforce who are specialized in their area of work. These organizations tend to be grouped into functional departments, with centralized authority and a very narrow **span of control**. All decision making follows the **chain of command** and all activities within the organization are strictly controlled by rules and regulations.

Bureaucratic costs

Bureaucratic costs arise in an organization as a result of problems related to coordination and motivation. Typically, bureaucratic costs arise from:

B

- supervisory monitoring;
- motivational problems;
- coordination activities;
- opportunism;
- information distortions.

There are bureaucratic costs associated with the internalizing of activities; ultimately businesses may face a point where the costs of continuing to undertake all bureaucratic activities (both required and those which have grown out of control) outweigh the transaction-cost savings that would be afforded them by **outsourcing** certain functions.

Business capabilities

The term 'business capabilities' refers to the unique characteristics of a business. It is these capabilities which should determine the direction in which the business goes in its activities and dealings with markets.

Its expertise, knowledge or positioning in the market are typical forms of business capabilities. In using its capabilities, which may have been developed over a number of years, the business seeks to achieve a **competitive advantage**.

Business level strategy

Business level strategy is based on three key considerations:

- customer needs (*what* is being satisfied);
- customer groups (*who* is being satisfied);
- distinctive competence (*how* customer needs are to be satisfied).

Customer needs can be satisfied through the characteristics of a business's products or services. Product differentiation can be seen as the process of creating a **competitive advantage** in designing product characteristics to satisfy those customer needs.

Identifying customer groups, in essence **market segmentation**, involves grouping customers according to important differences in their needs or preferences so as to gain a competitive advantage. There are three approaches:

- concentrate on the average customer and not segment at all;
- develop products or services specifically for each identified group;
- only serve selected segments.

Further, a business may decide to develop different versions of a given product or service in order to attract customers from different groups, and then focus on the most profitable groups.

The third issue regarding business strategy is to decide what type of distinctive competence to pursue in order to satisfy customer needs. Some businesses may focus on their production technology (developing distinctive manufacturing competences), others may focus on technological competence or sales and marketing competence. In all cases, the business needs to combine and organize its resources to pursue this competence in order to gain and retain a competitive advantage.

Finlay, Paul, *Strategic Management: An Introduction to Business & Corporate Level Strategy.* London: Financial Times, Prentice Hall, 2000.

Business model

There are many different forms of business model, but all seek to explain the functions, and inter-relations of those functions, as a descriptor of how a business operates, or should ideally operate.

A typical business model is shown in Figure 16.

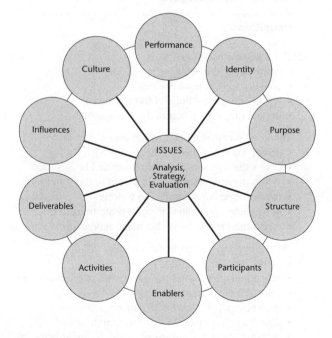

Figure 16   A typical business model

The different aspects of the business model can be further explained, beginning with the inner circle, as in Table 8.

Table 8   The business model's inner circle

Aspect	Definition
Analysis	Analysis involves an assessment of the issues facing the business. Any measurement of an issue needs a definition, a risk assessment and access to relevant information.
Evaluation	The degree to which the skills of the business are being exploited. Appraisal of systems, responses, benchmarking, inter-industry comparisons and other comparisons.
Strategy	Attaining specific goals, which are measurable, authorized, realistic and have clear time-frames, in addition to being feasible and attractive to the business.

The outer circle requires more definition, as can be seen in Table 9.

Table 9   The business model's outer circle

Aspect	Definition
Identity	The 4 key elements are: • name (what the business is known as); • constitution (its legal position); • reputation (perceptions of the business); • impact (the impression of the business).
Purpose	There are 6 key elements, which are: • *raison d'être* (purpose of the business), • core values (essential uncompromised beliefs); • vision (how the business sees itself in the future); • mission (moving towards the vision); • key policies (guidelines for corporate behaviour); • target markets (who the business serves as customers).
Structure	There are 6 key elements, which are: • physical deployment (location); • functional composition (departments of the business); • roles (jobs/staff duties); • workplaces (where work is carried out); • reporting structures (line of command); • external infrastructure (relations with outside groups).

Table 9 The business model's outer circle (*continued*)

Aspect	Definition
Participants	There are 9 key elements, which are: • owners (the actual shareholders or stakeholders); • managers (planning and control); • workers/employees (all other staff); • channels (how products and services are brought to customers); • customers (the end-users); • suppliers (providers of products and services); • partners (cooperative arrangements); • neighbours (who are affected by the business's operations); • indirect participants (those dependent on the business).
Enablers	There are 8 key elements, which are: • land and buildings; • technology; • intellectual property; • information (data); • skills; • core competences (capabilities of the business); • relationships (contacts); • financial resources (cash/investments).
Activities	There are 5 key elements of this aspect, which are: • line of business (producing products and services); • support functions; • management (planning and control); • compliance (legal requirements); • incidentals (all other activities).
Deliverables	The 2 key elements of this aspect are: • products (tangible items); • services (intangible items or activities performed on behalf of the customers).
Influences	There are 4 key influences, which are: • constraints and pressures (which restrict the business's actions); • risks and threats (which may destabilize the business); • opportunities (which the business can use to its advantage); • competitors (who are attempting to take the business's customers).

B

⇒

Table 9 The business model's outer circle (*continued*)

Aspect	Definition
Culture	There are 5 key aspects of business culture, which are: • management style; • rules and customs (acceptable behaviour); • social behaviour (interactions within the business); • benefits and perks (rewards for compliance); • personal development (scope for career advancement and growth).
Performance	The 5 key elements of performance are: • scale (size, throughput or output, and performance); • efficiency (ease and speed); • empathy (treatment of participants); • innovation (change-making ability); • finance (the soundness of the business's financial position).

Business plan

Business plans are not only used to attract new investment, but can also be used by a business to frame proposals for future developments (which may involve the business needing to secure additional finance).

The content of a business plan tends to evolve over time and few actual ventures end up bearing any relation to the predicted path outlined in the business plan. The primary purpose of the business plan is to provide a snapshot which aims to:

- illustrate that there is a market;
- illustrate that there is a solution;
- illustrate that the writers of the plan are in a position to bring the product or service to the market;
- illustrate the opportunities for growth.

It is normally considered to be the case that business plans need not exceed some 20 pages. Above all, the business plan needs to be written in such a way as to be matched to the audience (at an appropriate level, using suitable language and technical detail), and to be clear, concise and accessible.

Although there are many different styles of business plan, a common format (for the majority of cases) is detailed in Table 10.

Barrow, Paul, *The Best-laid Business Plans: How to Write Them, How to Pitch Them.* London: Virgin Books, 2001.

Table 10   A typical business plan

Business plan section	Description and content
Business case/cover sheet	Working title for the business or venture and a clear statement of the classification of the document (i.e. confidentiality).
Executive summary	Maximum of 2 pages, containing: • purpose of the business plan; • purpose or opportunity for which the funding is required (level of funding, estimate of shares available in return for the investment), likely exit routes; • problem which the opportunity addresses and unique selling points; • barriers to competitors; • market for activity; • financial projections/critical milestones; • management, operational and marketing strategies; • synopsis of management team's CVs; • business philosophy/mission statement; • alliances/collaborations.
Table of contents	Page numbers related to sections.
The business	• Notes on the originator's experience, track record or capabilities. • Origin of the idea for the opportunity, and description. • Unique selling proposition of the business as a whole. • Has the business a dominant or monopoly position, and if so for how long, and how long will the position take to establish? • Barriers to others entering the market: is there a patent protection, reputation, knowledge or capability barrier? • Activities and responsibilities, whether the business or a parent business will carry out various functions. • Summary of the intellectual property position (including patent numbers if relevant). • Scope for subsequent products and services. • Manufacturing routes, costs etc.

B

⇒

Table 10 A typical business plan (*continued*)

Business plan section	Description and content
Summary of market surveys	Ideally diagrams rather than text, on the current market and how the business expects the market to develop: • geographic breakdown; • size and growth of markets; • pricing details of similar/competing products and services; • summary of major competitors; • nature of the markets; • ease of access to the markets; • identification of key customer types.
Competition and SWOT analysis	One of these is required for each activity which will be undertaken by the business: • monopoly position (patent, reputation, knowledge, capability, equipment); • competition (direct and indirect); • **SWOT analysis** (current operations and solutions); • unique selling point (for each activity); • activity and corporate strategy fit.
Operations, staff and organizational structure	• Priorities. • Management/staff issues (experience of management and/or technical staff, vacancies, contracts and legal aspects of employment), organizational structure (a chart). • Salary structure. • Location of operations. • Accommodation requirements. • Structure of business (legal, investment requirements and structure of that investment, valuation and shareholding, non-executive positions).
Collaborations/alliances and partnerships	• Identification of partners. • Why partners have been chosen. • Nature of links with partners. • Links back to parent company (if applicable).
Marketing and pricing	Must be detailed for each activity: • target markets; • services and products (special arrangements for targets);

$\Rightarrow$

B

Table 10   A typical business plan (*continued*)

Business plan section	Description and content
	• identification of markets; • branding; • business philosophy; • pricing and sales figures.
Financial data	Assumptions regarding market share or value of sales, and likely exit strategies: • timeline of expenditure and income; • survey of overall expenditure and revenue over a 5-year period; • liquidity issues, equity and debt raising; • cash flow statement; • balance sheet; • profit and loss statement. Details of the following: • income (by named activity or product group); • direct costs (related to raw materials, manufacturing, etc.); • running costs (including advertising, accounts, consumables, depreciation, distribution, insurance, legal fees, rent, repairs, research, salaries, services, training, travel and utilities).
Risk analysis	A risk table could outline the various risks associated with the venture. Also included are the likely severity of those risks and any contingencies required. The risks should be linked to the financial data section.
Action plan	A **Gantt** chart could be used to show the product/service launch and at least the first 2 years of operations. All of the critical milestones should be identified and explained.
Appendices and supporting data	• Patents. • Technical papers. • Letters of support from collaborators. • Staff CVs. • Support from other funding bodies. • Future – where research is leading and new applications. • Details of market survey.

B

Business process

Business processes are the activities undertaken by a business which allow it to function. The business processes within an organization carry its operations forward in a smooth and, hopefully, profitable manner. Frequently, business processes are grouped by department or division, such as:

- Procurement – obtaining resources;
- Product development – planning, designing and refining products and services;
- Production – the manufacturing or providing of products and services;
- Delivery – receiving, fulfilling and tracking shipments;
- Accounting – the tracking of transactions and investments;
- Human resources – the hiring and firing of employees and the management of payroll and benefits;
- Marketing – the promotion of products or services;
- Customer service – the solving of customer problems.

Managers actively contribute to the business process by identifying and eliminating potential inefficiencies and bottlenecks in the business. They are actively involved in:

- the elimination of flaws in the systems;
- the reduction of time spent on particular tasks;
- cost reduction;
- reduction in the use of resources;
- improvements in efficiency;
- improvements in quality;
- increasing customer satisfaction;
- increasing employee satisfaction.

Smith, Howard and Fingar, Peter, *Business Process Management (BPM): The Third Wave*. Tampa, Florida: Meghan-Kiffer Press, 2003.

B

Business strategy

As Alfred P. Sloan, the Executive Officer of General Motors, stated in 1945: 'The strategic aim of a business is to earn a return on capital, and if in any case the return is not satisfactory, the deficiency should be corrected or the activity abandoned.'

Typically, a business strategy involves the art of conducting a business campaign on a broad scale focused on achieving a specific (and well defined) goal or series of outcomes. All this needs to be achieved within a specified time-frame. The features of business strategy inevitably involve:

- a means by which the business can achieve its objectives;
- a means of galvanizing staff, supplies and stakeholders to meet those objectives;
- a drive for both growth and profits.

Business strategies tend to have a time-frame of between three and seven years, within which **business plans** covering between one and three years are reviewed and updated. The business strategy aims to provide a framework for the tactics which need to be employed to achieve the business's goals. In essence, it becomes the foundation for future activities and provides a practical context in which the following are addressed:

- pressures;
- urgencies;
- opportunities;
- threats.

Business strategy can be exemplified as in Figure 17.

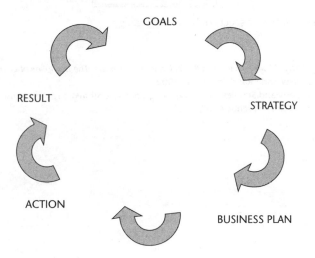

Figure 17   Business strategy

A more refined version of this figure directly associates the various aspects of business strategy, as in Figure 18.

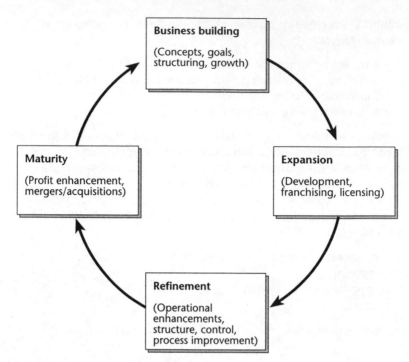

Figure 18 Various aspects of business strategy

Bossidy, Larry, Charan, Ram and Buck, Charles, *Execution: The Discipline of Getting Things Done*. New York: Random House, 2002.

Johnson, Gerry and Scholes, Kevin, *Exploring Corporate Strategy: Text and Cases*. London: Financial Times, Prentice Hall, 2001.

B

Capable competitors

'Capable competitors' is a term associated with the existence of other businesses that can supply products or services which directly compete with a business in terms of quality, delivery and service (and many other aspects).

The existence or non-existence of capable competitors often determines the **business strategy** of an organization, such as in the following cases:

- Non-existence of capable competitors enables a business to be an *aggressive sole provider* of a product or service. This is because imitation may be difficult, the business possesses the required skills and resources, and there are suppliers of complementary products.
- *Passive multiple licensing* is possible when there are capable competitors, when the **barriers to imitation** are low, but the other businesses lack the skills and resources required.
- *Aggressive multiple licensing* (combining licensing with aggressive positioning) can take place when the businesses have the required skills and resources, the barriers to imitation are low, and there are several capable competitors.
- *Selective partnering* occurs when the barriers to imitation are high, other businesses lack the required skills and resources, but there are potentially several different capable competitors.

Capacity control strategy

Simply, capacity is the maximum rate of output for a given process. It is usually measured in output per unit of time. Businesses will tend to use different units of time in order to calculate their capacity, such as per minute, per hour, per day or per shift. In truth, the maximum capacity is much better described as being the demonstrated capacity, as this is the true level of capacity which has been achieved. Some organizations and analysts will attempt to calculate a theoretical capacity, which is largely based on the capacity of the machines involved and rarely takes into account any variables which may affect the capacity. Businesses will try to operate at their optimum capacity. This means attempting to reduce costs, or loss of capacity associated with waiting time.

Capacity management is best described as being the maximum output, content or performance of a given system or component. Capacity management is often applied to the information technology area, describing or defining in both business and technical terms the requirements of a business's information technology capacity. An efficient information technology infrastructure must be able to deliver, at the optimum cost, the ability to deal with specified levels of capacity. 'Capacity', in its simplest form, describes the probable volume of activities which the information technology infrastructure must be able to cope with given normal circumstances. Clearly, capacity management needs to ensure that there is sufficient capacity, plus additional reserve capacity.

Capacity requirements planning (CRP) is the process of determining the short-term output demands on either an organization or one of its production processes. CRP is a computerized system that projects the load from a material requirements plan (MRP) onto the capacity of the system and then identifies underloads and overloads. CRP is used by an organization to assess whether it can start new projects in the future, or whether it can produce an immediate order for a customer. Normally CRP will require information about when orders are needed, and details of the equipment and labour required, as well as any orders already in the pipeline. The CRP will then be able to provide the organization with a profile for each operation in the production system. It will make a comparison of the work that needs to be completed and the work already in progress, in relation to the system's capacity. CRP relies on accurate information, defining capacity as a sum of the following formula:

Number of machines or employees × number of shifts × utilization of machines and workers × efficiency

CRP is therefore used to calculate the ability of the organization to meet its orders.

Capital budget

A capital budget is a fund which is earmarked by a business in order to assist it in the acquisition of long-term fixed assets.

Capital investment appraisal

Capital investment involves a business purchasing capital assets. The capital assets, which may take the form of machinery or plant, are essential in a manufacturing industry for example, which will rely on these capital assets to produce products. Theoretically the overall expenditure on capital investment in a given economy reflects the state of that economy. Higher expenditure on capital investment indicates a fast-growing economy, whereas low capital investment indicates either reluctance on the part of businesses to invest in new plant and machinery, or a general downturn in the economy itself.

Capital investment's primary goal is for the business to achieve a greater financial return, in terms either of capital gain or of income. In many respects capital investments can be viewed as a form of financial investment which leads to savings for the business. In making a capital investment a business is indicating its desire to produce more efficiently and to replace perhaps outdated and inefficient plant and machinery. The desire in making a capital investment is to become more profitable. The level of capital investment is often used as a primary measure by which the government assesses overall business confidence.

Chisholm, Andrew, *An Introduction to Capital Markets: Products, Strategies, Participants.* New York: John Wiley, 2002.

Capital structure

Capital structure is a means by which the balance between a business's debt and its equity can be expressed.

Cash cow

Cash cows are part of the **Boston growth matrix** and represent well established products or services which are likely to be in the mature phase of their product life cycle. Cash cows are well entrenched, with sales that have grown to a stable level.

Cash cows are considered to be profitable products or services which are making positive contributions to the business's cash flow. Businesses that have the advantage of having a cash cow or a number of cash cows as part of their portfolio are often encouraged by the income to consider the launch of product variants on the theme of the cash cow. This often ends in failure as it only serves to fragment the market and undermine the general sales and profitability of the cash cow. Instead, many businesses use the cash generated by the cash cow to develop and launch new products and services. They will inevitably target growth markets, while they continue to support the cash cow and its hard-won market share.

Some businesses also attempt to strengthen the position of their cash cows but this is often a costly and unsuccessful strategy, leading to businesses recognizing that they need to set an upper limit on the support, providing they maintain the market position.

Cash cows are vulnerable to cheaper substitute products which offer better or equal benefits. Equally, cash cows, being older than more modern substitutes, may have less technically developed means of production. This can make the unit costs of the cash cow less attractive than those of the newcomers. If a new competing product is successful, the cash cow's product life cycle will be shortened, reducing its financial return.

See also **Boston growth matrix.**

Cash flow

'Cash flow' is a term used to describe the net funds that have flowed through an organization over a period of time. Traditionally, cash flow is usually defined as earnings. The identification of when those earnings were received and when payments have to be made defines the parameters of cash flow management. Cash flow is often complicated by the actual value of the cash received in a given period. Cash flow does not take into account expenses that may have been incurred by the organization prior to the period the cash flow covers, yet during this period the organization is benefiting from those costs in the past. Equally, the reverse is true: payments may now be due over the cash flow period on equipment or stock from which the organization has already profited and which has been noted on a previous cash flow account.

Cash flow also has a difficulty in dealing with outstanding debts and money owed by creditors. These do not appear on the cash flow, as neither has been paid, yet they are important considerations, as they may have a negative or positive effect on the available working capital of the organization. The available funds, which are calculated and identified within the cash flow, have enormous implications for the business, particularly as the available working capital determines the organization's ability to pay debts promptly and to make necessary investments.

Graham, Alistair, *Cash Flow Forecasting and Liquidity*. Glenlake: Fitzroy Dearborn, Publishers, 2000.

Category management

Category management involves the identification of interchangeable or substitute products which could reasonably replace products required by a customer. The identified groups of products are brought together under one category so that they can be offered to the customer as alternatives, should the specific product demanded be unavailable, or if it has been superseded by another product in that category. Category management can be differentiated from alternative means by which products are managed. In many cases businesses will manage products individually and there will be clearly identifiable differences between the products offered by that business. In this respect it is difficult for customers to perceive the level of substitution of alternative products offered by the same business.

Nielson Marketing Research, *Category Management: Positioning your Organization to Win*. Chicago, IL: Contemporary Books, 1997.

Centrality

'Centrality' is usually taken to mean the importance of a particular part of a business, perhaps a department or division, in terms of its involvement in the activities of other parts of the organization.

Centrality, therefore, measures or identifies key functional or service areas of a business upon which the rest of the organization may rely. Typically, divisions or departments with a high level of centrality are at the heart of resource transfers in the business.

Centralization/devolution

Centralization is a measure of how concentrated the decision-making processes are within an organization. The greater the concentration, the more centralized the organization is considered to be.

Chain of command

The chain of command within an organization is a feature typically associated with a business that has a hierarchical structure. The chain of command is the formal line of communication, beginning with the board of directors, or managing director, who passes instructions down to departmental managers, section heads and then to individual employees. The chain of command typifies a pyramid-shaped organization, where increasingly down the pyramid more individuals have to be informed of decisions and instructions. Effectively, the chain of command of the board of directors or the managing director encompasses every individual underneath them in the hierarchical structure. Similarly, the chain of command of a section head consists merely of the immediate employees who work under that individual's supervision. The term 'chain of command' is closely associated with **span of control**.

Keuning, Doede and Opheij, Wilfred, *Delayering Organisations: How to Beat Bureaucracy and Create a Flexible and Responsive Organisation*. Woodslane, Australia, 1994.

Chaining strategy

The term 'chaining strategy' has different meanings in different contexts. One of the most basic definitions relates to a business which establishes a number of linked outlets that are so interconnected and reliant upon one another that they are able to function cooperatively as a single business entity.

W. C. Jordan and C. S. Graves (1995) suggested a form of chaining strategy which would allow businesses (particularly in manufacturing) to create flexible configurations. These flexible configurations combine, or chain, the stages of production effectively, helping to eliminate inefficiencies. Their approach suggests that chaining strategies are ideal in dealing with multi-stage supply chains through which raw materials, components and finished goods pass.

Jordan, W. C. and Graves, C. S., 'Principles on the Benefits of Manufacturing Process Flexibility', *Management Science*, 41(4) (1998), pp. 577–94.

Champy, James

James Champy has written extensively on the re-engineering of corporations and leadership. Champy's arc of ambition specifically relates to ambition in the leadership sense and its importance in determining achievement. Champy identified three archetypal figures, as listed in Table 11.

Table 11 Archetypal figures

Archetypal figure	Description
Creators	True innovators who pioneer new technology. They make previous modes of operation obsolete.
Capitalizers	Users of new ideas who will configure an organization's infrastructure to accommodate the new ideas. They find use for innovation.
Consolidators	Professional managers who make new innovations actually work in a practical sense, in a constant manner and profitably.

Champy, James, *X-Engineering the Corporation*. London: Hodder & Stoughton, 2002.

Champy, James and Nohria, Nitin, *The Arc of Ambition: Defining the Leadership Journey.* New York: John Wiley & Sons, 2001.

www.perotsystems.com/newsroom/bios/james_champy.htm

Changeability

Business changeability is a measure of an organization's agility or flexibility. The flexibility of a business is measured by the degree to which the organization can adapt its operations to changes in the market. A generic changeability or agility diagram is shown in Figure 19:

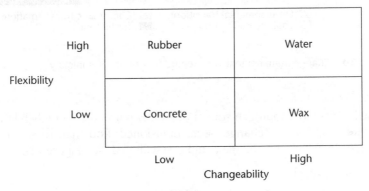

Figure 19   A changeability or agility diagram

As the diagram implies, organizations with low flexibility and changeability characteristics resemble concrete in that they do not have the capacity for movement and are inflexible. Those with high scores on both counts resemble water, being able to flow and adapt as required.

Change management

There are many theories regarding change management. Many focus upon the way in which a business thinks about change and the way it drives change. As there are a number of different theories, it is perhaps prudent to focus on just some of the ways in which change management can be achieved. Although change may not necessarily be driven by a human resource department, it is often the role of the department to manage the intricacies and complications arising out of change. There are innumerable theories not only on the way change affects individuals and groups within a business, but also on the ideal ways of managing that change.

Doug Stace and Dexter Dunphy took the view that change management could be packaged in terms of its size and complexity and then organized accordingly, as can be seen in Figure 20.

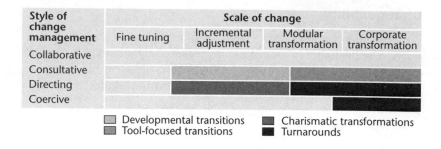

Style of change management	Scale of change			
	Fine tuning	Incremental adjustment	Modular transformation	Corporate transformation
Collaborative				
Consultative				
Directing				
Coercive				

☐ Developmental transitions   ■ Charismatic transformations
▨ Tool-focused transitions   ■ Turnarounds

Figure 20   Change management with regard to size and complexity

Sheila Costello's approach sought to set the parameters purely by the size and scope of the change being envisioned, and then to suggest strategies by which the change could be facilitated (see Figure 21).

Size of change	Planning and action implications
Developmental	Enables ideas to be generated from and developed by affected employees and involves them in implementation planning.
Transitional	Management needs to be clear about the change and identify similarities and differences between the current and the new procedures. Targets and objectives should be set and progress monitored and reported on. Employees should be acknowledged for their efforts and any successes.
Transformational	The change must be communicated throughout the organization with no possibility of ambiguity or misunderstanding. Employees must be educated as to why the change is occurring, how it will affect them and what the new vision is.

Figure 21   Change management in terms of size and scope

Paul Bate, on the other hand, considered the whole process of change to be a cycle which had clearly identifiable phases, as can be seen in Figure 22.

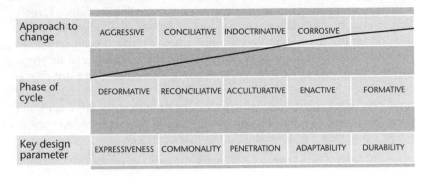

Approach to change	AGGRESSIVE	CONCILIATIVE	INDOCTRINATIVE	CORROSIVE	
Phase of cycle	DEFORMATIVE	RECONCILIATIVE	ACCULTURATIVE	ENACTIVE	FORMATIVE
Key design parameter	EXPRESSIVENESS	COMMONALITY	PENETRATION	ADAPTABILITY	DURABILITY

Figure 22   The cycle of change

Bate, Paul, *Strategies for Cultural Change*. Oxford: Butterworth-Heinemann, 1995.
Costello, Sheila, *Managing Change at Work*. New York: Irwin Professional, 1994.
Stace, Doug and Dunphy, Dexter, *Beyond the Boundaries: Leading and Re-creating the Successful Enterprise*. New York: McGraw-Hill Education, 2002.

Change options matrix

The change options matrix links the main areas of human resource activity. The three main areas of strategic change are work, cultural and political change. The change options matrix was developed by Michael Beer, Russell Eisenstat and Bert Spector (1990) when they provided a six-point plan on how best to proceed with change:

- mobilize commitment through joint diagnosis;
- develop a shared vision of how to organize and manage for competitiveness;
- create a consensus for the new vision along with the competence and cohesion to act on it;
- revitalize departments by pressure from senior management;
- ensure change through the adoption of policies, systems and structures;
- monitor and adjust strategies as required.

Beer, Michael, Eisenstat, Russell A. and Spector, Bert A., 'Why Change Programs Don't Produce Change', *Harvard Business Review*, November 1990.

Channel management

Channel management involves the selection and motivation of distribution channel members and the periodic performance evaluation of their efforts and commitment.

A manufacturer, for example, may wish to agree performance targets (in terms of quotas, delivery times, lost or damaged goods procedures, promotion and marketing agreements, training, and overall service to customers). The manufacturer will periodically review these arrangements and be prepared to take remedial action when there are deviations from the agreed performance standards. In most cases, the producer or ultimate supplier controls or significantly influences the channel members, who are subordinate to the producer on account of the fact that they are dependent upon that producer.

Forsyth, Patrick, *Channel Management*. Oxford: Capstone Express, 2001.

Clarity of expectations

Sound planning not only ensures focus, but it also ensures clarity of expectations. In this sense, clarity of expectations is an integral part of the structuring of tasks and the setting of deadlines. 'Clarity of expectations' refers to managers being precise regarding their instructions and communications in order to ensure that subordinates comprehend what is expected of them and what the likely outcome of a task is expected to be with regard to performance.

Clarity of expectations is an integral part of enhanced communications, information sharing, and **delegation**.

Coercive power

Coercive power was one of the five different forms of power suggested by J. P. R. French and B. Raven in 1960. Their theories refer to the different types of power exercised or wielded by managers. The five types of power are summarized in Table 12.

French, J. P. R. Jnr, and Raven, B., 'The Bases of Social Power', in D. Cartwright and A. Zander (eds), *Group Dynamics*. New York: HarperCollins, 1974.

Cognitive bias

Essentially, cognitive bias is the tendency for individuals, however intelligent or well-informed, to do the wrong thing.

Because certain issues or occurrences come to the mind more easily than others, individuals tend to use these occurrences as benchmarks for decision making rather than a better and more efficient alternative.

The human brain, it is said, is built for interpersonal relationships rather than statistics. Because of cognitive bias, managers need discipline, tools and quantitative methods in order to make the correct decisions.

Table 12   Coercive power

Power type	Description
Coercive	In forcing employees to do things against their will, physical threats can be used. Typically, the manager is dictatorial or a bully. The principal goal is compliance; managers will make examples of those who do not comply. Rewards can be withheld and individuals can be socially excluded.
Reward	Providing employees with what they want in exchange for compliance and obedience. Rewards can be withheld as a means of ensuring compliance.
Legitimate	Seen to be the acceptable face of raw power. Managers have legitimate power by virtue of their position in the business. Employees obey the position in the organization, not the manager as such.
Referent	Power derived from employees liking and wanting to emulate the manager. Charisma is a key factor; it can be used to exclude or coerce. Social leaders can direct others to exclude or shun individuals.
Expert	Power based on knowledge and skills, common in businesses which promote technically able individuals into management positions. Power revolves around experience and understanding, to which others defer.

Kahneman, Daniel and Tversky, Amos, 'Subjective Probability: a Judgement of Representativeness', *Cognitive Psychology*, July 1972.

Commission system

Commission-based pay is an incentive-based pay structure, which is widely believed to produce better results from employees than a traditional pay structure. Typically, sales staff are placed on commission-based pay. Their income is directly related to their performance and in most cases there is no ceiling to the amount of money that they can earn. Commission-based structures are seen as a viable means of identifying those who are under-performing and who may require either redeployment or training. One of the many associated problems, however, with commission-based pay structures is that employees tend to focus on the sale of items which provide them with the largest return in relation to the time spent. Commission-based salaries tend to work when the products or services sold by a business have few variations. This means that employees tend to focus on building relationships with customers in order to provide steady commission payments.

> Torkelson, Gwen E., *Contribution Based Pay: Tools to Identify, Measure and Reward Performance.* iUniverse.com, 2001.

Communication barrier

A communication barrier is a problem in the communication system or stream which effectively blocks either the communication itself or the understanding of that communication between the relevant parties. Communication barriers can take a number of different forms, such as:

- lack of sufficient or effective training of employees;
- lack of information needed to make a decision;
- personal relationship problems;
- faulty or inadequate systems or procedures;
- noise or other messages which can confuse the transmission and receiving of the message.

Communication models

The **organizational structure** will determine the channels through which communication is regularly made. Communication channels need to ensure that information flows freely throughout the organization in order that the right information meets the right person, at the right time. Open communication channels tend to take the following forms:

- notice boards;
- newsletters;
- minutes of meetings;
- non-confidential internal mail;
- multi-user computer systems;
- email.

Communication channels also have to pass information of a confidential or security-restricted nature and the organization will restrict access to this information in a variety of ways, including passwords for computer systems.

An organization will select the most effective method of communication for transmitting information both internally and externally, although taking into account considerations such as speed, cost, feedback requirements or written documentation needs. Figures 23 and 24 identify the main methods of communication, in both written and verbal format.

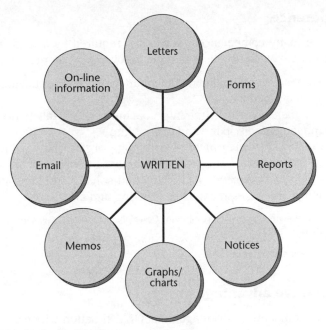

Figure 23   Methods of written communication

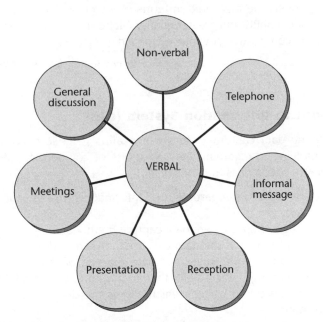

Figure 24   Methods of verbal communication

Competence

There are many competences (key skills) required by a manager, but these can be typified as falling into the following categories:

- *Job management* – including time management, prioritization, planning and scheduling
- *Team management* – training, coaching, appraisal, performance management, discipline and counselling.
- *Relationship management* – listening, organizing, giving clear instructions, giving and receiving unbiased information.
- *Thought management* – identifying and solving problems, decision making, risk assessment, clear thinking and analysing.

Winterton, Jonathan and Winterton, Ruth, *Developing Managerial Competence*. London: Routledge, 1999.

See also **core competence**.

Competitive advantage

The term 'competitive advantage' refers to a situation where a business has a commercial advantage over the competition by being able to offer consumers better value, quality or service. Normally, a competitive advantage would be measured in terms of lower prices, though in the case of more benefits and greater quality, higher prices are possible as a result of the competitive advantage enjoyed.

Porter, Michael E., *Competitive Advantage: Creating and Sustaining Superior Performance*. New York: Simon & Schuster, 1998.

Competitive Information System (CIS)

A marketing data capture system which aims to collect, collate and assess intelligence regarding the operations of competitors. Ideally, a CIS needs to encompass the following:

- A clear decision regarding the information that needs to be collected.
- The design of appropriate data capture methods.
- A system by which the data can be analysed and evaluated in a timely manner (note that aged data may be of little value or, at worst, may suggest strategies that are no longer appropriate).
- A communications system which allows the dissemination of the information.
- The incorporation of the data into the decision-making process,

coupled with an ability to assess the quality of the data collected so that systems can be refined.

See also **sustainable competitive advantage.**

Competitive intelligence

Competitive intelligence (CI) is increasingly seen as a distinct business management discipline, which provides an input into a whole range of decision-making processes. There are four stages in monitoring competitors, known as the four Cs:

- Collecting the information.
- Converting information into intelligence (CIA: Collate and catalogue it, Interpret it and Analyse it).
- Communicating the intelligence.
- Countering any adverse competitor actions.

www.bidigital.com/ci/Documentation

Competitor profile analysis

Competitor profile analysis is a market research method which seeks to quantify the key success factors in a given industry or market, incorporating the same criteria for major competitors. By assigning a score to the most important or closest match, for both the industry and the competitor, an aggregate score is derived (see Table 13). These scores indicate the key determinants of success and show how well suited, or perhaps vulnerable, a given competitor may be. Obviously an extension of this profiling analysis would be to carry out a similar exercise with your own business.

Complementors

The power of complementors arises when the value of a business's products or services depends upon the availability of others. Toothpaste on its own, for example, would have no value without toothbrushes. Complementors directly influence the profitability of a given market. In the absence of the correct complementors, or in the case of the slow development or poor quality of those complementors, profitability can be harmed.

The concept of complementors was probably first introduced by Andy Grove of Intel.

Grove, Andrew, *Only the Paranoid Survive*. New York: Doubleday, 1998.

Table 13 Competitor profile analysis – key success factors

Success factor	To industry (A)	To competitor (B)	Score (C)
Product quality	1 2 3	1 2 3	1 2 3 4 5 6 7 8 9
Product mix	1 2 3	1 2 3	1 2 3 4 5 6 7 8 9
Price	1 2 3	1 2 3	1 2 3 4 5 6 7 8 9
Distribution dealers	1 2 3	1 2 3	1 2 3 4 5 6 7 8 9
Promotion ability	1 2 3	1 2 3	1 2 3 4 5 6 7 8 9
Manufacturing operations	1 2 3	1 2 3	1 2 3 4 5 6 7 8 9
Overall cost situation	1 2 3	1 2 3	1 2 3 4 5 6 7 8 9
Financial strength	1 2 3	1 2 3	1 2 3 4 5 6 7 8 9
Organization structure	1 2 3	1 2 3	1 2 3 4 5 6 7 8 9
General management ability	1 2 3	1 2 3	1 2 3 4 5 6 7 8 9
Human resource quality	1 2 3	1 2 3	1 2 3 4 5 6 7 8 9

Total weighted score

A – The scale of importance is 3 = high, 2 = moderate, and 1 = low.
B – The scale for the rating is 3 = strong, 2 = moderate, and 1 = weak.
C = A × B.

Compliance

A compliance approach is effectively a review or audit of human resource practices, with the intention of determining whether they conform to the business's stated policies. An integral part of this is to consider whether human resource practices comply with legal standards. A compliance approach can also encompass an audit of managerial compliance.

Concentrated marketing

'Concentrated marketing' is a marketing strategy which sees a business focusing primarily on obtaining a brand leadership or market dominance in a single market or a small number of markets. All marketing activities will be concentrated on having the maximum impact on these markets and the business will be less active in other markets as a result.

Concentration ratio

The concentration ratio measures the fraction or percentage of total sales in a given market which is controlled by a specified number of the industry's largest sellers. Many of the concentration ratios calculate the share of an industry's total market sales made by between three and five of the largest businesses in that market. In the UK, for example, data is collected by the Office of National Statistics, and in the cases of tobacco products, petroleum and fuels the totals are almost 100%. On average, however, the markets the concentration ratio measures are dominant to the extent of between 40% and 60% in areas such as metals, office machinery, computers, televisions, communication equipment and motor vehicles.

Conceptual skills

Conceptual skills are one of the three broad skill types which are identified in different occupations, the other two being technical skills and human skills. The comparisons between the three generic types of skills are shown in Table 14.

Managers tend to be more replete in human skills, followed by conceptual skills and finally technical skills.

Conflict aftermath

See **conflict management.**

Table 14 The three skill types

Generic skills	Description	Examples
Technical	Related to methods, procedures or techniques.	Software, computer-aided manufacture, networking, computer programming, project planning, cost management.
Human	Associated with the individual's behaviour.	Leadership, creativity and analytic skills, self-learning and flexibility, communication, team working, strong sense of commitment.
Conceptual	Related to the individual's perception of the business's environment.	Strategy and planning, vision for the business, vision globally.

Conflict management

Conflict management involves situations where there may be opposition, incompatible behaviour and antagonistic interaction, or the blocking of individuals from reaching their goals. Conflict behaviour can range from questioning or doubting, to a desire to annihilate the opponent.

Typically, conflicts will arise out of disagreements, disputes or debates. Conflict is not always a negative aspect for a business and there is no specific need to reduce all conflicts, as they ebb and flow and become an inevitable part of organizational life. Indeed, many consider conflict to be essential for growth and survival. Therefore, conflict management includes both decreasing conflict and increasing it.

There are various forms of conflict but they can be broadly distinguished as being either functional or dysfunctional. Functional conflict, or constructive conflict, was first suggested in 1925 by **Mary Parker Follett**. It increases information and ideas, encourages innovative thinking, allows different points of view to be raised and reduces organizational stagnation.

Dysfunctional conflict, on the other hand, usually arises from tensions, anxieties and stresses. It reduces trust, and often poor decisions are made because of distorted or withheld information. Management tends to be obsessed with dysfunctional, high-conflict situations.

There is also a sub-division, which is dysfunctional low conflict, which again is negative in the sense that few new ideas are presented, and there is a lack of innovation or sharing of information, all of which leads to stagnation.

Conflict management also involves three levels of conflict. Clearly there could be conflict between or within the organization itself. There is also group conflict within the organization and individual conflict between individual members of the groups.

Generally it is considered that there are three kinds of conflict episodes, these are:

- latent conflict – which is behaviour which starts a conflict episode;
- manifest conflict – which is the observable conflict behaviour;
- conflict aftermath – which is the end of a conflict episode, and can become the latent conflict for another episode in the future.

Clearly, conflict management appears between the manifest conflict and the conflict aftermath, which seeks to lower the level of the conflict itself. A more complete view of the conflict episodes and the place of conflict management within this system can be seen in Figure 25.

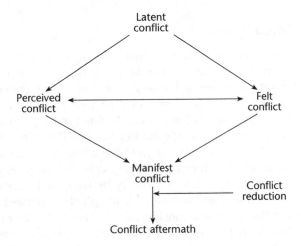

Figure 25   Aspects of a conflict episode

As can be seen in the diagram, perceived conflict occurs when individuals become aware that they are in conflict. Conflict can be perceived even when no latent conditions exist. A prime example is the misunderstanding of another indivudal's position on an issue. Felt conflict is the emotional or personalizing part of the conflict and is exemplified by oral or physical hostility. These are the hardest episodes for managers to control.

The various episodes may link the conflict aftermath to future latent conflict, and effective conflict management breaks this connection by discovering the latent conflicts and removing them. An ideal conflict management model, which would seek to maintain conflict at functional levels, would include the following:

- no complete elimination of conflict;
- an increase in dysfunctional low conflict;
- choosing a desired conflict level based on perceived conflict requirements;
- a tolerance towards conflict.

Mayer, Bernard S., *The Dynamics of Conflict Resolution: A Practitioner's Guide*. New York: Jossey Bass Wiley, 2000.

Congruence

See **goal congruence**.

Consolidated industry

Consolidation is a measure often applied to the study of particular industries. In the UK, for example, some 85 per cent of all retail sales are achieved by just 500 different businesses. It is therefore imperative for businesses to understand that in a competitive environment it is vital to understand the dynamics of the market. Highly consolidated industries are typified by a dominance of the market by a handful, relatively speaking, of businesses, which may appear to the consumer to be a broader range of businesses than they actually are. Consolidation has gradually been achieved in many areas of industry by large multinational businesses through mergers and acquisitions. In order to continue to present the perception that there is a considerable degree of choice and competition in a marketplace, these businesses have tended to retain old company names and continue to trade under these company names, despite the fact that they are enjoying all the **economies of scale** associated with a larger business enterprise.

Consumer-orientated business

Consumer or customer orientation is a marketing principle that aims to describe a business which views its entire operations in terms of the end-user. All product development, production, distribution and marketing are aimed at fulfilling consumer needs and wants. This is a marketing concept that is diametrically opposed to a product or production orientation, which seeks to find markets and persuade consumers to buy existing products and services that have not been initially designed to match their needs and wants.

Contingency approach

Robert Tannenbaum and Warner Schmidt were amongst the first researchers to look at and identify the various factors which influenced a manager's choice of leadership style. They decided that situational factors influence the form of leadership, in as much as the managers take into account practical considerations before making a management decision.

The contingency approach recognizes that managers need to distinguish between different sorts of problems. Some problems need to be resolved by themselves and others require a degree of collaboration. Tannenbaum and Schmidt suggested that there were three main forces that had an impact upon the leadership style of a manager:

- Personal forces – which include the manager's background, experience, inclinations and confidence.
- Subordinate characteristics – including their willingness to accept responsibility and to make decisions for themselves.
- Situation – which could include time pressures, the type of task, corporate culture or normal style of work.

They believed that, in effect, decisions could be made on a form of continuum which ranged from a very autocratic and authoritarian management style at one extreme, to a far more democratic style which allowed greater freedom for subordinates. As a consequence, decisions, according to the contingency approach, ranged from the manager making all the decisions, to the other extreme where the manager allowed subordinates an almost complete freedom of action.

Tannenbaum, R. and Schmidt, W. H., 'How to Choose a Leadership Pattern', *Harvard Business Review*, May–June 1973.

Continuity plan

A continuity plan, as the term suggests, is a form of contingency plan which aims to place the business in a position to recover quickly in the event of a disaster. Disasters could range from severe damage or destruction of the business and its information systems, to the loss of a vital or pivotal member of staff.

Business continuity plans aim to support the business and are an integral part of an ongoing risk assessment and risk management with the purpose of ensuring that the business could continue should these risks materialize. A continuity plan is not simply concerned with disaster recovery; it could affect the continuity of a business in many different situations, such as a staff shortage in a specialist area. Continuity means that the business needs to continue to deliver, and move towards its business objectives, even if things do go wrong.

Normally a business will appoint a Continuity Management Coordinator, who will understand how the business is structured and the people involved, and will have good communication and interpersonal skills. Obviously any continuity plan, often known as a business continuity plan (BCP), must be endorsed by the senior management and tested on a regular basis. The key stages of business continuity management are:

- to understand the business;
- to formulate continuity strategies;
- to develop a response;
- to implement a continuity culture;
- to test the plan through maintenance and auditing.

www.business-continuity-world.com

Core competence

Core competences have two specific definitions. The first is the identification of the key skills, knowledge and experience required of an individual to perform a specific job role.

The other definition refers to the ability of employees or managers to be adaptable in the sense that they could work in an alternative, remote location, such as abroad. In these cases core competences examine the adaptability and resourcefulness of the managers when operating in what may be an unknown overseas environment.

Stone, Florence M. and Sachs, Randi T., *High-value Manager: Developing the Core Competences Your Organization Demands.* New York: Amacom, 1996.

See also **competence**.

Corporate culture

Corporate culture is taken to be the beliefs, values, norms and traditions of an organization which directly affect the behaviour of its members. Each organization has its own unique culture and many businesses are conscious of this culture, which may be based on a sense of community or another fundamental driving force. It is widely believed that there are five different forms of diverse corporate culture, as shown in Table 15.

Table 15   Forms of corporate culture

Corporate culture orientation	Explanation
Individual versus collective	The business determines the appropriate level at which behaviour needs to be regulated.
Power distance	How less powerful members of the organization accept and adhere to the distribution of power within the organization.
Uncertainty avoidance	The degree to which rules, long-term employment prospects and the possibility of progression exist and whether employees are unsure of how to deal with particular situations.
Dominant values	Whether a formal structure, based on well-defined roles, is at variance with employees' desire to have quality relationships, job satisfaction and work flexibility.
Short-term versus long-term	Whether the focus is upon short-term performance or longer-term relationships, and the desire to take an extended view of achievement.

Schein, Edgar H., *The Corporate Culture Survival Guide*. New York: Jossey-Bass, 1999.

See also **Hofstede, Geert.**

Corporate strategy

Corporate strategy can be seen as an overarching strategy put in place by a business, encompassing the deployment of its resources. Corporate strategy is used to move the business towards its goals in the various areas of its activities, including production, finance, research and development, personnel and marketing.

Lynch, Richard, *Corporate Strategy*. London: Financial Times, Prentice-Hall, 2002.

Cost leadership strategy

Cost leadership strategy, although it is regarded more as a generic marketing strategy, has considerable implications for human resource management. Cost leadership strategy aims to provide the business with a competitive advantage by lowering the costs of its operation. This can inevitably mean that since the drive is towards increased profitability, via the reduction in costs, leading to a reduction in prices, there will be pressure on employees in many different areas of their work. Clearly, either a policy can be adopted which seeks to reduce the overall demands on the business in terms of pay, which can involve a reduction in the workforce, or it may require each individual to show a higher level of productivity and a greater contribution towards profit. Another inevitable implication is the use of outsourced labour in order to provide products and services at a lower cost than could be achieved by employing a workforce directly. Businesses will seek to find means by which the human resource department can identify cost savings, either by reducing staff numbers, by job enlargement or by **multi-skilling**.

Pohlmann, Randolph; Gardiner, Gareth S. and Heffes, Ellen M., *Value Driven Management: How to Create and Maximize Value over Time for Organizational Success.* New York: Amacom, 2000.

Cost–benefit analysis

Cost–benefit analysis is a technique which seeks to assess the value of the benefits of a particular course of action and then subtract any costs associated with it. The majority of benefits are received over a period of time, whilst costs may be either one-off episodes or ongoing costs. In effect, cost–benefit analysis allows a business to work out a payback period for a particular course of action.

In its simplest form, cost–benefit analysis can use only financial costs and financial benefits. This would make it easy for a business to assess and analyse the costs and benefits associated with any particular scheme. Restricting the analysis to purely financial aspects does not mean that all costs and benefits have been assessed, as there may be human-resource, environmental, production, or a host of other costs and benefits which have not been taken into the equation. Therefore a more sophisticated approach to this form of analysis can attempt to put a financial value on what would be intangible costs and benefits, although this is notoriously subjective.

Cost–benefit analysis can be a powerful tool, particularly if the intangible items are incorporated within the analysis.

Brent, Robert J., *Applied Cost-Benefit Analysis*. Aldershot: Edward Elgar, 1996.

Cost-plus pricing

The cost-plus pricing method is one of the most common forms of pricing policy, it is also one of the more straightforward forms. The pricing methodology simply involves adding a predetermined percentage or gross figure to the costs of production or purchase, thereby creating a price point for the product or the service.

This basic form of pricing does not individually take into account current market conditions and is in many cases considered to be too prescriptive in its structure for standard use. Despite this, many base prices are calculated on this cost-plus assumption.

Counter measure

Counter measures are steps which a business may choose to take in order to offset a negative impact on business operations. Businesses will inevitably have assessed particular risks or the likelihood of particular events occurring, such as the arrival of a new and vigorous competitor in a particular market. Counter measures seek to provide the basis for a measured response to a particular risk or threat to the business. Whilst these may have been framed already, the business needs to be sure that the counter measures being considered are appropriate in the particular circumstances which now present themselves.

Covey, Stephen

Stephen Covey, a management and leadership guru, is perhaps best known for his book *The Seven Habits of Highly Effective People*, which has sold over 1.5 million copies. His seven habits are highly applicable to managers. They are:

- Being proactive, in the sense that the managers need to control their own environment, using self-determination and the power to respond to various circumstances.
- Always looking towards the end of a situation – this means that the manager needs to be able to see the desired outcome and concentrate on activities which help in achieving that end.

C

- Organization – in the sense that managers need to personally manage themselves and implement activities which aim to achieve the second habit – looking to the desired outcome. Covey suggests that everything should begin with that second habit and then move to this third habit – organization.
- Seeing the benefits for all – Covey suggests that this is the most important aspect of interpersonal leadership because most achievements are based on cooperative effort, therefore the aim needs to be win–win solutions for all.
- Understanding – by developing and maintaining positive relationships through good communications, the manager can be understood, and can understand the subordinates.
- Synergy – Covey cites this as being creative cooperation, in the sense that collaboration often achieves more than could be achieved by individuals working independently towards attaining a goal.
- Self-renewal – learning from previous experience and encouraging others to do the same. Covey sees development as one of the most important aspects in being able to cope with challenges and aspire to higher levels of ability.

Covey, Stephen, *The Seven Habits of Highly Effective People.* New York: Fireside, 1989.

www.franklincovey.com

Crisis management

For most organizations, crisis management is unavoidable in situations where the business's survival or well-being is threatened by an unexpected problem. Most organizations will have established a series of contingency plans in order to ensure that specific steps have been outlined to deal with similar, predicted situations. In most cases the business will appoint an individual, probably from the board or senior management, to deal with the situation. This individual will be given the full support of the board and may be granted considerably more sweeping authority in order to deal with the crisis. Swift decision making is essential in crisis management as immediate remedies are required in order to ensure the business's continued survival.

Fink, Steven, *Crisis Management: Planning for the Inevitable.* Lincoln, NE: Universal Publishers, 2000.

Critical path analysis

A critical activity is a major event on a critical path. A critical chain is a means by which an organization can look at the full duration of a particular project, and is considered to be somewhat more all-inclusive than a critical path. The critical chain not only addresses the issues which a critical path considers, but also takes into account any factors relating to the supply of products or components prior to the commencement of the production process itself. A critical chain would consider start and finish times, as well as any slack periods. The longest total time through these stages is known as the critical path. The critical chain seeks to assign the resources required for each part of the process and recognizes the fact that the next stage cannot be undertaken until the resources required for that task are made available. The critical chain then identifies all of the stages in the process until the schedule has been completed. In this respect, a critical chain is somewhat longer than a critical path. In addition, the critical chain incorporates time buffers, with the aim of protecting the activities on the critical chain from beginning later than is desirable.

Alongside a critical chain, a non-critical chain would also be constructed, to ensure that activities which could have an impact on the critical chain are planned in such a way that they do not cause an interruption.

A critical path is the longest possible path through which a project has to pass in order to be completed. The critical path identifies crucial activities in the stages of dealing with, or managing, a particular project, identifying in effect the worst case scenario in order to make a clearer estimation of the time a project will take to complete. The critical path aims to focus the organization's attention on the activities which are essential to ensure the completion of the project.

The critical path method (CPM) begins with the start time for a particular project. It then proceeds to identify the earliest possible start times and finish times for each activity which is required to complete the overall project (see Figure 26). Once this has been completed, the CPM seeks to work backwards from the date by which the project needs to be completed and amends the start times of all of the activities in relation to this date. The critical path is the pathway which has the minimum amount of slack time. This critical path is then given priority in terms of attention and allocation of resources, aiming to reduce the overall project time.

The CPM should also assist the business in being able to identify aspects or activities in the process which can be either rolled together or speeded up in order to have a positive impact on the overall project completion time.

C

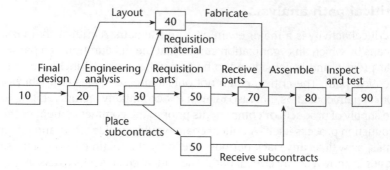

Figure 26 Example of a critical path

Busch, Dennis H., *New Critical Path Method: CPM – The State-of-the-Art in Project Modeling and Time Reserve Management*. Chicago, IL: Probus Professional Publishing, 1990.

Latino, R. J. and Latino, K. C., *Root Cause Analysis: Improving Performance for Bottom Line Results*. Boca Raton, FL: Interpharm CRC, 1999.

Leach, Lawrence P., *Critical Chain Project Management*. London: Artech House, 2000.

Critical success factors (CSFs)

A business may identify critical success factors (CSFs) as a means by which it can help determine its own strategic objectives. Each of the major objectives has associated CSFs, which in theory should be achieved *en route* to the principal objective or objectives. In other words, these CSF criteria are major milestones along a continuing process towards the objectives as identified by the business.

Sashkin, Molly G. and Sashkin, Marshall, *Leadership that Matters: The Critical Factors for Making a Difference in People's Lives and Organizations' Success*. San Francisco, CA: Berrett-Koehler Publishers, 2003.

Current ratio

The current ratio is used as an indicator of whether a business has the ability to meet its short-term debt obligations. Typically, it is calculated by dividing the current assets by the current liabilities.

The current assets include all cash, or assets which can be easily converted into cash (stock, debtors etc.). By dividing the current assets by the current liabilities, a business will be able to assess the amount of coverage it may have available to meet its short-term debt obligations.

For example, a business may have current assets valued at £950,000 and its current liabilities may run to £450,000. Using the current ratio, the business can then calculate the following:

$$\frac{950,000}{450,000} = 2.11$$

This figure can be expressed as 2.11:1. The ratio shows that the business has £2.11 of current assets for every £1.00 of current liabilities. If the industry standard current ratio was, for example, 2:2, then this business would be considered to have a satisfactory current ratio.

Fridson, Martin and Alvarez, Fernando, *Financial Statement Analysis: A Practitioner's Guide.* New York: John Wiley & Sons, 2002.

Temple, Peter, *Magic Numbers: The 33 Key Ratios that Every Investor Should Know.* New York: John Wiley & Sons, 2001.

Customer defection rate

According to the American Management Association, the majority of profits of a business are earned from their loyal customers and typically loyal customers account for 65% of an organization's revenue. They further suggest that a cut in the customer defection rate of 5% could lead to a profit increase of between 25% and 85%. In other words, by reducing the number of customers lost to competitors, a business could double its growth in a year.

Given the fact that new customers cost five times as much to obtain as the cost of retaining a current customer, businesses are increasingly concerned with customer retention figures. Having said this, the vast majority of businesses do not know their own customer defection rate.

Typically, businesses will put off improving their services to customers until it looks as if the customers are going to defect to another business; usually by this time it is too late and the decision has already been made. As a result, database marketing seeks to identify average customer behaviours and, in effect, set up a 'trip-wire' event which will lead the business to believe that a customer is considering defecting to a competitor.

Customer relationship management (CRM)

Customer relationship management is based on the assumption that there is a relationship between the business or the brand and the customer. This is a relationship that needs to be managed, both through the individual buying stages and in the longer term.

CRM is very much related to fostering customer loyalty and, in the longer term, customer retention.

CRM can be used in call-centre support and direct marketing operations; software systems assist in the support of customer service representatives and give customers alternative means by which they can communicate with the business (such as mail, email, telephone etc.). Some sophisticated CRM software programs have email response systems which process incoming emails and determine whether they warrant a personal response or an automated response. Recent figures indicate that systems such as this can handle around half of the requests from customers (typically, requests for additional information or passwords, and responses to emails sent by marketing departments).

Other CRM software systems allow customer representatives to take part in live chat rooms or co-browsing, offering the business a less formal environment in which to make contact with customers. CRM software can also queue customers on the basis of their profiles, by requesting that the customer logs into the website; it is then possible to pass the customer on to individuals in the customer service team who may be better suited to deal with customers who share similar profiles. CRM software also provides the means to maintain and update a database of information about each customer (in other words, a case history).

Customer response time

Customer response time is a measure of a business's ability to provide products or services to its customers. Customer response time is also known as 'waiting time in line' (WTIL). Waiting time in line describes the usually non-productive time which customers have to wait before being served or processed. There are, essentially, three costs that must be balanced in a waiting-line system: the cost of service and the cost of waiting as well as the cost of a scheduling system. Theoretically, a scheduling system is a management strategy designed to avoid waiting lines.

In cases where the cost of service and the cost of waiting are known and measurable, the organization can attempt to determine the optimal, or close to optimal, waiting-system configuration and rate of service. However, the cost of service has a positive relationship with the rate of service; conversely, the cost of waiting has a negative relationship with the rate of service. In other words, the faster the service rate, the higher the cost of service, and the faster the service rate, the lower the cost of waiting. The opposite applies with a slower service rate, meaning a lower cost of service but a higher cost of waiting.

Chen, H. and Yao, D. D., *Fundamentals of Queuing Networks: Performance, Asymptotics and Optimization* (Applications of Mathematics). New York: Springer-Verlag, 2001.

Dshalalow, Jewgeni H. (ed.), *Advances in Queuing: Models, Methods and Problems*. Boca Raton, FL: Interpharm CRC, 1995.

Customer responsiveness

Customer responsiveness is a measure of a business's ability not just to identify, but also to satisfy the needs or requirements of its customers. Various reports suggest that up to 40% of businesses fail to respond to even simple customer requests. In a survey carried out by RDMP in 2003, 250 of the top 500 FTSE businesses, including those in finance, insurance, communications, utilities and manufacturing, who had collectively spent £16.5 billion a year on advertising, failed in basic consumer responsiveness measures. Some 92% failed to re-contact a customer who had made an initial enquiry, and only 24% of enquiries were replied to within 24 hours. In spite of the rise and importance of websites, some 66% of these businesses failed to respond to consumers who had requested information or asked questions via their websites.

www.computerweekly.com/article122826.htm

Customization

Customization is a trend that has been slowly developing over recent years, and aims to create bespoke products and services which more closely match the exact needs and wants of the customers.

Traditionally, customization and low costs were mutually exclusive; the period of mass production meant that unit costs could be driven down at the expense of providing specifically for customer needs. Uniformity was the key word. In order for customers to purchase bespoke products and services, a premium price was charged by specialists or small suppliers.

Interactive technologies, such as the Internet, now allow customers to purchase products and services to their own specifications by automated systems. This means that customers can be encouraged to specify their exact requirements, for which an additional, but not crippling, extra charge is levied. This allows marketing activities to revolve around this aspect of the offering, focusing on the personalized nature of the product or service. The process has also become known as 'mass customization' as, in point of fact, the specifications are often prescriptive and the variations from the norm not as wide as one would expect to be the case.

Kelly, Sean, *Data Warehousing: The Route to Mass Customisation*. Chichester: John Wiley, 1996.

Dd

Day's sales outstanding

The day's sales outstanding (DSO) is calculated by dividing the total amount owed to a business by the sales achieved per day. Businesses simply calculate the daily sales by dividing their annual sales (on credit) by 365.

If a business has a yearly turnover of £1,000,000 then the daily sales figure is £2,739.70. If the business is currently owed some £10,000 then the calculation is:

$$\frac{10,000}{2,739.7} = 3.65$$

Should the business improve this DSO then it simply multiplies the amount still owed by the percentage improvement in the collections. It would then subtract the resulting figure from the amount still owed, before repeating the DSO calculation.

In the US, DSO is calculated per quarter, in which case the formula is: the accounts receivable divided by the sales and then divided by 91.

Debt to assets ratio

The debt to total assets ratio seeks to measure the extent to which lenders and creditors are contributing to the financing (of the assets) of a business. The debt to total assets ratio is:

$$Debt/total\ assets = \frac{Total\ debt\ (long\text{-}/short\text{-}term)}{Total\ assets\ (fixed\ and\ current)} \times 100$$

A business may have a total debt of some £2,100,000 and fixed and current assets currently valued at £5,700,000. Its ratio looks like this:

$$\frac{2,100,000 \times 100}{5,700,000} = 36.84\%$$

This particular ratio reveals that lenders and creditors are contributing nearly 37% of the total funds which the business has used to finance the purchase of its assets.

Fridson, Martin and Alvarez, Fernando, *Financial Statement Analysis: A Practitioner's Guide*. New York: John Wiley, 2002.

Temple, Peter, Magic Numbers: *The 33 Key Ratios that Every Investor Should Know*. New York: John Wiley, 2001.

Debt to equity ratio

The debt to equity ratio is primarily concerned with the relative contribution of debts and equities (for ordinary shareholders) in financing the operations of a business. The ratio is:

$$Debt\ to\ equity\ ratio = \frac{total\ debt\ (long\text{-}\ and\ short\text{-}term\ liabilities)}{total\ equity\ (ordinary\ share\ capital\ plus\ reserves)}$$

If a business had a total debt of some £2,100,000 and a total equity of £3,600,000 then the ratio would be:

$$Debt\ to\ equity\ ratio = \frac{2,100,000}{3,600,000} = 0.58$$

This means that for every £1 which has been contributed by equity shareholders, the lenders and creditors have contributed £0.58. The higher the ratio, the less protected the lenders.

Fridson, Martin and Alvarez, Fernando, *Financial Statement Analysis: A Practitioner's Guide*. New York: John Wiley, 2002.

Temple, Peter, *Magic Numbers: The 33 Key Ratios that Every Investor Should Know*. New York: John Wiley, 2001.

Decentralization

Decentralization involves a gradual dispersal of decision-making control across an organization. Integral to the dispersal of decision making is the movement of power and authority from the higher levels of management, or a single headquarters unit, to various divisions, branches, departments or subsidiaries of the organization. At its very core, decentralization implies **delegation**, by transferring the responsibility and power from senior management to individuals at lower levels. The purpose of decentralization is to encourage flexibility and, above all, assist faster decision making, which, in turn, means faster response times.

Decentralization is also strongly associated with the concept of empowerment, affording to frontline staff the power, authority and responsibility of making immediate decisions without reference to senior management.

D

Decision support system

Decision support systems are usually a computerized series of flexible menus which include models and decision aids that can be used in conjunction with current and relevant data. These support systems are designed to assist managerial decision making at all levels of an organization.

Decision tree

Decision trees are tools which assist managers in deciding between several different courses of action. As graphical representations of the options, they can be used to investigate the outcomes that would be associated with the choosing of different options. Decision trees can therefore be used to form a balanced picture.

In order to create a decision tree, a small box is drawn at the left-hand side of the page. Lines are then extended to the right, which relate to each possible solution or option. The name or description of the solution is written along the line. At the end of each line a circle may be drawn if the result of taking that decision is unclear. Alternatively, if the initial option leads to another decision needing to be made, another square is drawn and the procedure is repeated and continued. Squares on a decision tree represent decisions, and circles represent uncertain outcomes.

It is now possible to note on each of the lines what each of the options means. All of the possible options can now be compared. Normally a business or a manager would assign a cash value or a score to each possible outcome. At each of the points represented by a circle, an estimate of the probability of the outcome needs to be calculated. These can either be fractions which add up to 1, or percentages.

Once the value of each of the outcomes has been calculated, the actual values of the decisions or options can be calculated in monetary terms. An example of a decision tree is shown in Figure 27, offering answers to the question: Should we open a new outlet in London or refurbish our existing one?

The calculations therefore are:

Full refit
$$0.6 \times £150,000 = £90,000$$
$$0.2 \times £100,000 = £20,000$$
$$0.2 \times £50,000 = £10,000$$
$$\overline{£120,000}$$

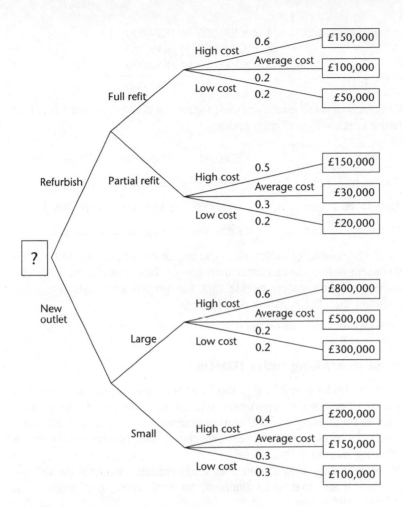

Figure 27 Example of a decision tree

Partial refit   0.5 × £50,000 = £25,000
                 0.3 × £30,000 = £9,000
                 0.2 × £20,000 = £4,000
                                  ─────────
                                  £38,000

Large new outlet   0.6 × £800,000 = £480,000
                    0.2 × £500,000 = £100,000
                    0.2 × £300,000 = £60,000
                                     ─────────
                                     £640,000

Small new outlet
$$0.4 \times £200,000 = £80,000$$
$$0.3 \times £150,000 = £45,000$$
$$0.3 \times £100,000 = £30,000$$
$$£155,000$$

Using the following maximum-cost figures, it is now possible to calculate the cost savings of each option:

Full refit   £150,000 – £120,000 =   £30,000

Partial refit   £50,000 –   £38,000 =   £12,000

New large outlet   £800,000 – £640,000 = £160,000

New small outlet   £200,000 – £155,000 =   £45,000

Clearly, the new large outlet offers the greatest cost savings, but the full investment is four times higher than any of the other alternatives. The business may ultimately decide that the investment costs are more significant than the apparent cost savings.

www.mindtools.com/dectree.html

Decision-making units (DMUs)

A decision-making unit is a group of people, usually taken to mean a business or perhaps a department, who make collective decisions with regard to purchasing. A DMU can, of course, be a household, although the term is usually more closely associated with business-to-business marketing and sales.

Stereotypically, a DMU would have individuals who fulfil the following roles: a specifier, an influencer, an authorizer, a gatekeeper, a purchaser and a user.

D

Decline stage

This is the final stage of the standard product life cycle. As sales decline, the business has several options:

- maintain the product, possibly by adding new features and finding new uses;
- try to reduce costs and continue to offer the product, possibly to a loyal segment;
- discontinue the product, selling off any remaining stock (if it is a product) or selling it to another business that is willing to continue the product.

An alternative to accepting the inevitable end of a product's life cycle is to consider re-launching the product, perhaps with a new image or identity. Many businesses will, however, either consider terminating the product entirely, or perhaps take the option of dumping the product (often continuing its production) in another country.

De-layering

De-layering is a concept primarily related to the 1990s, which saw businesses move to 'flatten' their **organizational structure**. This is achieved by effectively stripping out a number of layers of management in the organization. It became synonymous with a reduction in bureaucracy, faster decision making, shorter communication channels and fostering high-involvement management.

The majority of organizations considered that in de-layering they would cut their overheads and for many this was the principal motivation. For others, the flatter organization represented **teamwork** and high-involvement working practices.

Flatter organizations are achieved by:

- eliminating or automating management activities (which leads to these posts becoming redundant);
- reducing and reallocating unnecessary and costly overlaps of accountability.

There is no ideal way of undertaking the process, but the key influencing factors are:

- the pace of the de-layering;
- the extent of the imposition of the de-layering;
- the degree of employee involvement in the process;
- the degree of organizational re-design and analysis required.

The major aspects in attaining the benefits of de-layering are:

- form should follow function;
- provided de-layering eliminates situations where management does not add value, the process is credible;
- loss of hierarchies could mean that new hierarchies must take their place;
- new accountabilities must be clarified;
- the commitment of employees must be won;
- performance indicators must be in place, and pilot de-layering is desirable;

D

• management delivers the de-layering, but is also the target of it, and will require additional support.

Keuning, Doede and Opheij, Wilfred, *Delayering Organisations: How to Beat Bureaucracy and Create a Flexible and Responsive Organisation.* Woodslane, Australia, 1994.

Delegation

Delegation is not only an issue for management in general, but also of considerable importance to the management of human resources, as it involves the active use of the skills and experience of employees in subordinate positions. Delegation usually begins with the identification of an individual suitable to perform a particular task. This person needs to be prepared, and, above all, given the authority, to carry out the job properly. Delegation does mean that the manager needs to support and monitor progress and, once the task is completed, to acknowledge that the job has been completed successfully.

Delegation is a means by which pressured key members of staff can reduce their workload in the certain knowledge that vital tasks will still be performed. It is not always possible to delegate all tasks to other individuals, but delegation can mean greater efficiency, increased **motivation**, skill development and, above all, a more equitable distribution of work throughout a team.

Smart, J. K., *Real Delegation: How to Get People to Do Things for You – and Do Them Well.* New York: Prentice Hall, 2002.

Deming, William Edwards

William Edwards Deming was born in Sioux City, Iowa, on 14 October 1900. In 1921, he graduated in electrical engineering. In 1925, he received an MSc at the University of Colorado, and in 1928, a PhD from Yale. Deming is perhaps best known for his work in Japan; from 1950 he taught management and engineers methods of managing quality. He died in 1993.

Deming's 'fourteen points' aimed to identify key success drivers derived from industry leaders. The fourteen points are designed to be applicable to any situation and any type of business. They are, therefore, applicable to both manufacturing and service-based industries. The fourteen points are:

1 Create constancy of purpose towards improvement of products and service, with three aims: to become efficient and profitable; stay in business; and provide employment.

2 Recognize that the business is operating in a new age (as indeed it always is to this day). Management needs to be aware of these challenges and adopt a policy of leading change.

3 Eliminate the policy of inspection in order to achieve quality. Build quality into the product from the earliest stages in order to eliminate the need to carry out inspections.

4 Instead of making outsourcing and supplier decisions purely on the basis of price, aim to minimize total costs. This can be achieved by forging a long-term relationship based on loyalty and trust, with one or a few suppliers.

5 Improve production and service levels, and productivity and quality will follow and also reduce overall costs.

6 Introduce on-the-job training as a means to increase productivity, job satisfaction and quality.

7 Introduce leadership by ensuring that anyone in a supervisory or management position focuses on helping the workforce to do their jobs more effectively.

8 Ensure that there is no fear in the organization, as this does not assist the workforce in performing effectively, as they are concerned about their jobs and how they are treated by the management.

9 Encourage cross-departmental cooperation by breaking down barriers; all areas should work as a team in order to see problems before they occur.

10 Eliminate demands for zero defects, as the causes of defects are often beyond the power of the employees. Zero-defect demands are empty statements if not supported by the management through ensuring that the workforce has materials of sufficient quality. Zero-defect demands simply lead to adversarial relationships.

11 Eliminate work standards such as quotas and substitute effective leadership. Eliminate concepts such as management by objectives, numbers or numerical goals and substitute these with effective leadership.

12 Eliminate the use of quotas in relation to the performance of hourly paid workers as this robs them of any hope of being able to display craftsmanship. Substitute this with the concept of quality rather than numbers. Equally, eliminate annual or merit ratings base on productivity and substitute with rewards for sustained quality.

13 Ensure that the entire workforce has an opportunity to improve their knowledge, skills and education.

14 Ensure that the entire workforce is involved in transforming the business; transformation is not a management responsibility or interest alone.

These points have achieved a level of reverence commensurate to that accorded the Ten Commandments; their corollaries are Deming's seven deadly sins:

1 lack of constancy of purpose;
2 emphasis on short-term profits;
3 personal review systems;
4 mobility of management;
5 use of visible figures only for management;
6 excessive medical costs;
7 excessive costs of liability.

These rules together are used in what is called a 'plan, do, check and act (PDCA) cycle'.

Deming, W. Edwards, *Out of the Crisis: Quality, Productivity and Competitive Position.* Cambridge, MA: MIT PRESS, 2000.

The W. Edwards Deming Institute: www.deming.org/

Departmentalization

Many organizations use departmentalization in order to concentrate specific expertise or operational functions into a single, common structure. Many departmentalized organizations have somewhat centralized authority and tend to have a rather bureaucratic view of decision making. Within each department there is a recognized hierarchical structure, which controls aspects such as personnel or marketing for the whole of the organization. In effect, a department could be considered to be an individual operating unit which has full responsibility for its own management. This latter version of departmentalization implies that the organization is somewhat **decentralized** in as much as the department has power and authority to carry out its functions without necessarily referring to senior management.

DePree, Max

Max DePree has written extensively on leadership, notably in *Leadership is an Art*. DePree suggests that the most effective leaders are those who promote:

- empowerment;
- teamwork;
- coaching.

He sees these aspects as the corner-stones of knowledge management.

DePree, Max, *Leadership is an Art*. New York: Bantam Doubleday, Dell Publishing Group, 1990.

www.depree.org

Deskilling

Deskilling is the process by which division of labour and technological development may lead to a reduction of the scope of an employee's specialized tasks. Work becomes fragmented and employees lose the integrated skills and knowledge associated with a craftsperson. Deskilling has been seen as a negative impact of technology whereby a process or machine can perform a task better than the human hand.

Harry Braverman wrote a Marxist critique of capitalism and, in particular, the organization of work under 'antagonistic' social relations. He was concerned with the loss of craft skills in the organization of work. He was one of the first theorists to define the term as 'deskilling', which he described as being the effective separation of mental work and manual work. Deskilling is closely associated with scientific management and is seen as a means by which management can closely control the labour process, in the sense that it removes the skills, knowledge and science of the labour process and transfers these to management. An additional concern is that it can mean that manual and mental workers feel diametrically opposed to one another.

Braverman went on to suggest that deskilling leads to decomposition (the dispersal of the labour process across numerous sites and time) and that as such, deskilling increases the opportunities for management to exploit labour and reduce the capacity of workers to resist their control.

Both Frederick Taylor and Henry Ford were deeply involved in early attempts to deskill and initiate decomposition. As scientific management practitioners they attempted to transform the organization of work to improve profitability and to reduce craft skills' control of work. The terms 'Fordism' and 'Taylorism' are closely associated with the use of the assembly-line. Fordism itself attempts to harmonize the dual desires of mass production and mass consumption.

Deskilling therefore involves the following:

1 the maximum decomposition of the labour process as a series of work tasks across time and space;

2 the separation of direct and indirect labour;
3 the minimization of skill in any work task;
4 the creation of standardized products;
5 the use of specialized machine tools (as opposed to general purpose machine tools);
6 the use of the assembly-line and methods of continuous production (at a pace set by management and not by the workforce).

Braverman, Harry, *Labor and Monopoly Capitalism: The Degradation of Work in the Twentieth Century*. New York: Monthly Review Press, 1999.
Taylor, Frederick Winslow, *The Principles of Scientific Management*. Mineola, NY: Dover Publications, 1998.

See also **labour process approach.**

Dialectic enquiry

Where there are irreconcilable analyses of situations, a formal structure known as 'dialectic enquiry' can be employed. Aided by facilitators, the group concerned can identify the assumptions behind their options, and then all of the participants will attempt to arrive at a negotiated settlement or conclusion. In effect, this is a compromise, preferably a synergistic synthesis of opinion which integrates all the differing viewpoints.

Attempts to reconcile the opinions will fail if the manager intentionally, or unintentionally, encourages the continuance of the holding of diametrically opposed views, with no compromise.

Mitroff, I. I., Emshoff, J. R. and Kilmann, R. H., 'Assumptional Analysis: a Methodology for Strategic Problem Solving', *Management Science*, 25 (1979), pp. 583–93.

Diamond

See **Porter's diamond.**

D

Differentiated marketing

Differentiated marketing is a partner strategy to differential pricing, as it provides the means by which different markets or customer groups that are offered the same product at different prices, learn about the product. Differentiated marketing is also a broader issue as it addresses a business's need to target several markets simultaneously and create versions of the same product or service for each of those market segments.

Differentiation strategy

The purpose of differentiation strategy is to achieve a **competitive advantage** by creating a product or service that is, essentially, perceived to be unique in some way. In achieving differentiation, a business is able to charge a premium for its products and services.

Businesses which seek to produce differentiated products or services tend to aim for a high level of differentiation and produce a wide range of these products and services. Differentiation can also be achieved with innovation, technological competence, superior after-sales service, distribution and other key customer service functions.

Differentiation has the following advantages:

- Potential entrants to the market must develop unique products to compete.
- Differentiated businesses have a high level of **brand loyalty**.
- The threat of competitors is only based on their ability to produce truly substitute products and services.

The following disadvantages relate to differentiation:

- The business must maintain the perception of uniqueness in the eyes of the customer.
- The business must continue to innovate in order not to be caught by its competitors.
- Uniqueness could be eliminated as a factor by a change in customer tastes and demands.
- The business needs to be aware of new marketing opportunities at all times, to exploit its uniqueness.

Aaker, David A., *Brand Portfolio Strategy: Creating Relevance, Differentiation, Energy, Leverage and Clarity*. New York: Free Press, 2004.

Discounted cash flow

Discounted cash flow is an investment appraisal method which seeks to investigate capital investment projects and compare their income as depicted in forecasted **cash flows**, together with their present and future costs in comparison with other equivalents. These other equivalents, or current equivalents, aim to take into account the fact that any future incomes are less valuable than current receipts. This is due to the fact that the interest which could be earned on current receipts could be used to offset any current payments. Discounted cash flow seeks to discover whether capital outlays will generate positive cash inflows in the future. Each of the cash inflows is multiplied by a discount factor which is set between 0 and 1 (because money at a future date is worth less to the business than the same sum of money, should they have it to hand now). The business may have to wait a considerable time for any future inflows of capital, which inevitably means that these future sums are worth less than the equivalent amount of money in the present day.

Once the business has discounted these figures the future cash flows can be totalled. This gives the business the opportunity to assess the capital outlay by deducting this figure to give the net present value of the project. If the figure arrived at is positive, then comparatively speaking the project is a viable one. If it is a negative figure, then the business should seriously consider whether the project is worth pursuing.

In the following example, which incorporates both the discount factor and the discounted cash flow, these assumptions can be made:

- A new printing press has cost the business £2 million.
- It has been estimated that the printing press will be a viable asset for four years.
- In each year the printing press will cost £200,000 to run, but will save the business £800,000 in labour costs.
- The business has assessed that the interest rate and therefore the discount factors run at 10%.

It is therefore possible to assemble a table in order to complete the calculations (see Table 16).

Table 16 Sample cash flow table

Year	Cash in (£)	Cash out (£)	Net cash (£)	Discount factor	Net present value (£)
Current	–	2,000,000	(2,000,000)	1.00	(2,000,000)
1	800,000	200,000	600,000	0.91	546,000
2	800,000	200,000	600,000	0.83	498,000
3	800,000	200,000	600,000	0.75	450,000
4	800,000	200,000	600,000	0.68	408,000
					(98,000)

In this case, once the business has made the calculations as to the possible income and expenditure and adjusted these figures to take account of discounted cash flow, the project over the four-year period entailing the purchase of the new printing equipment is shown to represent a loss of £98,000. This would make the purchase of the printing machinery somewhat difficult to justify.

Wright, Maurice Gordon, *Using Discounted Cash Flow in Investment Appraisal*. London: McGraw-Hill Education – Europe, 1990.

Diseconomies of scale

Diseconomies of scale are said to be the point at which a manufacturing process simply becomes too large and the normal rule of **economies of scale** ceases to apply. In certain cases, as capacity continues to increase, the manufacturing organization may encounter the problem of average unit costs increasing, rather than falling. There are usually three reasons for this:

- Different stages within the manufacturing process may have already reached their optimum capacity and be unable to produce any more products, thus causing difficulties for other stages which are capable of a higher rate of production. This means that various sections of the production process are literally starved of parts and components by these bottlenecks.
- As the organization grows, there are attendant difficulties related to the coordination of activities. To support the manufacturing process there is an increase in administration and a proliferation of bureaucratic procedures which may inhibit the production process itself, whilst adding indirect costs to each unit of production.
- On the assumption that the capacity levels of the organization could, up to a point, be met by other organizations within a viable geographical area, as production increases the manufacturing organization may need to cast its net wider in order to secure a sufficient supply. It may also need to make compromises as to the lead times, quality and delivery costs of supplies from the additional suppliers. All of these issues will add costs overall, which in turn are applied to each unit of production.

Diseconomies of scale, therefore, occur as a mixture of internal and external diseconomies.

Distinctive competency

The term 'distinctive competency' is usually used to describe any specific specialisms or advantages which a manufacturing organization may possess. It is these distinct competences or abilities which mark the organization as having a competitive edge in a specific aspect of its operations.

Diversification

Diversification involves the movement of a business into a wider field of activity, with the primary objective of spreading the risks and reducing dependence on a single market or product range. Diversification can be achieved in a number of different ways, including the purchasing of other businesses already servicing targeted markets.

Businesses which are involved in diminishing markets, such as tobacco, or seasonal markets, such as ice creams, are keen to move into new areas in order to ensure their continued growth. Strategic decisions are made to either diversify through purchase or diversify through development of new areas within the business itself.

The key advantages include the improvement of the long-term survival prospects of a business, the movement away from a saturated marketplace in order to ensure sustained growth, and the provision of new opportunities for the business's existing skills and resources.

There are also clear disadvantages attached to diversification, which could include the business's failure to understand its new customers and market or the nature of the new competition. Diversification may also bring about **diseconomies of scale**, through being involved in too many different areas to enjoy true efficiency in any one aspect of the businesses operations. A business may also find that diversification weakens its core business, as it may be required to divert resources away from traditional areas in order to support the new business activities.

Dividend yield

The dividend yield is, in effect, the annual dividend per share, but expressed as a percentage of the current market price of that share. Given the fact that the share price fluctuates in the marketplace, a share which increases in value will see a proportionate fall in yield. Dividend yields are an important consideration for those who seek an income from their shares. The normal formula used is:

Dividend per share/market share price × *100* = *dividend yield*

If a share which has an average value of £20 over a given trading period pays out a dividend of £1, then using the formula the dividend yield is 5%. However, if the share falls to £10, yet still pays out £1 in dividends, the dividend yield has in fact increased to 10%. Conversely, if the share increases in value to £40, yet still pays out £1 in dividends, the dividend yield has fallen to 2.5%. It is normally the case that more established companies offer higher dividend yields, whilst younger companies that are still growing offer lower dividend yields. It is also the case that many smaller, growing businesses are unable to offer a dividend yield at all to their investors.

Spare, Anthony and Ciotti, Paul, *Relative Dividend Yield: Common Stock Investing for Income and Appreciation*. New York: John Wiley, 1999.

Division of labour

The term 'division of labour' refers to rigid and prescriptive allocation of work responsibilities. Formerly skilled employees were allocated specific job roles, and because of the complexity of their work, it was difficult to assign individuals who did not have the same degree of skill to those particular roles. Equally, the skilled individuals were keen to avoid any moves by the management to deskill their work and thus undermine their position. Division of labour therefore became a system by which different employees within a manufacturing organization could be identified and compensated in different ways. As the process of **multi-skilling** has swept manufacturing, coupled with the introduction of more complex technology, many of these former divisions have either disappeared or become blurred over time. None the less, division of labour can still be typified as instances where specific groups or teams of employees are allocated specific roles, and where only these individuals carry out that work.

See also **deskilling** *and* **labour process approach**.

Document management

Document management is an integral part of many businesses' desire to become a truly paperless, or document-less, office. Document management involves the transition from paper-based documentation to an electronic format. The system requires the availability of optical scanners and optical character recognition systems to convert paper-based documentation into an equivalent electronic format. Document management also requires a sophisticated form of database management, as an integral part of the transition from paper to digital document holding is the facility to search those electronic documents for key words, phrases and numerical sequences.

Dog

'Dog' is the label applied to one of the four parts of the **Boston growth matrix**. Poducts sold into segments in which the business is not one of the leaders, and in which the market is not growing, are classified as dog products. These products are likely to be in the mature phase of their product life cycle. Their markets exhibit slow, static or even negative growth. There will be little new business to compete for and any strategic moves to increase market share are likely to provoke vigorous competitive reaction.

Dogs may be linked to low profits, and the prognosis for investment is generally low. Unless some new competitive advantage can be introduced it is likely that these products or businesses will not be able to compete and will not attract the resources necessary to improve the product's position within the market. If future market demand is considered likely to last for some years, then the commercial risk of building market share may be worthwhile. Generally however, alternative more attractive investments could probably be found elsewhere. Therefore dogs should remain within the portfolio only so long as they contribute something to the business. Dog producers should provide:

- a positive cash flow;
- a contribution to overhead expenses;
- a strategic need.

If (as is often the case with dog products) the opportunity is moribund, decisive action should be taken, such as:

- diverting attention and resources to other segments that will provide a better return;
- focusing attention and resources on other segments which can be ring-fenced;
- maximizing cash flow from the product by reducing to a minimum all production and marketing costs;
- disposing of the product, selling the rights to the product or the business;
- dropping the product from the portfolio.

See also **Boston growth matrix**.

Double loop learning

Double loop learning was proposed by **Chris Argyris** and it relates to learning to change underlying values and assumptions. He believed that in solving complex and ill-structured problems, individuals can change the way in which they problem solve. In effect, double loop theory is based on the ability to learn while doing. Whilst the manager may be concentrating on the specific tasks in hand, or on carrying out the role of a leader, he or she is actually learning about the skills involved in leadership and management. Thus double loop learning means that a secondary learning process is being undertaken while the duties of a manager are being carried out. Effective problem solving is learned, provided the manager is involved in situations where there is an opportunity to examine and experiment with different ways of solving problems.

A simplistic managerial double loop learning experience is shown in the diagrams in Figure 28.

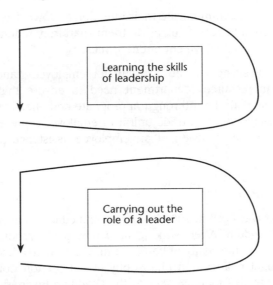

Figure 28 Double loop learning

Argyris, Chris, *Increasing Leadership Effectiveness*. New York: John Wiley & Sons, 1976.
Argyris, Chris and Schon, D., *Theory in Practice: Increasing Professional Effectiveness*. San Francisco, CA: Jossey-Bass Wiley, 1992.

See also **Argyris, Chris**.

Downsizing

The term 'downsizing' refers to an organization's need to streamline its activities, perhaps involving the closure of certain operations, along with the associated loss of employees engaged in those areas. Vital in the concept of downsizing is the quality, as opposed to the quantity, of employees.

The downsizing process needs planning by the human resource management as the implications are that some employees will be offered voluntary redundancy. Inevitably those that opt to take this method of dismissal will be those that are valued by the organization because they have the qualifications, skills and expertise that will potentially make them more attractive to competing organizations. Within the process of planning for downsizing, the human resource management would have to consider:

- the legal implications with regard to redundancy;
- the implications to the organization of losing key members of staff to competitors;
- how they will communicate their intention to downsize;
- what alternatives are available to them apart from redundancy, e.g. retraining or redeployment of employees.

Fear of downsizing can be stressful for employees, and the staff in the human resources department need to ensure that they are communicating with them through appropriate and effective channels. Certainly consultation with trade union or employee representatives is essential, as is the provision of an employee assistance programme (EAP).

Drucker, Peter

Peter Drucker was born in 1909 in Vienna and educated in Austria and the United Kingdom. After working as a newspaper reporter and an economist for an international bank, he moved to the United States in 1937. He taught politics and philosophy at Bennington College, then became professor of management at the Graduate Business School of New York University.

Since 1971 he has been Clarke Professor of Social Sciences at Claremont Graduate University (the graduate management school there was named after him in 1984). Drucker has received several honorary doctorates and is the Honorary Chairman of the Peter F. Drucker Foundation for Non-profit Management.

In the words of Peter Drucker, 'marketing is the entirety of the business from the perspective of the customer'. He also wrote that 'Marketing is so basic that it cannot be considered a separate function. . . . It is the whole business seen from the point of view of its final result, that is from a customer point of view.'

Drucker's main point is that marketing should be effective enough to make the process of selling superfluous.

Drucker, Peter, *The Essential Drucker: The Best Sixty Years of Peter Drucker's Essential Writings on Management*. New York: HarperCollins, 2003.

The Peter Drucker Foundation for Non-Profit Management can be found at www.pfdf.org

Dumbsizing

'Dumbsizing' refers to attempts by organizations to streamline, or engage in a **de-layering** process which strips out levels of management. Dumbsizing, whilst attempting to cut the fat from an organization, which would benefit the business in terms of cost saving, actually only succeeds in cutting out some of the organization's muscle in respect of critical functions and responsibilities no longer being covered.

Dumbsizing is also known as 'flattening' and can have serious and negative impacts on the business's ability to operate. It is also typified by a gradual, but severe, reduction in the overall workforce of an organization to such an extent that the business becomes not only inefficient but also unprofitable. It is a radical restructuring process which breaks many of the rules of considered and logical restructuring exercises.

D

Economies of scale

Strictly speaking, 'economies of scale' is an economics-related issue. However, it has considerable implications for operations management and production. The basic concept revolves around the fact that a business needs to build up a critical mass. Once a business has reached a point where it is a larger trading entity, it can enjoy many of the benefits associated with larger-scale production or distribution. In other words, as the size and scope of the business increases, the generally held view is that the unit costs are driven down. The corollary is that having achieved economies of scale, it has a greater amount of funds available to further improve the market position and efficiency of the business.

Jackson, Dudley, *Profitability, Mechanization and Economies of Scale*. Aldershot: Ashgate Publishing, 1998.

Economy of scope

'Economy of scope' is an economics term which puts forward the proposition that a business will enjoy a lower unit cost as it increases the variety of products it offers. Rather than receiving benefits associated with the basic form of **economies of scale**, the business derives advantages from the synergies (similarities) of the production of similar products. The unit costs are driven down by the fact that several products share the same resources and a number of components may be used which have a commonality, to produce this variety of products.

Ashton, John Kevin, *Cost Efficiency, Economies of Scale and Economies of Scope in the Retail Banking Sector*. Bournemouth: Bournemouth University School of Finance and Law, 1998.

Efficiency

Efficiency is measured by comparing the average time taken to carry out a particular process on a production line against a standard processing time. In other words, if a particular process normally has a standard time of 30 minutes per production unit and the current production time is actually 25 minutes, then the efficiency of that part of the process is $30/25 = 1.2$, which is normally expressed as a percentage, in which case this would be 120%.

Coelli, Tim, Prasada Rao, D. S. and Battese, George E., *An Introduction to Efficiency and Productivity Analysis*. Dordrecht: Kluwer Academic Publishers, 1997.

Wheelwright, Steven C. and Clark, Kim B., *Revolutionizing Product Development: Quantum Leaps in Speed, Efficiency and Quality*. New York: Free Press, 1992.

Embryonic industry

An embryonic industry is typified as being an industry which is only in its first stages of development. In the past, tourism, information technology, recycling, forestry management and a host of other industrial and service areas were described as being embryonic. If a business is considering entering an embryonic industry, this can represent a difficult situation. Often there are few rules, the expectations of customers are unclear and the exact extent of the competition is unknown.

Businesses that are part of an embryonic industry, therefore, have no distinct benchmarks upon which to base their structure or their business operations. Inevitably businesses tend to adopt approaches borrowed from industries that are broadly similar in some respect to their own business. Equally, existing or emerging embryonic industries tend to cluster around a specific area in a given country in order to enjoy **synergies** between businesses and to engage in **strategic alliances** where appropriate.

Emotional intelligence

The idea of emotional intelligence first hit businesses in the mid-1990s with Dan Goleman's books *Emotional Intelligence* and *Working with Emotional Intelligence*. Broadly, emotional intelligence is concerned with the intelligence that individuals have which assists them in understanding, managing and motivating others.

E

Currently Peter Salovey and John Mayer have studied personal, emotional and social abilities in relation to emotional intelligence, Howard Gardner has developed at least seven different types of intelligences, of which emotional intelligence is one. But it was Daniel Goleman's books, written by a psychologist and behavioural scientist, that noted that emotional intelligence was as important as IQ.

Goleman, Daniel, *Working with Emotional Intelligence*. London: Bloomsbury, 1999.

Goleman, Daniel, *The New Leaders: Emotional Intelligence at Work*. New York: Little Brown, 2002.

Empathy

An empathetic manager attempts to listen to and respect a subordinate's feelings and values. This requires managers to be flexible, experimental and creative in the way in which they deal with subordinates. Empathy also implies a suggestion of equality, in as much as the subordinate does not feel inferior; spontaneity, in terms of communication; a problem orientation, which allows the managers to deal with problems as they arise; as well as managers being descriptive, in the sense that they are clear about their perceptions and describe situations in a fair manner.

Empowerment

The term 'empowerment' refers to an individual employee being allowed to control his or her contribution within the organization. This means that they are given the authority and responsibility to complete tasks and attain targets without the direct intervention of management. The benefits to the organization of empowerment are that it reduces the importance of repetitive administration and the number of managers required at the various levels of the structure. The streamlining of management levels often increases the effectiveness of communication. From the employees' point of view, empowerment increases their creativity and initiative, as well as their commitment to the organization, by allowing them to work with autonomy.

Engagement

The term 'engagement' can actually be applied to both employees and customers. Engaged employees are encouraged to use their natural talents in order to assist the business in having a competitive edge. It is believed that, collectively, efforts involving employee engagement can actually assist in the engagement of customers themselves. Employee engagement requires that employees have an understanding, not only of the business but also of the management and what they both hope to achieve. Managers within organizations must assist employees in realizing their expectations, which have been learned by the subordinates as being the primary motivators of the business itself.

Employee engagement, therefore, involves the mobilization of the talent, energy and resources of employees. If done effectively, employee engagement delivers the following:

- It contributes to the development of a healthy and sustainable business.

- It assists the business in identifying the needs of customers and their solutions.
- It creates opportunities for dialogue with the business's stakeholders.
- It provides leverage for the business in the sense that it strengthens relations with stakeholders and leads to partnerships.
- It uses resources more efficiently.
- It allows for the development of skills and personnel.
- It is an asset for leadership and team development.
- It assists in bringing any form of corporate culture into sharp focus, building morale, loyalty and pride in the workforces.
- It assists in the establishment and maintenance of the business's reputation.

Axelrod, Richard H., *Terms of Engagement: Changing the Way we Change our Organizations*. San Francisco, CA: Berrett-Koehler Publishers, 2000.
Buckingham, Marcus and Coffman, Curt, *First, Break All the Rules*. New York: Simon & Schuster, 2001.

Entrepreneur

An entrepreneur is an individual who is associated with a degree of risk-taking and a flair for identifying potential business opportunities. Entrepreneurs exist in almost every area of business activity and seek to identify gaps in the present market provision which can be filled with a new means by which the products or services can be delivered, often in a way radically different from that in which the market already operates. Entrepreneurs place a great emphasis on innovation and will seek to design an entirely new business model, rather than relying on tried and tested business practices.

Environmental scanning

Environmental scanning is the process of monitoring and detecting external changes in the environment. In essence, environmental scanning can be seen as a way of identifying new, unexpected, major and minor possible impacts on the business. Environmental scanning, however, needs to be systematic for two main reasons. First, indiscriminate collection of information is somewhat random and it may not be possible to distinguish the relevant from the irrelevant. Secondly, it provides early warnings for managers of changing external conditions in a measured and paced manner.

The key objectives of environmental scanning are:

E

- To detect scientific, technical, economic, social and political trends and events of importance.
- To define the potential threats, or opportunities, of changes implied by those trends and events.
- To promote future thinking in both management and staff.
- To alert the management to trends which are converging, diverging, speeding up, slowing down or interacting in some manner.

At the heart of environmental scanning is the notion that decision-makers need to be aware of the environment in which they operate. In this respect environmental scanning provides the business with strategic intelligence which can help it frame organizational strategies. Environmental scanning should help a business to forecast in the light of the expectation of change (see Figure 29).

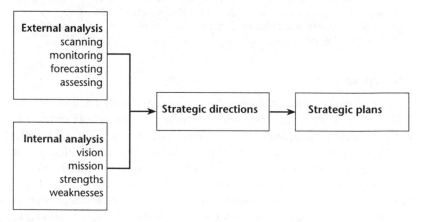

Figure 29   The role of external analysis in strategic planning

Halliman, Charles, *Business Intelligence Using Smart Techniques: Environmental Scanning Using Text Mining and Competitor Analysis Using Scenarios and Manual Simulation.* Houston, TX: Information Uncover, 2001.

Morrison, J. L., 'Environmental Scanning', in M. A. Whitely, J. D. Porter and R. H. Fenske (eds), *A Primer for New Institutional Researchers.* Tallahassee, Florida: Association for Institutional Research, 1992, pp. 86–99.

Ethics

Ethics and social responsibility related to marketing have become increasingly important and much-debated issues in recent years. Essentially, there is an inherent conflict between the desires of the business, the industry, society in general and the consumer. All may have mutually exclusive goals and objectives. Ethical issues arise when one group's values conflict with those of another. In many cases there are multiple levels of conflict arising out of different sets of values.

The marketing industry has sought to pre-empt governmental intervention by establishing professional associations and accrediting bodies who are concerned with self-regulation. An example of these is the American Marketing Association (AMA), which suggests that marketing behaviour should follow the rules set out in Table 17.

There is considerable conflict between the main purposes of marketing, the ethical criteria as stated by organizations such as the AMA, and the goal of making a profit. Given that the major promotional objectives include accentuating the value of the product, the provision of information, the stabilization of sales, the stimulation of demand, and the differentiation of the product, it is clear from these inherent marketing responsibilities that it is difficult to retain an ethical balance.

Table 17 Recommendations for marketing behaviour

Guidelines	Description
Responsibility	The AMA urges those involved in marketing to accept responsibility for the consequences of their actions and activities. They are asked to consider their decisions, recommendations and subsequent actions in the light of satisfying and serving all stakeholders.
Honesty and fairness	The AMA urges marketers to show integrity, honour and dignity as professionals.
Rights and duties	The AMA suggests that there should be an inherent relationship between businesses and their customers firmly based on the notion of trust. Products and services should be safe and fit for the uses for which they were intended. They also stress that marketing communications should be truthful and that products and services should be sold in good faith. In the case of disputes, a grievance procedure should be established.
Organizational relationships	The AMA also suggests that those involved in marketing should be clearly aware that their actions are intended to influence the behaviour of others. In this respect, given their persuasive role, they should not encourage unethical behaviour or apply undue pressure on those they target.

E

Robin, D. P. and Reidenbach, R. E., 'Social Responsibility, Ethics and Marketing: Closing the Gap between Concept and Application', *Journal of Marketing*, 51 (January 1987), pp. 44–58.

Expatriate managers

Businesses involved in international trade, and specifically those who set up operations abroad, tend to use expatriate managers for the following reasons:

- to control and coordinate operations;
- to transfer skills and knowledge;
- for general managerial development.

Employing managers from the originating country has been estimated to cost between three and four times as much as employing a local individual. Traditionally, expatriate managers who had taken overseas assignments could expect promotion on their return, but increasingly the larger financial packages are disappearing as organizations move towards equalizing the terms and conditions between locally employed staff and expatriates. In the past, expatriates could expect to be either on domestic salaries or better, often in countries where the cost of living was considerably lower than in their home country.

Expectancy theory

See **Vroom, Victor.**

Expected value

Expected value can be calculated as the sum of the products of each possible outcome of a situation and the relative likelihood that any of these will occur. Typically, expected value can be applied when making the necessary calculations for a **decision tree**.

Fey, James T., Phillips, Elizabeth D. and Anderson, Catherine, *What Do You Expect: Probability and Expected Value*. Dale Seymour Publications, 1996.

Experience curve

The term 'experience curve' has had a direct application for many businesses over a number of years, in as much as it describes improved performance of both the organization and individuals within that organization, over a period of time, as they repeat and become competent in tasks. Experience curve analysis is the study of this phenomenon and indeed it has an additional dimension in terms of international trade, with the experience curve being steeper in the sense that there is more to learn and understand and then practically demonstrate when businesses deal with overseas markets.

It has been proved that there is a direct and consistent relationship between growth in product volume and the reduction in unit product cost. Each time production doubles, costs decline between 20% and 30%. The experience curve itself relates the cost per unit output to the cumulative volume of output since a production process was first begun. The cost per unit of production declines as the cumulative volume of output increases. The production process, repeated time after time, allows the business and employees to learn from experience and adjust the production process in accordance with their acquired knowledge, thus reducing costs.

Numerous studies suggest that these costs tend to decline by a relatively stable percentage each time the cumulative volume produced is doubled. Clearly, the experience curve, or learning curve, of the organization and its employees have different dimensions, particularly in the case of setting up production facilities abroad. None the less, the fundamental phenomenon of the experience curve and its cost-saving implications are still ultimately enjoyed.

E

Factor endowments

'Factor endowments' refers to the primary factors of production of a given country. In essence this means the different ratios of capital to labour and the fact that goods differ in their input requirements, notably in terms of ratios between rents and wages and the fact that some goods require more capital per man hour than others. Primarily the endowment factors include labour, capital, land and, in some cases, natural resources. The concept of factor endowments is very much based on the Heckscher–Ohlin model. A similar model, known as the Stolper–Samuelson theorem, states that as the price of goods goes up, the return on the factors used intensively in their production goes up by a larger percentage, while the return on other factors of production falls.

Lal, Deepak, *Unintended Consequences: The Impact of Factor Endowments, Culture and Politics on Long-Run Economic Performance*. Cambridge, MA: MIT Press, 1998.

Fayol, Henri

In 1916 Henri Fayol, a French industrialist, wrote his views and theories about the problems commonly encountered by organizations. His view was that many of the root causes of industrial failure were down to management and personnel. Fayol was a '**top–down**' theorist (see Figure 30), who believed that change must begin with the board of directors or the managing director.

Fayol began by identifying the three main aspects of management, which are:

- the activities of the organization;
- the elements of management;
- the principles of management.

Fayol identified the six main categories of activities of a business organization as being:

- *Technical activities* – which include production, manufacture and adaptation.

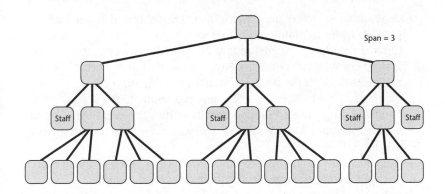

Figure 30 Top–down management

- *Commercial activities* – which include buying, selling and exchanging.
- *Financial activities* – which include the seeking of finance and deciding the best use of that finance.
- *Security services* – which include the protection of the organization, its employees and its property.
- *Accounting services* – which include the production of balance sheets, costings, statistical data and stock inventories.
- *Managerial activities* – which include forecasting and planning, organization, giving instructions, coordinating and controlling employee activity.

Fayol then identified fourteen elements and principles of management which were key qualities and functions:

- *Division of work* – ensuring that all employees know what their duties are.
- *Authority* – the ability to give clear, complete and unambiguous instructions.
- *Discipline* – to be rigid and firm when appropriate but always to ensure understanding.
- *Unity of command* – to ensure that all aspects of management within the organization are uniform.
- *Unity of direction* – to ensure that the business has a clear corporate strategy.
- *Subordination* – the ability to put the organization first, and personal needs and commitments second.
- *Remuneration* – the need for a fair wage for a fair day's work.

F

- *Centralization* – to ensure that tasks are concentrated and not duplicated in order to maintain cost effectiveness.
- *Clear scalar chain* – to ensure that all individuals within the organization know their position. Fayol suggested that this could be achieved through the production of an organization chart.
- *Internal order* – to strive to avoid internal conflict.
- *Equality* – to ensure equal opportunity within the organization and avoid discrimination by age, sex, sexual orientation, disability or religion.
- *Stability of tenure* – to ensure that employees feel their job is secure so that they are not concerned about their own security.
- *Initiative* – to encourage idea creation and to accept ideas from employees, without necessarily enforcing senior management input.
- *Esprit de corps* – to encourage a company spirit where individuals are proud to support the objectives of the business.

Fayol also identified some rules which he considered management should follow. He wrote that an individual who specialized would become more skilled, efficient and effective, but also considered that the manager should have the ultimate accountability for the employees.

Boje, David and Dennehy, Robert, *Managing in the Postmodern World* (3rd edition) September 2000, at http://cbae.nmsu.edu/~dboje/mpw.html

Summary of Fayol's work at www.comp.glam.ac.uk/teaching/ismanagement/manstyles1f.htm

Feedback

The definition of the word 'feedback' relates to any information that helps to evaluate the success or failure of an action that has taken place.

Felt conflict

See **conflict management**.

Fiedler, Fred

Fiedler wrote on leadership style and the relationship between that style and particular situations. His model depends upon the leadership style being described in terms of task or relationship motivation. The form of leadership depends upon three factors:

- the relationship between the leader and the members, which is concerned with how the leader is accepted and supported by the members of the group;

- the structure of the tasks and whether they are defined, with clear goals and procedures;
- position power, which details the leader's ability to control subordinates through punishment and reward.

Fiedler suggested that high levels of these three factors give the most favourable situation and low levels the least favourable. Leaders who are relationship-motivated are most effective in moderately favourable situations, whilst task-motivated leaders are most effective at either end of the scale. Fiedler recognized that while it is difficult for leaders to change their style, what they must attempt to do is to change their situation in order to achieve effectiveness.

First-mover advantage

The term 'first-mover advantage' is most closely associated with the competitive edge gained by a business which is first, or early, into a new market. Whilst businesses moving into a new market face the risks of failure, since neither they nor any other businesses have experience of that market or those modes of operation, when successful they have a substantial competitive edge over those who wish to emulate them.

In internet business, not only were both eBay and Amazon keen to establish clear distribution, promotion and fulfilment, but they were also concerned with measures to successfully combat competitors who sought to enter or emulate their own market. In both cases these businesses have successfully used their first-mover advantage, being first into the market, and remaining the most dominant businesses.

Five Forces model

Michael Porter developed a five forces model for industrial analysis. He maintained that industries are influenced by five forces and that the model enables businesses to understand the industry context in which the business operates. Porter's five forces consisted of:

- The barriers to entry – including cost advantages, access to raw materials and components, **economies of scale**, switching costs and access to distribution channels.
- Buyer power – price sensitivity, brand identity and buyer concentration and volume.
- Degree of rivalry – concentration of industry, exit barriers, product differences, diversity of rivals and industry growth.

F

- Supplier power – concentration of suppliers, switching costs, possibility of forward integration, importance of buyer to supplier.
- Threat of substitutes – inclination of buyer to purchase substitutes, relation of price to performance compared with substitutes, switching costs.

Porter went on to suggest that generic strategies could be followed in order to counter the impact of the five forces. He suggested that strategy could be formulated at three different levels:

- corporate level;
- business unit level;
- functional or departmental level.

His three generic strategies were:

- **Cost leadership strategy** – which was applicable in an industry-wide context.
- **Differentiation strategy** – which again was applicable industry-wide and rested on the uniqueness of the product.
- Focus strategy – which was largely applicable in market segments based on the offering of low costs and product differentiation.

Porter, Michael, *Competitive Advantage: Creating and Sustaining Superior Performance.* New York: Free Press, 1985.

Fixed assets turnover ratio

The fixed assets turnover ratio measures how effectively a business uses its fixed assets in order to generate sales. The ratio is:

$$Fixed\ assets\ turnover\ ratio\ = \frac{Sales}{Fixed\ assets}$$

Normally, the end-of-year assets figure is used. In other cases businesses may prefer to use the opening and closing fixed assets figures and take an average (this is useful for an expanding business).

Assuming a business generates £3,200,000 in sales, with fixed assets of some £1,900,000, then the calculation is:

$$\frac{3,200,000}{1,900,000} = 1.68\ times$$

The ratio reveals that for every £1 invested in fixed assets, the business generates with those fixed assets £1.68 in sales.

Clearly, assets which have depreciated will lead to a higher figure, yet the assets may still be effective and efficient in generating sales potential. It is therefore possible for two identical businesses with identical sales figures to have radically different fixed assets turnover ratios, as one of them may have aged and depreciated fixed assets whilst the other is using new fixed assets valued at or near their purchase price.

Oberuc, Richard, *Dynamic Portfolio Theory and Management: Using Active Asset Allocation to Improve Profits and Reduce Risk.* New York: McGraw-Hill Education, 2003.

Flat structure

A flat organizational structure is a **hierarchical structure** in the sense that it is in the shape of a pyramid, but it has fewer layers. Often a hierarchical structure can be de-layered in order to create a flat structure. This **de-layering** process often allows decisions to be made more quickly and efficiently because each layer is able to communicate more easily with the others. This enables the organization to become less bureaucratic, and gives a simpler structure often used by organizations operating from a single site. The directors and other major decision-makers are readily available for consultation with employees, who often find that they feel more a part of the process. This encourages motivation, particularly amongst junior managers, who are likely to be given more responsibility through delegation from the senior management level of the structure.

Flexible manufacturing technology

Theoretically, a flexible manufacturing system is an integrated group of machines which have the capacity for automated handling between them. In other words, they share an integrated information system which automatically passes part-finished products between the machines for the next stage of the process to be carried out.

Gunasekaran, A., *Agile Manufacturing.* Oxford: Pergamon, 2001.
Kidd, P. T. and Karwowski, W. (eds), *Advances in Agile Manufacturing: Integrating Technology, Organization and People.* Amsterdam: IOS Press, 1994.

F

Follett, Mary Parker

In her 1995 book *Mary Parker Follett: Prophet of Management*, Pauline Graham describes Mary Parker Follett as being the prophet of management. Follett was born in the mid-nineteenth century and died in the 1930s. During the 1920s, her most productive period, she wrote extensively on leadership, power, conflict, behaviour, empowerment, teams, networking, relationships, authority and control. Her ideas were considerably ahead of her time and she has, quite rightly, been identified as one of the most influential management writers, or creators of theory models.

Graham, Pauline (ed.), *Mary Parker Follett: Prophet of Management*. Boston, MA: Harvard Business School Press, 1996.
Tonn, Joan C., *Mary P. Follett: Creating Democracy, Transforming Management*. Newport, CT: Yale University Press, 2003.

See also **conflict management.**

Force field analysis

See **Lewin, Kurt.**

Forecasting

There are a number of associated terms related to forecasting, but forecasting itself is an attempt to predict the future of a variable. Businesses will attempt to forecast the demand for their products or services in order to plan both their stock and manufacturing requirements. The accuracy of a forecast very much depends upon the reliability of the data upon which the forecast has been based and, indeed, the length of time into the future which the forecast is expected to encompass. Generally a manufacturing organization will seek to forecast demand slightly in excess of its average manufacturing lead time. The further into the future a forecast is projected, the more chance there is of a significant error, as variables become far more unpredictable as a result of other, unknown variables having an influence upon them.

Formal organization

F

A formal organization is typified by a business which is bound to its organization chart, its hierarchies, rules, policies, procedures and regulations. This is not necessarily to imply that a formal organization is ineffective; nor does it mean that formal organizations are not profitable. It is simply a way of describing what could be considered to be a rather more traditional form of business.

The term 'formal organization' can also refer to a business's organizational **architecture**. Formal organizations can be typified, and compared with other forms of organization, as can be seen in Figure 31.

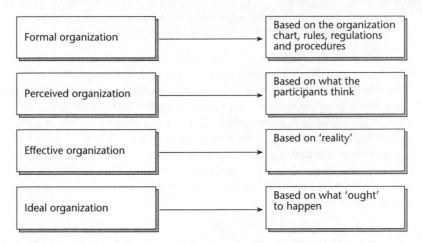

Figure 31 Comparison of organizational types

Forward integration

Forward integration is a downstream form of integration in which a business seeks to acquire other businesses, which under normal circumstances it would supply. In effect the business is seeking to control more of the supply or **value chain**. In Figure 32 the shaded boxes indicate the integration, or lack of integration, of a business concerned with assembly.

Fragmented industry

A fragmented industry is an industry or market which is not dominated by any large businesses. The market typically consists of a large number of small to medium-sized businesses. None of these businesses are in a position to be able to dominate the market in any way. In many respects a fragmented industry, both in concept and in reality, is the reverse of the situation measured by a **concentration ratio**.

F

Free cash flow

Free cash flow is another means by which the general health of a business can be assessed, as it is concerned with the amount of cash a business has to hand after it has dealt with its expenses and made any necessary investments. In many respects, free cash flow reveals the actual working capital of a business. Free cash flow is used as a financial measurement tool, particularly in the US, where it has an associated ratio:

*Operating cash flow (net income + depreciation + amortization
– capital expenditure + dividends = free cash flow)*

Many financial analysts consider free cash flow to be a prime indicator
of the way in which a business is being run and of its overall financial
condition. Free cash flow, however, can be misleading in some respects
since many growing businesses plough back the majority of their earnings directly into new investments. This would obviously reduce their
amount of free cash flow. Therefore a negative free cash flow does not
necessarily mean that the business is in trouble, but it may reveal that
the business is not earning a sufficiently high rate of return on the
investments it has made. This may indicate that the business is simply
spending too much.

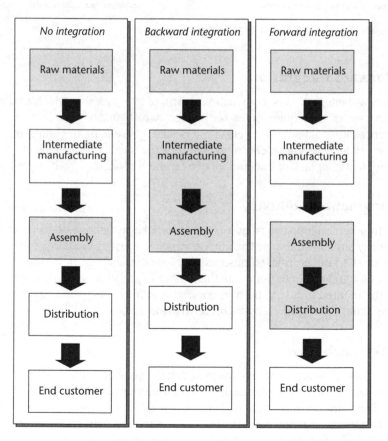

Figure 32   Business integration

Full integration

Full integration may be the ultimate desire of a truly multinational or multi-domestic business. In order to become fully integrated, a business needs to control all of its own inputs into its core business operations. In other words, this requires the business to acquire suppliers of raw materials and components which were previously independent suppliers to the business. In addition, the business is also concerned with the acquisition of distributors and ultimately retailers, who will be able to sell its products and services straight into the market, without the requirement of involving any other external operation or business. In essence then, full integration involves both forward and backward integration, so that a business controls all of its inputs and the disposal of all of its outputs through its own operations.

Functional authority

Functional authority, unlike line authority, is not necessarily exercised by every single manager. Typically, functional authority is exercised by managers who have specialist functions. They will have the right to instruct other managers as to what to do and how to do it with regard to their area of specialism. A finance director, for example, may not only be responsible and ultimately liable for the conduct of the financial matters of the business, but will also have the functional authority to insist that other managers follow the business's financial procedures and policies. Functional authority detracts from the power of line managers and their ability to act on their own discretion. However, having specialist guidance through functional authority enables the line managers to fulfil their responsibilities, being guided in the correct direction when required.

See also **functional structure.**

F

Functional structure

A functionally based organizational structure is designed around specific sections of the organization, usually those that produce, market and sell the organization's product or service. Functional structures can be a substructure of both **hierarchical structures** and **flat structures**, and will similarly be controlled by a managing director supported by relevant senior function or departmental managers. The creation of positions and departments around specialized functions is an integral part of the functional structure. There will be common themes, in terms of function or process, within each department, enabling management to concentrate on specific issues within their own technical area of expertise. This form of organizational structure has a number of advantages and disadvantages over other types of structure, as shown in Table 18.

Table 18 Functional structure evaluation

Advantages	Possible disadvantages
Promotes skills specialization and reduces duplication of resources.	These organizational structures tend to limit the organization to a relatively short-term horizon.
There is a clear career progression route.	Managers of each department could become parochial, thus limiting career advancement.
There are clear lines of communication, which could lead to higher productivity and performance within the department.	There is a chance of restricted communication between departments.
	If one department does not reach expectations, this has a knock-on effect on other departments.

Sutherland, Jon and Canwell, Diane, *Organisation Structures and Processes*. Harlow: Financial Times, Prentice Hall, 1997.

F

Gg

Game theory

Game theory is essentially a branch of mathematics which has been developed to study decision making in conflict situations. The conflict situations are circumstances where two or more decision-makers have different objectives. Game theory seeks to provide the optimum strategy in the face of opponents who may have their own strategies.

In essence, game theory takes the following steps or assumptions:

- Each of the decision-makers (players) has at least two choices or sequences of decisions (plays) available.
- Every combination of the plays available to the players leads to a situation which can be defined as win, lose or draw.
- The pay-off for each player is associated with an end state or a zero-sum game, which means the sum of all the pay-offs is zero.
- Each player should understand the game and the pay-offs of the other players.
- All decision-makers are considered rational, in the sense that given two choices, they will choose the one with the biggest pay-off.

Unfortunately the last two assumptions make game theory difficult to apply to real-life situations, but it continues to be used for management analysis and enquiry.

Vega-Redondo, Fernando, *Economics and the Theory of Games*. Cambridge: Cambridge University Press, 2003.

Gantt, Henry

The Gantt chart was developed as a production control tool by Henry L. Gantt in 1917. Gantt was a US engineer and social scientist, and developed a type of horizontal bar chart which is now commonly used to illustrate many different types of schedule.

Gantt charts are also used in **project management**. They provide a graphical illustration of a schedule, which assists the planning, coordination and tracking of each task within an overall project. Gantt charts can be simplistic horizontal bar charts, drawn on graph paper, or, as is now more common, can be created using proprietary software, such as Microsoft Project or Excel.

Gearing ratio

Gearing ratios measure the level of debt within a business's capital structure and are a generally accepted indicator of the level of financial risk an investor may face in becoming involved with the business. One of the two most used gearing ratios is the **debt to equity ratio**, which examines the relationship between the long-term debt and the total equity or shareholders' funds.

The other form of gearing ratio is known as the gearing percentage. This ratio has a slightly different structure:

$$Gearing\ percentage = \frac{Long\text{-}term\ debt}{Shareholder\ funds\ +\ debt \times 100}$$

The higher the gearing level, the more speculative the investment may be. In the US, gearing is referred to as 'leverage', which similarly investigates the relationship between debt and equity in the form of a ratio and more generally examines the degree to which a business is utilizing borrowed funds. It is considered to be the case that highly geared or leveraged businesses are more likely to fail, as they may be unable to continue to make their debt payments. Equally, these highly geared or leveraged businesses may find it difficult to convince new providers of finance to make an investment in the business.

Fridson, Martin and Alvarez, Fernando, *Financial Statement Analysis: A Practitioner's Guide.* New York: John Wiley & Sons, 2002.
Temple, Peter, *Magic Numbers: The 33 Key Ratios that Every Investor Should Know.* New York: John Wiley & Sons, 2001.

Gilbert, Tom

G

In Tom Gilbert's book *Human Competence: Engineering Worthy Performance*, he described a series of techniques designed to improve the performances of average or below average employees. He called this a Behaviour Engineering Model (BEM); the six identified factors were:

- information;
- resources;
- incentives;
- knowledge;
- capacity;
- motivation.

Table 19 explains in detail the full nature of the six factors.

Table 19 The Behaviour Engineering Model

Factor	Description
Information	What is required of the job role, clear and accurate guidelines, data for employees to track their own record, and frequent feedback.
Resources	Equipment/materials to optimize the job, sufficient time and staff to do the job, and organized work loads and processes.
Incentives	Financial and non-financial reward systems, removal of competing incentives, tailoring incentives to motivate individuals and a clear idea of the consequences of continued poor performance.
Knowledge	Systematic training to match each job and continuous opportunities for training.
Capacity	Effective recruitment and ongoing support in terms of the physical, intellectual and emotional capacity of employees.
Motivation	Personalized schemes in position, backed up by the correct selection procedures to identify the right candidates.

Gilbert, Tom, *Human Competence: Engineering Worthy Performance.* Silver Spring, MD: International Society for Performance, 1996.

Gilbreth family

Frank and Lillian Gilbreth were pioneers in time and motion studies. They developed a view of management that was contemporary with, but independent of, that of **F. W. Taylor**. They analysed the components of a specific job, breaking down each activity into separate parts. They then judged the most efficient means of carrying out each of those components, added the ideal times assigned to each of these components and arrived at an aggregate time for the whole activity.

www.gilbrethnetwork.tripod.com

Global matrix structure

A global matrix structure is essentially a **horizontal differentiation** along product divisions and geographical divisions. In other words, to visualize the organization structure, product groups are on a vertical axis and the foreign divisions are on the horizontal axis. It allows businesses to reduce costs by increasing efficiency, and to differentiate their activity with innovation and responsiveness.

The feature of the global matrix structure is that it involves a dual decision-making responsibility, as there is both a divisional and an area hierarchy. The system is not without its problems, as many organizations consider this form of structure to be rather clumsy and bureaucratic. There is also the question of slow decision making and a rather inflexible form of organization. Several international businesses have sought to overcome the problems by basing their organizational structure on wide networks with a shared culture and vision and stressing that the informal structures are more important than the formal structure itself. These forms of organizational structure are known as 'flexible matrix structures'.

Egelhoff, W. G., 'Strategy and Structure in Multinational Corporations: a Revision of the Stopford and Wells Model', *Strategic Management Journal*, vol. 9 (1988), pp. 1–14.

Globalization of markets

The term 'globalization of markets' is in stark contrast to more familiar views of global marketing. The globalization of markets suggests that many international businesses no longer consider individual national markets to be distinct entities. Given the fact that, until recently, many nations were closed by virtue of the fact that it was difficult to trade there, now that trade barriers have been removed these national markets are merging. Concerns regarding transportation, distance to market and even culture are being subsumed as international businesses increasingly treat national markets in a similar manner to markets in which they already trade.

Globalization of production

The term 'globalization of production' refers to the trend in international businesses, notably multinationals, towards choosing to disperse their production processes across the world. In essence these multinationals take full advantage of specific countries' factors of production in order to frame their global manufacturing policy.

Weiss, John, *Industrialisation and Globalisation: Theory and Evidence from Developing Countries*. London: Routledge, 2002.

Goal congruence

Goal congruence occurs when the objectives of two **stakeholders** in an organization have been met. In other words, the goals or objectives of those two stakeholders, such as the management and the shareholders, have both been reached through the joint or several actions of the two parties.

Goals down, plans up

'Goals down, plans up' is a term associated with the development of key performance indicators (KPI) and change management. When launching KPIs there are four usual stages:

- *Goals down, plans up* – which requires the KPIs to be cascaded down to the operational teams. The KPIs are the goals and the teams develop their relevant KPIs through the plans they develop to achieve these goals.
- *Individual performance plans* – which require management and team leaders to create their own KPIs from the organizational plan.
- *Documentation development* – all KPIs are logged and a process for updating the next planning cycle is organized.
- *Training* – both 'hard' and 'soft' skills are developed in terms of group training, and individual skills training for both technical and functional skills (hard skills) and behavioural performance (soft skills) are included.

Goals down, plans up is also used in change management models such as the example in Figure 33. In this sense the goals are paramount and the plans are simply there to ensure that the goals are achieved.

McCalman, James and Paton, Robert A., *Change Management: A Guide to Effective Implementation.* Thousand Oaks, CA: Sage Publications, 2000.

Smith, Jeff, *The KPI Book: The Ultimate Guide to Understanding the Key Performance Indicators of Your Business.* London: Insight Training and Development, 2001.

Godin, Seth

Seth Godin is the author of five books on permission marketing, business ideas, websites, change management and business transformation. Godin suggests, on permission marketing, that once customers volunteer their time it is the business's chance to establish a long-term relationship. In *The Big Red Fez* he suggests that website visitors are like monkeys; they want to be able to find what they are looking for, and quickly, or they will move on.

In *The Purple Cow*, Godin offers innovative ideas on marketing. In his *Unleashing the Idea Virus* he writes on creating a customer-to-customer buzz about products and services and how this network can be beneficial

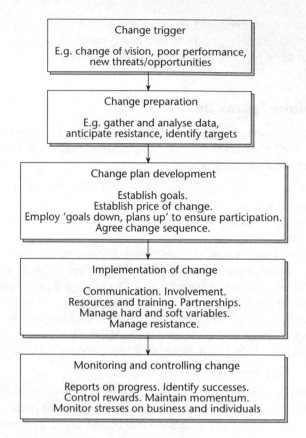

Figure 33 Change management model (example)

to the business. Godin's *Unleashing the Idea Virus* continues the theme of permission marketing, suggesting that strong products or service ideas benefit immensely from the word-of-mouth networks of customers.

Survival is Not Enough suggests that evolution and change should be grasped and used to a business's advantage, and that in change there are opportunities for even greater profits.

Godin, Seth, *Unleashing the Ideavirus*. New York: Simon & Schuster, 2002.

Godin, Seth, *Permission Marketing: Strangers into Friends into Customers*. New York: Free Press, 2002.

Godin, Seth, *The Big Red Fez*. New York: Free Press, 2002.

Godin, Seth, *Purple Cow: Transform Your Business by Being Remarkable*. Portfolio, 2003.

Godin, Seth, *Survival is Not Enough: Shift Happens*. New York: Free Press, 2003.

www.sethgodin.com

Golembiewski, Robert

Robert Golembiewski has authored or edited some 60 books. He is particularly famed for his theories on change management. Of particular interest is his study on corporate stress and burnout. He and his team of researchers interviewed some 40,000 individuals in 20 countries and predicted a huge rise in stress-related problems for managers over the next 10–15 years.

Golembiewski, Robert, *Ironies in Organizational Development*. New Brunswick, NJ: Transaction Publishers, 1989.

Governance mechanisms

The three key aspects of governance mechanisms are:

- ownership structure;
- monitoring and controlling mechanisms;
- management performance.

Governance mechanisms deal with the ways in which the management structure, as determined by the ownership and overall structure of the business, both monitors and controls the business while at the same time it is monitored and controlled itself.

The governance mechanisms cover the board structure and composition, disclosure standards, financial accounting and standards, risk management and the monitoring and control of information and transactions.

Monks, Robert and Minow, Nell, *Corporate Governance*. Oxford: Blackwell Publishers, 2001.

Grapevine

Grapevine communication is an informal method of passing on messages, allowing it to be one of the speediest forms of communication. Often considered to be gossip and rumour, grapevine communication can be extremely unreliable, however. Snippets of information get passed from one individual, or group of individuals, to another and the message can become extremely distorted. Grapevine communication is not a method to be encouraged by managers, who should attempt to inform employees in a more formal way, stating facts rather than part-truths. A high degree of grapevine communication within an organization, if it is not adequately dealt with by management, can lead to low morale. Although this method of communication is quite natural and prevalent in all organizations, it should be tackled in such a manner that employees hear the message from the appropriate level and through the appropriate channels.

Greenleaf, Robert

Robert Greenleaf (1904–90) wrote extensively on management, organizations and power. In 1970 he wrote an essay entitled 'The Servant as Leader', which suggested that an individual spurred on by vision and a servant ethic could make a considerable contribution to society in general. He went on to suggest that leaders are chosen, and that they should have several characteristics:

- awareness;
- foresight;
- listening skills;
- the ability not be coercive, manipulative or over-persuasive.

Greenleaf was a pragmatist and strongly believed that 'management is the study of how things get done'.

Spears, Larry, *Reflections on Leadership: How Robert K. Greenleaf's Theory of Servant Leadership Influenced Today's Top Management Thinkers*. New York: John Wiley, 1995.

Green-mail

The term 'green-mail' is most closely associated with the pursuing of shares in another business and the profits which can be achieved by re-selling these shares under certain circumstances. The process usually works in the following manner:

- A business secretly begins buying shares in another business.
- The purchasing business then announces that it wishes to take over control of the second business and acquire a majority shareholding.
- The board of directors of the business under threat, thinking that they will lose control of their business, invest or borrow money to purchase as many shares as they can from the market to protect their position.
- The business which originally purchased the shares is happy to sell the shares back to the directors at a profit.

Greiner's model

Larry Greiner (1972) suggests that organizations go through five stages of growth and need appropriate strategies and structures to cope.

The stages of the growth of organizations and the various crises and solutions are:

1 Growth through creativity – ideas and creativity are the driving force and therefore a simple entrepreneurial structure is all that is required. The organization reaches a stage where it cannot cope and a revolutionary crisis of leadership leads to a need for direction.

2 Growth through direction – the new systems and procedures provide direction through a functional structure. The procedures eventually smother creativity; this leads to a crisis of autonomy as the systems cannot cope with individuality.

3 Growth through delegation – a new decentralized decision-making system allows more autonomy. Employees can use their initiative to quickly make and take decisions. The organization has adopted a form of 'holding company' structure, but if the decision-makers in the units begin to move in their own direction then there is fragmentation leading to a crisis of control. The decision-makers can be brought back into line through a process of re-centralization, but this simply takes the organization back to the problems which led to autonomy being granted in the first place. The answer is to proceed to Phase 4.

4 Growth through coordination and monitoring – controlled centrally through a divisional structure which allows the decision-makers free operation but within the overall controls of the organization. Coordination needs to be at arm's length, otherwise a crisis of red tape can occur.

5 Growth through collaboration – a matrix structure develops to facilitate the use of small teams to accomplish tasks; however, new crises may occur.

Greiner, Larry E., 'Evolution and Revolution as Organizations Grow', *Harvard Business Review*, July–August 1972.

Gross profit margin

The gross profit margin ratio is one of several ratios which help to assess the overall operating performance of a business. The ratio itself expresses the gross profit as a percentage of sales. The ratio is:

$$Gross\ profit\ margin\ = \frac{Gross\ profit \times 100}{Sales}$$

If a business generates some £700,000 in gross profit on a total sales revenue of £3,200,000, then the following calculation is made:

$$\frac{700{,}000 \times 100}{3{,}200{,}000} = 21.87\%$$

This indicates that the business earns £0.218 or £0.22 in gross profit for every £1 of sales.

Group think

The term 'group think' was coined by Irving Janis, who related the term to a phenomenon within groups. Janis considered that group think occurs when a group of individuals are so determined to make a decision that they ignore all major considerations and alternatives, as well as any disagreements within the group, in order to achieve this. Groups suffering from group think are often thought to be over-cautious and to lack necessary creativeness. They bond with each other and the individuals see themselves as secure because they belong to the group. The group members have little doubt about the effectiveness or invulnerability of the group and consider the views of anyone not involved within the group to be those of insignificant outsiders. According to Janis the symptoms of group think are:

- invulnerability, in that they consider they cannot be touched;
- inappropriate rationale, in that they consider things are unlikely to happen to them;
- morality, in that they think they know what is best;
- stereotyping other groups by considering them all to be less effective than they are;
- pressurizing other groups;
- exerting an element of self-censorship by not communicating all information to other groups or relevant individuals, but selecting what they consider to be appropriate;
- unanimity, by assuming a consensus when no individuals speak up;
- mind-guards – referring to the fact that they do not allow any other thoughts to contradict what they have already decided.

Suffering from group think can make groups ineffective. Janis considered that management would have to encourage the individuals within the group to:

- consider and examine all alternatives;
- feel able to express their own doubts within the group;
- listen to criticisms from outside the group;
- challenge those who have firmly held beliefs;

- actively seek feedback, advice and information from outside the group;
- create sub-divisions within the group;
- avoid **grapevine** communication.

Group think can lead to ineffective decision making through insufficient attention to alternatives and risks.

www.aFirstlook.com/archive/groupthink.cfm

Growth share matrix

See **Boston growth matrix**.

Hamel, Gary

Gary Hamel is an author and consultant and wrote the highly influential *Leading the Revolution*. In a nutshell, Hamel suggests that innovation comes from those who dare to think differently. He urges organizations to recognize and nurture different thinking. Change, he believes, is the key to business success, otherwise the business will be overtaken by 'revolutionaries' in other businesses.

Hamel, Gary, *Leading the Revolution*. Watertown, MA: Harvard Business School Press, 2000.

www.garyhamel.com

Hammer, Michael

Michael Hammer is perhaps best known for his work in business process re-engineering, notably in his book *Reengineering the Corporation*. In his own words:

In order to achieve the performance levels that customers now demand, businesses must organise themselves around the axis of process; moreover, they must apply the discipline of process even to the most creative and heretofore chaotic aspects of their operations.

He believes that collaboration across the supply chain can be enabled by the deployment of robust and innovative technologies.

Hammer, Michael and Champy, James, *Re-engineering the Corporation: A Manifesto for Business Revolution*. London: Nicholas Brearley Publishing, 2001.

www.mastersforum.com/archives/hammer/hammerf.htm

Handy, Charles

Charles Handy's main areas of research have been centred around organizations and how they are structured, particularly with regard to their cultures and progression, together with the progression of individuals within an organization.

In 1985 Charles Handy was concerned with career development from the point of view of both the organization and the individual's ability to plan the right moves for success. He described the process of planning for career development as a 'human hurdle race', with often too many hurdles to make it achievable, even for highly motivated employees. The added complication, according to Handy, is that if one of the hurdles, during the early stages of development, is considered a failure, then the individual has little chance of re-attempting it. Added to this is the speed of the expectation of success, and often individuals are so focused on the next hurdle that they become blinkered in their outlook and disregard anything that is not appropriate to the achievement of the next stage of development.

Handy linked the relevance of the **organizational culture** and **organizational structure** as being a determining factor in an individual's ability to gain promotion or see any success in the development of his or her career. The result, from an organizational point of view, of the lack of appropriate planning for career development could be high levels of labour turnover. From an individual point of view, being employed by an organization that fails to plan for career development and promotion could restrict the individual's progression.

Handy, C. B., *Understanding Organizations*. London: Penguin Books, 1999.

www.leadertoleader.org/leaderbooks/handy

Hard management

The fundamentals of hard management can be closely associated with a quote from **Peter Drucker**: 'Doing the right things is more important than doing things right.' This seems to be the fundamental ethos behind hard management, in as much as the primary role of all private businesses is to be competitive and to produce a profit. All other considerations, as far as hard management is concerned, are subservient to this.

Hard management would, therefore, transcend all areas of the business, including human resources, and rather than focusing on employees' job satisfaction, **motivation** or even employee retention, the drive is to achieve a competitive advantage, make the best return on investment and meet or exceed the organization's objectives. Proponents of hard management believe that if this holistic approach is adopted, then management will do the right thing, which may mean that particularly valued employees are not only well rewarded but also well treated. Hard management is to be distinguished from **soft management** by virtue of the fact that the latter focuses on human resource factors on a basis equal to that of the other objectives and strategies of the business.

Harvest strategy

See **asset reduction.**

Hersey, Paul and Ken Blanchard

Paul Hersey and Ken Blanchard were involved in the study of situational leadership. They linked task and relational behaviour. The task behaviour focused on the definition of roles and responsibilities, and the relational behaviour was concerned with providing support to teams and subordinates. They suggested that the extent to which situational leadership is used ultimately depends upon managers' maturity in their post and whether they feel secure. In essence, situational leadership, as far as Hersey and Blanchard were concerned, was a question of **delegation**, participation, the selling of decisions, or the simple dictating of decisions.

See also **Blanchard, Ken.**

Hersey, Paul, Blanchard, Kenneth H. and Johnson, Dewey E., *Management of Organizational Behavior: Leading Human Resources.* New York: Prentice Hall, 2001.

Herzberg, Frederick

Frederick Herzberg developed his two-factor theory, which included his hygiene factor and his motivator factor, during his investigation of accountants and engineers in the USA. This brought about his angle on the theory of leadership, motivation and management. According to Herzberg, the major motivating factors are:

- Achievement – employees have the need to feel that something has been accomplished by their labours.
- Recognition – an employee has the need to feel that management and others realize that the role the employee is playing within the organization is an important and appreciated one.
- The work itself – the employees have the need to feel that they have enough freedom to make their own decisions and that their job role meets or reaches their own potentials.
- Advancement – the employees have the need to feel that they have a chance of promotion and that their skills and performance warrant such a promotion.

The hygiene factors that Herzberg identified are features of the workplace, or the organization itself, that help to make the employees feel good about themselves, and include:

H

- wage or salary paid;
- bonuses/commissions paid;
- working conditions;
- quality of supervision;
- the working environment;
- job security.

The hygiene factors do not motivate employees, who can never reach a stage of either complete satisfaction or of complete dissatisfaction, but remain in a neutral zone.

Herzberg's motivators are concerned with the work that the employees undertake and their performance within each task (see Figure 34). An employee cannot be motivated if the organization is not offering any of the following, and will remain in the neutral zone:

- attainment;
- advancement;
- responsibility.

Motivators	Varied work Control of own work Gross pay
Demotivators	Isolation Poor working conditions Continual pressure

Figure 34 Herzberg's motivational hygiene model

Herzberg, Frederick, *Work and the Nature of Man*. E. Rutherford, NJ: New American Library, 1978.
Herzberg, Frederick, *Motivation to Work*. Somerset, NJ: Transaction Publishers, 1993.

Hesselbein, Frances

Frances Hesselbein holds no less than sixteen honorary doctorates. She is considered to be one of the leading thinkers on management and leadership in non-profit organizations. Her principal areas of expertise include leadership, multicultural and diverse organizations, and organizational change and development.

Hesselbein, Frances, *Journey to Leadership and Lessons Learnt Along the Way*. New York: Jossey-Bass Wiley, 2002.
Hesselbein, Frances, Goldsmith, Marshall and Beckhard, Richard (eds), *The Organization of the Future*. New York: Jossey-Bass Wiley, 2000.

Hierarchical structure

A hierarchical organization structure is best imagined by use of an image of a pyramid. At the top are the major decision-makers, who are few in number, and further down the pyramid the shape of the organization broadens as more employees become involved at the lower levels. At the base of the pyramid are the majority of the workers.

Power, responsibility and authority are concentrated at the top of the pyramid and decisions flow from the top downwards. An organization would choose this form of structure when decisions need to be made by those who have expertise and experience, together with the authority to ensure that decisions are implemented.

The most common version of this form of structure is the steep pyramid, where there are many different layers of management, possibly within an organization that operates in several different locations, needing to fulfil different administrative functions. Equally, organizations of a complex nature may choose this structure.

There are some disadvantages for those lower down the hierarchical structure in that if the pyramid is too multi-layered and complex, they often find difficulty in understanding how and why decisions are made. The organization may also find itself too bureaucratic in nature and the result could be that the decision-making process becomes too complicated and time-consuming because there are too many layers involved.

See also **chain of command.**

Hierarchy of resources

'Hierarchy of resources' refers to the various levels of both internal and external resources required to carry out a specific task or series of related tasks. It is, perhaps, typified by what is known as the Kirkpatrick model, which was outlined by Donald Kirkpatrick in relation to training. He identified that there were four levels of hierarchy and related evaluation:

1 The goal at Level 1 is to measure the participants' reaction to the training material which is presented. This can be considered to be the Level 1 of the hierarchy of resources – the training materials themselves.

2 This is an evaluation which measures whether the participants actually learned from the material presented in the training. Usually this would take the form of a pre-test or a post-test assessment. This measures the quality of the resources which have been put into the training programme.

3 This measures any changes in behaviour as a result of the training. Although this is an individual-by-individual measure, it shows whether the resources that went into providing the training, and covering for the individual while they were training, was well spent.
4 The fourth level measures the overall impact of the training on the effectiveness of the organization itself. It shows whether the resources which were deployed in the training programme as a whole have had a positive impact on the business.

Kirkpatrick, Donald, *Managing Change Effectively: Approaches, Methods, and Case Examples*. Oxford: Butterworth-Heinemann, 2000.

Hock, Dee

Dee Hock is the founder of the Chaordic Alliance, which aims to disseminate and implement new concepts in organizational set-up and operations. Hock was also the founder of Visa USA and Visa International.

In his book *Birth of the Chaordic Age*, Hock claims to have been the first to recognize the future and potential of electronic exchange, upon which Visa International's business is based, linking some 20,000 financial institutions, 14 million merchants and over 600 million customers in 220 countries. He believes that hierarchical bureaucracies stifle innovation:

Success will depend less on rote and more on reason; less on authority of the few and more on the judgement of the many; less on compulsion and more on motivation; less on external control of people and more on internal discipline.

Hock, Dee, *Birth of the Chaordic Age*. San Francisco, CA: Bennett-Koehler, 2000.
Hock, Dee, *The Chaordic Organization*. San Francisco, CA: Bennett-Koehler, 2000.

Hofstede, Geert

Geert Hofstede is best known for his dimensions theory, which relates to cultural differences. His main findings are summarized in Table 20.

A fifth dimension was later added, namely long-term v. short-term orientation. In the US, for example, there was a tendency towards the short term, as results were wanted immediately. Japan is on the other end of the extreme and takes a longer view.

Hofstede, Geert, *Culture's Consequences: International Differences in Work-related Values*. London: Sage Publications, 1980.
Hofstede, Geert, 'National Cultures in Four Dimensions', *International Studies in Management and Organizations*, 13 (1983).
Hofstede, Geert, *Cultures and Organizations*. New York: McGraw-Hill, 1991.

See also **corporate culture.**

H

Table 20   Findings of Hofstede's dimensions theory

Key dimension	Findings
Individual v. collectivism	Were employees and managers more concerned with personal responsibilities or rewards, or focused more on group/organizational responsibilities and success?
	The US and UK ranked highly on individualization. Indonesia and West Africa were high on collectivism.
Power distance	Was there a strong separation of individuals based on their ranking in the organization?
	Power distance was high in Arab and Latin American businesses, but lower in most of Europe and the US.
Masculinity v. femininity	Masculinity was typified as being competitive, whilst femininity focused more on harmony within the organization and issues such as environmental protection.
	Japan ranked as a masculine country, the US was inclined towards masculinity. The most feminine country was the Netherlands.
Uncertainty avoidance	This measured the extent of structured rules as opposed to ambiguous circumstances. Countries which had lower uncertainty avoidance were more tolerant of risk taking.
	Japan ranked highly in uncertainty avoidance, the UK ranked in the middle of the scale and the US tended towards the lower end.

Horizontal differentiation

Horizontal differentiation involves the division of a multinational business into a series of sub-units, usually on a nation-by-nation basis.

Horizontal integration

Horizontal integration occurs when a business establishes new markets for its existing products or introduces new products into its current market. The business is not necessarily doing anything particularly new, but is playing to its strengths in order to achieve **economies of scale** or **economies of scope**.

The term is also used to describe the purchase of a business which broadly operates in the same area of industry as the buyer. Specifically, it would refer to a retailer purchasing a competitor retailer, or a manufacturer purchasing another manufacturer. This is a more common form of take-over or merger, or acquisition, as the business is still effectively operating at the same level in the distribution chain. If a retailer was to purchase a manufacturer, then this would be known as **vertical integration**, as the businesses have moved up or down the distribution chain.

Horizontal merger

Essentially, a horizontal merger is the joining together of two businesses with similar product lines or range of services. Governments are concerned with the regulation of horizontal mergers as they may create a monopoly, either nationally or regionally. There are, therefore, rules and regulations which govern horizontal mergers that might be considered to be against the interests of the country and the consumers. In actual fact, horizontal mergers can result in two radically different outcomes:

- Higher prices, as a result of the newly merged business effectively controlling the market as a virtual monopoly.
- Lower prices, as a result of lower future costs and/or better products. Less has to be spent on protecting market share through marketing and advertising.

www.dti.gov.uk/ccp/topics2/mergers.htm

www.usdoj.gov/atr/public/guidelines/horiz_book/hmg1.html

www.ftc.gov/bc/docs/horizmer.htm

House, Robert

Robert House is a highly respected management thinker and writer in the fields of leadership, motivation, personality and performance, and cross-cultural organizational behaviour.

House was one of the theorists who developed the path–goal theory of leadership. An effective leader was described as having the following characteristics:

- The ability to identify, and communicate to subordinates, the path they should follow to achieve both personal and organizational objectives.
- The willingness to assist subordinates on this path.
- The willingness to remove obstacles on the path.

House also wrote on charismatic leaders, suggesting that they communicate the imagination and energies of the subordinate; they create an image of success and competence and set values that they support through their own actions; and they have high expectations of their subordinates and retain a high level of confidence in their own and their subordinates' abilities.

House, Robert, 'A Path Goal Theory of Leadership Effectiveness', *Administrative Service Quarterly,* September 1971.

House, Robert and Mitchell, T., 'Path–Goal Theory of Leadership', *Journal of Contemporary Business,* Autumn 1974.

House, Robert J., Hanges, Paul J., Javidan, Mansour, Dorfman, Peter W. and Gupta, Vipin, *Leadership, Culture and Organizations: The GLOBE Study of 62 Societies.* New York: Sage Publications, 2004.

Hubris hypothesis

In 1986 Richard Roll argued that bidding businesses have a tendency to overstate the value of any economic benefits they would acquire as a result of a merger. In other words, the bid premium may be overstated as a result of a valuation error. This becomes all the more significant if the bidding business is dealing with a potential overseas acquisition. Managerial over-confidence, as exemplified in the hubris hypothesis, suggests the pursuit of the maximization of personal utility rather than the maximization of shareholder wealth.

Roll, Richard, 'The Hubris Hypothesis of Corporate Takeovers', *Journal of Business,* 59 (1986), pp. 197–216.

Human resources

The role of management in the deployment and effectiveness of human resources within an organization is a vast concern, which has been much written about. Human resource management, as such, can be differentiated from personnel management in the sense that the latter has more to do with the practical aspects of recruitment, appraisal, training and other key issues. Human resource management itself is more strategic and is concerned with the overall deployment of the human resources which are available to the business.

Typically there are four main areas in which human resource management is concerned:

- The aggregate size of the organization's labour force.
- The amount spent on training the workforce in order to achieve targets, such as quality or production output.
- Relations with trade unions and other employee-based organizations.

- Human asset counting, which analyses the costs and financial benefits of different forms of personnel policy.

The broader approach to human resource management involves a number of concerns, which include the following:

- The implications of the management of change, in encouraging flexible attitudes to the acceptance of new work practices.
- Making a major input into the organizational development.
- Being prescriptive and initiating new activities as opposed to being responsive to employment law, which is the preserve of personnel management.
- Determining employee relationships by the establishment of a culture which is conducive to cooperation and commitment.
- Taking a long-term view to integrate the human resources of the organization into a coherent whole.
- Emphasizing the need for direct communication.
- Developing an **organizational culture**.
- Encouraging employee participation in work groups.
- Enhancing employees' capabilities in the longer term and not focusing purely on their current duties and responsibilities.

Bernardin, H. J. and Russel, J., *Human Resource Management: An Experiential Approach*. New York: McGraw-Hill, 2002.

Stroh, C. K. and Caliguiri, P. M., 'Strategic Human Resources: A New Source of Competitive Advantage in the Global Arena', *International Journal of Human Resource Management*, 9(1) (1998), pp. 1–17.

H

Illusion of control

Clearly, this term suggests what could be considered an unrealistic optimism in the sense that an individual believes he or she has more control over events than is the case.

The illusion of control significantly reduces performance and reduces the ability of a manager to be able to forecast with any clarity. The illusion of control leads to a simplification in the evaluation stage of strategic decision making in the following way:

- A process of partial representativeness leads to inaccurate predictions of the consequences of actions, by associating them with similar events in the past.
- Partially understood alternatives are rejected, even though they may be the best course of action.
- Inherent risks are inaccurately assessed.

If a manager has misconceptions of the control on resources, for example, then it is possible that the manager will over-value the ratio of success for a task.

Illusion of control revolves around notions of one's own efficiency, and over-confidence. Any self-perceived efficiency corresponds to the manager's capabilities in mobilizing the motivation, resources and courses of action needed for specific situations. Over-confidence occurs when the manager believes that his or her decisions are correct, when in actual fact they are not. Over-confidence leads to stress, ambiguity and more complex problems.

Bandura, A., 'Self-efficiency: Toward a Unifying Theory of Behavioural Change', *Psychological Review*, 84(2) (1977), pp. 191–215.

Starbucks, W. H. and Mezias, J., 'Opening Pandora's Box: Studying the Accuracy of Managers' Perceptions', *Journal of Organizational Behavior*, 17 (1996), pp. 99–117. 1996.

Inbound/outbound logistics

Logistics incorporates the planning and control of all materials and products across the entire production and supply chain system. Logistics is, in effect, a managerial function which deals with the flow of materials, including the purchasing, shipping and distribution issues before, during and after the completion of the finished product.

In international business, logistics can be far more complex as it may require particular elements which will be needed in the manufacture of products to be coordinated, as regards shipment and delivery from various parts of the world. Increasingly, raw materials and components are sourced from overseas locations and delivered, either to a single country or to a series of manufacturers within a multinational, for onward processing. Logistics therefore includes the shipment of raw materials, components, finished goods, machinery, packaging materials and innumerable other inputs into a manufacturing and packaging service.

Clearly, it is advantageous for multinational businesses to reduce the movement of heavy or bulky raw materials and components, but often the associated transportation costs are offset by the fact that these materials can be sourced at radically lower prices then could be achieved in the domestic market. This means that the logistical task of multinationals has become increasingly complex, particularly in cases where the business has chosen to locate parts of the manufacturing process across the world. Increasingly, multinationals have sought to acquire businesses which had hitherto been their suppliers, in order to have a firmer grasp and control of the logistics chain.

Christopher, Martin, *Logistics and Supply Chain Management*. London: Financial Times, Prentice Hall, 1998.

Incentive

The term 'inducement' covers pay, benefits and other intangible incentives which are part of an overall package offered by an organization in order to attract potential employees. The inducements represent the total benefits or compensations which the employee would expect to receive as a result of accepting a job offer from a particular organization.

The term 'fringe benefit' refers to any incentive given to employees as a reward in addition to their wage or salary. Fringe benefits can include:

- a company pension scheme;
- employee sick pay schemes;
- subsidized meals;
- company products or services at a discounted price;
- company cars;

- private medical or health insurance;
- counselling or mentoring services;
- occupational health screening;
- social and recreational facilities;
- legal and financial service support.

Fringe benefits are not necessarily related to merit, but often increase with the employee's status and length of service. They do not necessarily benefit all employees but are established and monitored after the initial analysis process. Once they are established, however, it is difficult for the organization to remove them as this could affect employee retention. Fringe benefits are considered important because they improve job satisfaction provided they are consistently and fairly administered.

Incremental innovation

Incremental innovation has been described as a familiar and reassuring process. Effectively, it is the continual process of making small improvements in either efficiency or performance within the fixed parameters of a product, a business model or perhaps a practice. Incremental innovations tend to be year-on-year improvements, allowing the business to continue to function using recognizable systems or procedures without the huge upheaval of a truly radical innovation. 'Incremental innovation' therefore refers to slow, gradual refinements which improve performance in steady stages.

Tushman, M. L. and Moore, W. L., *Readings in the Management of Innovations*. New York: Pitman Publishing, 1982.

Industry life cycle model

The industry life cycle model consists of four distinct stages: fragmentation, shakeout, maturity and decline. The four stages effectively track the process, in a basic form, of the development, the dominance and the eventual decline of any industry. A basic life cycle model can be seen in Figure 35.

The stages can be described in a variety of ways according to the exact nature of the industry itself; however, Table 21 summarizes the main aspects of each stage.

Frankl, Paolo and Rubik, Frieder, *Life Cycle Assessment in Industry and Business: Adoption Patterns, Applications and Implications*. Berlin and Heidelberg: Springer Verlag, 2000.

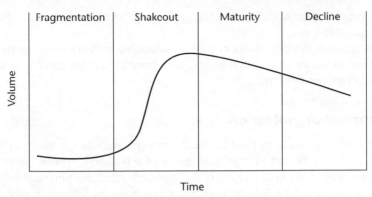

Figure 35   The industry life cycle model

Table 21   Stages in the industry life cycle

Stages	Description
Fragmentation	Entrepreneurs are the prime catalysts in developing a new industry. New industries arise when an entrepreneur overcomes the twin problems of innovation and invention and works out how to bring a new product or service into the market. The entrepreneur must secure financial capital, obtain market feedback and overcome any barriers to innovation.
Shakeout	A dominant model of how to run the industry emerges, efficiencies begin to be realized and the value of the industry quickly rises. Businesses learn how to adapt and use any new technology.
Maturity	Technological advances yield only incremental improvements. The efficiencies of the dominant business model give the organization a competitive advantage. Pricing, competition and cooperation take on complex forms.
Decline	Inertia may impede survival, wars of attrition between businesses may develop and those with heavy bureaucracies may fail. Demand may be fully satisfied or supplies may be running out. Equally, new technologies may promise more value.

Inert culture

If an organization has an inert culture it is considered to be inherently conservative, cautious and risk averse. An inert culture tends to impede the organization's ability to change, particularly when faced with a competitive threat.

In contrast, an organization with an **adaptive culture** tends to allow change in the strategy of the business in order to survive effectively in a changing environment.

Informal organization

Informal organizations tend to occur amongst employees, either at the same, or at different hierarchical levels of a business. These informal groups may develop as a result of background, ethnicity, personal affinities or even hobbies. Informal organizations have the following implications for a business:

- Management needs to understand the contribution these informal groups make to the business.
- Informal organizations can contribute to the stability of the business.

The characteristics of informal organizations have both positive and negative connotations. The positive ones include:

- They encourage support between employees – individuals are no longer 'strangers'.
- They help employees carry out their work, through verbal and informal support mechanisms.
- They enhance communications – when problems arise, situations can be dealt with 'unofficially'.

The negative characteristics are:

- Informal organizations may divert employees.
- Informal organizations may work against the management.
- Informal organizations may resist change, by silent dissent.

Informal power

Whilst managers and supervisors have clear formal power to assert their authority over subordinates, others are given informal power to operate and direct on behalf of those with formal authority. Informal power tends to occur in situations where an individual's **job description** does not explicitly give authority or power. Usually, by virtue of their age, experience or understanding of the processes and tasks required, certain individuals are granted informal power as a form of **delegation**, to exercise authority over peers.

Infrastructure

See **architecture**.

Initiating structure

The term 'initiating structure' refers to the orientation of a manager's behaviour towards structuring subordinate activities for the purpose of goal attainment. The implications of this approach are:

- It will add role clarity and will increase satisfaction.
- It will decrease satisfaction if the present structure is already adequate.
- The employees' performance will improve in cases where the task is unclear.
- The employees' performance will remain relatively unaffected when the task is clear.

Innovation

The innovation-adoption model can be applied both to consumers and to businesses. In consideration of its application to consumers, the innovation-adoption model charts the process of gradual acceptance of a new product. The key stages are: awareness, interest, evaluation, trial, and adoption for consumers.

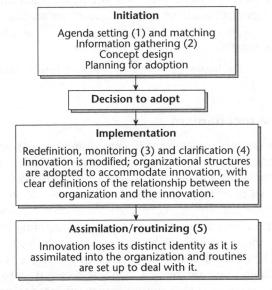

Figure 36   Innovation process stages

The innovation-adoption process in relation to businesses was developed by Everett Rogers and details the five stages of the innovation process, together with the associated activities at each of these stages, as can be seen in Figure 36.

Rogers, Everett M., *Diffusion of Innovations*. New York: Free Press, 2003.

Intangible resource

An intangible resource or an intangible asset is also known as an invisible asset. It is an asset which does not have a physical presence. In other words, intangible assets include goodwill, brand names, patents, trademarks, copyrights and franchises. Clearly, intangible resources are the opposite of **tangible resources**.

Interestingly, intangible resources can be more, or less, intangible. Brand names, trademarks or patents, for example, have, to some extent, a presence in the sense that they can be clearly identified as being an asset; other intangible assets are rather more ethereal. Goodwill is probably one of the most intangible assets as it has no supporting documentation and is of variable commercial value. For example, goodwill can be a very valuable intangible asset in the sense that it can offer a business, or a potential purchaser of a business, the opportunity to capitalize on future profits based on the work and relationships which have already been established and which constitute the goodwill.

There is, however, a slight distinction between some forms of intangible assets. Goodwill could be described as either an intangible or an invisible asset, whereas insurance policies, for example, are invariably referred to as invisible rather than intangible assets.

Donaldson, T. H., *The Treatment of Intangibles: A Banker's View*. Basingstoke: Palgrave Macmillan, 1992.

Integrating mechanism

For international businesses a well planned and considered means by which they can integrate their operations across several countries has become essential. Businesses that are involved in multi-domestic, international, global or trans-national business will seek to integrate their systems, usually through a more complex form of **organizational structure**. There are various different forms of integrating mechanisms; perhaps the most obvious is to have individuals from the parent company in direct contact with, or posted to, new overseas ventures in order to gradually integrate the new business enterprise into the overall organizational system. Other international businesses prefer interdepartmental liaison, in which selected individuals from key functional departments of the parent company are available to assist new overseas enterprises in integrating their systems into the parent's mechanisms. Other international businesses choose to create temporary task forces to speed up the integration process. They may well choose to site permanent teams with the new overseas enterprise, with a view to integrating the overseas business, but also to learn best practice from that overseas business, which can then be fed back to the parent company.

One of the most common forms of integrating mechanism is the creation of a **global matrix structure**, which effectively makes key functional departments in the parent company responsible for certain aspects of the overseas business's activities and helps ensure clearer integration and permanent liaison.

Intellectual capital

Intellectual capital is equal to business knowledge, expertise and relationships. It is considered to be the basis of being able to think, talk and do things which contribute to a business's earnings and performance. The main function of management is to convert intellectual capital into financial capital; it is only when the management and the increase of intellectual capital are correctly balanced that value can be created in the business.

Intellectual capital, arguably, consists of three different elements:

- *Human capital* – the skills, competences, knowledge and attitudes of the employees.
- *Structural capital* – the processes, systems and databases of the business.
- *Relationship capital* – the business's partnerships and relationships with customers, partners and suppliers. A sub-set of relationship capital includes brands, copyrights, patents and trademarks.

It has been estimated that intellectual capital contributes some 10 per cent of US gross domestic product, which equates to approximately $1 million. There are numerous other ways in which the exact nature of intellectual capital can be described. One such, although broader, set of definitions would include the following features:

- Brands – the identity and values of a business, representing its products and services and its place in consumers' lifestyles.
- Intellectual property and goodwill – which includes all trademarks, trade secrets, licences, patents, and the business's intellectual property strategy.

- Active intelligence – the energy and creativity of the business, its knowledge or know-how, information, data, and the ability to innovate.
- Corporate culture – the way in which the organization does business (its practices and rituals).
- People – the sum total of the abilities, talents and relationships of the management and employees.
- Experience and history – collectively known as the 'corporate memory'.
- Work product – the intellectual materials which create new products or services and new incomes.

Roos, Johan, Roos, Goran, Edvinsson, Leif and Dragonetti, Nicola C., *Intellectual Capital: Navigating in the New Business Landscape*. Basingstoke: Palgrave Macmillan, 1997.

Stewart, Thomas A., *Intellectual Capital: The New Wealth of Organizations*. London: Nicholas Brearley Publishing, 1997.

International strategy

Whilst strategy can be defined as being actions which the management of a business takes in order to meet the objectives of the organization, international strategy requires a more complicated and holistic view. International businesses which operate in different countries need to be aware of national differences, both in the markets in which they operate and in the potential advantages and disadvantages of establishing operations in those countries. They will often make a judgement as to the specific factors which can affect the performance of their activity in any given country. In each specific nation the strategy needs to be adapted in order to match the economies of the different locations.

One specific strategy could be the production or the offering of standardized products, but ultimately international expansion requires the business to attain specific competences in relation to each market. Multinational organizations can have a considerable advantage if they set up foreign subsidiaries and use the inherent skills in the marketplace in pursuit of their global strategy and objectives. Businesses will often look to find areas in which they can reduce costs and produce specific commodities where price is the main competitive weapon. Part of the successful strategy revolves around being locally responsive and reflecting consumer tastes and preferences whilst working within the peculiarities of an overseas nation's infrastructure and mirroring their traditional practices, using their distribution channels and being cognizant of the host government's policies and regulations.

Many multinational businesses will also consider that an integral part of their international strategy is the transference of skills and products into foreign markets which have been customized for local consumption. This means that the strategy aimed at customizing their products must include their overall business strategy in relation to that nation and the framing of appropriate marketing plans.

International businesses no longer consider simply replicating their domestic strategy in overseas markets. Indeed, to remain competitive and successful, they adopt a trans-national strategy which focuses upon cost reduction, the transference of skills and products, and stimulating local responsiveness.

Stonehouse, George, Hamill, Jim, Campbell, David and Purdie, Tony, *Global and Trans-national Business: Strategy and Management*. New York: John Wiley, 2001.

Intrepreneur

The term 'intrepreneur' was originally coined in the early 1980s and literally means an entrepreneur within an organization. The term is used to describe an individual with responsibility for developing new enterprises within the organization itself. Unlike standard start-up businesses, any new enterprise can enjoy the protection and financial benefits of the existing organization and usually has a far better opportunity to succeed.

Inventory turnover

Inventory turnover, or stock turnover, is equal to the cost of goods sold divided by the average investment in the inventory. Or, in other words, the cost of goods sold, divided by stock. The inventory turnover is the inverse of cycle time. Normally the inventory turnover increases in proportion to demand.

Investment strategy

Business investment strategy can be typified as having three primary exponents, namely exploration, exploitation and expansion. Investment strategy, be it internal or external, can involve strategic alliances, partnerships, acquisitions or mergers. Equally, investment strategy can move a business vertically, horizontally or laterally in terms of its involvement in a specific market or markets. Investment strategy is not for the risk averse, as higher-risk investments often offer longer-term advantages, assuming that the investment is a sound one. Clearly any form of investment strategy requires the diversion of resources from the core business area to a new, or allied, area of operation. Investment strategy therefore requires a sound technical capability, a tacit knowledge of the market and, above all, an understanding of the rapidly changing markets themselves.

Business investment does not mean having to secure ownership of all of a partner's or subsidiary's assets. It can involve a cooperative arrangement which seeks to enhance both businesses' competitive position. Businesses will seek horizontal mergers and acquisitions in the hope that they will capture a larger proportion of the market. They may also create new entities in order to reduce costs through **synergy** effects.

Businesses will look for the optimum business investment, which will not only minimize their transactional costs, but enhance their strategic objectives.

Bouchet, Michael Henry, Clark, Ephraim and Groslambert, Bertrand, *Country Risk Assessment: A Guide to Global Investment Strategy.* New York: John Wiley, 2003.

Ishikawa diagram

The Ishikawa, or fishbone, diagram was created by Kaoru Ishikawa and is, to all intents and purposes, a cause-and-effect graphic representation (see Figure 37). The diagram is designed to identify all the possible causes which lead to a specific effect.

An Ishikawa diagram is a graphic tool which is often used as a means to note the progress and content of a brainstorming session aimed at attempting to identify the causes of a problem.

The Ishikawa diagram is also known as a cause-and-effect or fishbone diagram. It is named after the inventor of the tool, Kaoru Ishikawa (1969). It is called a fishbone diagram because its shape resembles a fish skeleton, with the name of the basic problem being entered at the right of the diagram at the end of the main 'bone'. The causes of the problem are then drawn as bones off the main backbone.

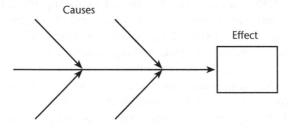

Figure 37   The Ishikawa diagram

Typically, four 'M's are used as a starting point, namely materials, machines, manpower and methods, although different categories can be used if needed. The main point of the exercise is to choose between three and six main categories which cover all of the possible influences.

Brainstorming allows the addition of causes to the main bones of the diagram and more specific causes to bones on the bones. The subdivision of the problems continues for as long as there are identified problems which can be subdivided.

Usually, the diagram has four or five levels, and when the fishbone has been completed, the individuals involved will be able to view a full picture of all of the possibilities relating to the root cause of the problem under discussion.

Ishikawa, Kaoru, *Guide to Quality Control*. Tokyo: Productivity, 1986.

Ivory tower planning

'Ivory tower planning' is a term used to describe the process of planning which is restricted purely to the responsibility of senior management. This form of planning is considered to take place in a vacuum, with little understanding of the business's operations, realities and external environment. Typically, senior management would not elicit assistance or information from managers actually operating the business, and might well develop a short- to long-term planning strategy which pays little regard to the actual realities of running the business itself.

Job analysis

Job analysis is a process which seeks to identify the component parts or elements of a particular job role. There are several different areas that provide sources of information regarding the exact nature of the job (see Table 22), which are integral to analysing a job successfully.

The process of analysing a job usually follows a fixed set of procedures, also known as a job analysis schedule.

Table 22 Sources of information used in job analysis

Information source	Questions answered
Work activities	What is actually done? What are the tasks which make up the job and what is their relative timing and importance? Are the tasks complex or simple?
Job context	Where is the job physically located? What are the working conditions? Is supervision necessary?
Work aids	What equipment, machinery or tools are immediately required to carry out the work?
How the job is performed	What are the precise operations involved? How are they measured and what standards do they need to conform to?
Personnel requirements	What experience, training, education, physical abilities, dexterity, aptitudes or social skills are required of the individual?
Job relations	How reliant is the job on cooperation? Is immediate supervision required? What advancement opportunities are there and what are the usual patterns of promotion?
Job tangibles and intangibles	In terms of tangibles, what resources are consumed or required by the job? With regard to intangibles, what services are required in order to facilitate the job?

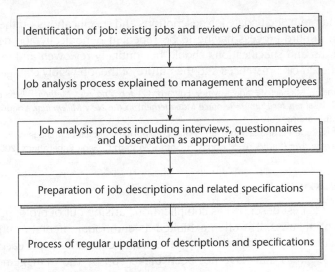

Figure 38   A job analysis scedule

Source: Adapted from Mathis and Jackson, *Human Resource Management: Essential Perspectives.*

A job analysis schedule is a multi-stepped process which aims to analyse the exact nature of a specific job. The chart in Figure 38 describes one way in which this may be achieved.

The steps are more clearly described in the following manner:

- Identify jobs and review existing documentation – typical documentation would include **job descriptions**, organization charts, and previous job analysis information. In identifying the job itself, analysis can take the form of analysing an individual job or specific job roles within a division or the whole organization.
- Explain the process to managers and employees – it is imperative that both managers and employees receive an explanation as to why the job analysis is under way, what steps will be involved and, if possible, the timescale. This will enable the analyst to encourage these individuals to participate, and identify who should be contacted when issues arise.
- Conduct the job analysis – typically, interviews may be conducted, observations made or questionnaires used to collect specific information.
- Prepare job descriptions and specifications – on the basis of the information collected, new job descriptions and job specifications can now be drafted. It is vital that existing employees and their managers are encouraged to participate and amend as necessary.

- Maintain and update job descriptions and specifications – rather than the entire process having to be repeated periodically, job descriptions and specifications should be routinely reviewed and updated should circumstances and the nature of the job visibly change.

Brannick, Michael T. and Levine, Edward L., *Job Analysis: Methods, Research and Applications for Human Resource Management in the New Millennium*. London: Sage Publications, 2002.
Mathis, Robert L. and Jackson, John Harold (eds), *Human Resource Management: Essential Perspectives* (2nd edn). Mason, OH: South-Western College Publications, 2001.

Job burnout

Burnout is best described as complications arising out of prolonged and substantial stress. It is often exhibited as emotional, mental or physical exhaustion in employees who have been exposed to unreasonable levels of stress that have not been picked up by the management or human resource department.

Burnout has been exacerbated by **downsizing** of businesses and the streamlining of operations in the constant search for ways in which to economize and improve profitability. Whilst these strategies are employed, businesses still seek to be as productive as they had been with larger workforces. Inevitably this places more strain on the remaining employees. The reasons for burnout can thus be described as a combination of increased work and the fear of being next on the list of dismissals.

Biggs, Richard K., *Burn Brightly without Burning Out: Balancing Your Career with the Rest of Your Life*. London: Thomas Nelson Publishers, 2003.

Job description

The main purpose of a job description is to define the job role and the intended tasks to be carried out within that role. It is vital to the success of the recruitment selection process that the job description is exact, both for the benefit of the organization and for the new employee. Typically, a job description would include the following:

- The title of the job.
- The location at which the work is to be carried out. This might be a branch of the organization, or the department or section within which the new employee will be based.
- The title of the new employee's immediate line manager.
- The grade of the job.
- The job titles of any subordinates of the new employee.

- The purpose of the job.
- The tasks to be carried out within the job role.
- Details of any equipment, machinery or other job- or skill-specific information.
- Details of any travel that may have to be undertaken as part of the job.
- Details of any additional work requirements, such as overtime, weekend work, shift work or dangerous working conditions.

Job rotation

Job rotation is a way of extending or enlarging the tasks carried out by employees. It involves the training, or retraining, of employees so that they are capable of exchanging jobs with one another, often on a regular and predetermined basis. Job rotation can often lead to increased job satisfaction because employees feel that they have a fuller picture of the related jobs and feel more involved in the organization as a whole. The employees also feel more versatile and consider that the scheme gives them a wider variety of tasks, as well as eliminating the need for them to carry out difficult or disliked tasks regularly, instead of only having to confront these tasks infrequently.

The main benefits to an organization of introducing a job rotation system are that there is constant cover for periods of holiday or sickness. Individual employees can, however, feel that they are constantly on the move and not given sufficient time for the development of specific skills, particularly if the process is carried out during times of high demand, when they often consider they have left a job with too many loose-ends not dealt with. Additionally, levels of competence have to be reasonably parallel; otherwise some employees could find themselves completing the bulk of the tasks involved in the job whilst other employees find little to do.

The question of **motivation** through job rotation is a questionable one as often employees are motivated at the introduction of the system, but once they have grasped the aspects of the new tasks involved, they find little reason to continue to strive. The job rotation scheme is an ideal system to be put in place by an organization employing large numbers of unskilled or semi-skilled workers.

Job specification

A job specification would be drawn up by an organization in order to identify a number of key issues relating to a post. Initially a **job analy-**

sis would be completed, and using this research into the nature of the job, the job specification would define:

- the qualifications required;
- the experience, knowledge and skills required;
- the personal qualities required;
- any other special demands the job might make.

The purpose of the production of a job specification is to enhance the interview stage of the recruitment process and to enable the interviewer to ask appropriate and enlightening questions of the potential new employee. It is vital that the level of qualification required is precise in the job specification and that the requirements are not pitched at either too high or too low a level. There are two recognized ways of analysing the information on a job specification: the seven-point plan and the five-point plan.

The seven-point plan was developed by Alec Rodger and covers:

- Physical make-up required – this looks at health, physique, appearance, bearing and speech issues.
- Attainments – this is where the education, qualifications and experience required will be stipulated.
- General intelligence – this is the intellectual level required.
- Special aptitudes – this is where considerations such as manual dexterity, communication or number skills, or those in the use of particular equipment or machinery, will be included.
- Interests – this section would identify whether the prospective emploee needs to be physically active, practical, artistic etc.
- Disposition – this section would identify whether the individual has to be of a certain nature, such as being steady, reliable, self-reliant, able to influence others, etc.
- Circumstances – this would relate to the individual's domestic circumstances and the occupations of his or her family.

Munro Fraser designed the five-point, or five-fold, grading system, which is often considered to be simpler and concentrates more on the previous career of the applicant. The five-fold system looks at:

- Impact on others – this looks at issues such as the potential employee's physical make-up, appearance, communication skills and general manner.
- Acquired qualifications – education, training, qualifications and, where appropriate, work experience carried out.
- Innate abilities – this aspect considers the potential employee's aptitude for learning and quickness of comprehension.

- Motivation – this aspect considers whether potential employees have set goals, aims, targets or objectives for themselves and whether or not they have achieved them.
- Adjustment – this consider issues such as emotional stability, ability to deal with stressful situations, and the individual's nature with regard to getting along with others.

Brannick, Michael T. and Levine, Edward L., *Job Analysis: Methods, Research and Applications for Human Resource Management in the New Millennium*. London: Sage Publications, 2002.

Johari window

In 1970 Harry Ingham and Joe Luft presented the Johari window, which illustrated relationships in terms of awareness. It has been used since to describe much about human relations. As can be seen in Figure 39, the Johari window consists of four quadrants marked I to IV.

Quadrant I refers to behaviour and motivations which are known to both the individual and others. Quadrant II refers to things that others can see in us but of which the individual is unaware. Quadrant III represents things the individual knows but does not reveal to others, such as hidden agendas. In quadrant IV are behaviours and motives which neither the individual nor others are aware of, yet some of these behaviours and motives influence relationships.

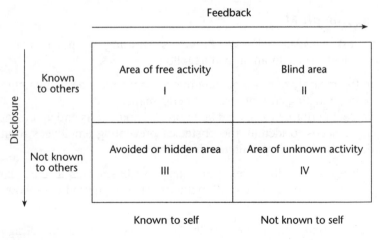

Figure 39 Johari window (basic)

Luft, Joe, *Group Processes: An Introduction to Group Dynamics*. Mayfield Publishing, 1970.

Joint venture

A joint venture is a long-term agreement by two or more separate business entities to cooperate and jointly control a separate business entity. Typically, a joint venture would involve a manufacturer and, perhaps, a distributor, in developing a new business venture which affords both parties the potential for profit and a more secure share of the market. A contractual arrangement, setting out the terms of the joint venture, forms the basis of the association between the two separate founding businesses.

The term 'joint venture' is also applicable to international business deals which see collaboration between organizations which are based in two different countries. They will contribute to a new business enterprise in which, in one way or another, ownership and control are shared.

Joint ventures may be described as being either populated or unpopulated. A populated joint venture is a legally independent business, with its own management and staff. An unpopulated joint venture is one that is typified by the concept of a shell company, in which the partner companies temporarily loan their management and staff to the joint venture.

Vermeulen, Erik, *The Evolution of Legal Business Forms in Europe and the United States: Venture Capital, Joint Venture and Partnership Structures.* New York: Kluwer Law International, 2003.

Juran, Joseph M.

Juran worked closely with **W. Edwards Deming** on people-based management issues. Juran argued as follows:

- In the majority of cases management concentrates on maintaining or perpetuating current levels of performance.
- Present performance should be improved and to this end, management needs to identify the obstacles preventing employees from doing this and then eliminate those barriers.

Juran also worked with Deming and Japanese businesses to enhance product quality through statistical methods. They suggested the following:

- It is important to ensure that the product conforms to the design specifications.
- It is necessary to use statistical quality control (SQC) and a form of process control to monitor quality during the production process or the delivery of the service.

- Work teams or **quality circles** can then concentrate on error reduction. While they are doing this, management must support them in their efforts.

Juran, J. and Gryna, Frank M., *Quality Planning and Analysis: From Product Development Through Use*, 4th edition. New York: McGraw-Hill, 2000.

www.juran.com

Just-in-time (JIT)

JIT is a philosophy which was developed in Japan, emphasizing the importance of deliveries in relation to the process of small lot-sizes. The philosophy emphasizes the importance of set-up cost reduction, small lot-sizes, pull-systems, level production and, importantly, the elimination of waste (*muda*).

JIT is designed to allow the achievement of high-volume production, whilst ensuring that minimal inventories of raw materials, work-in-process and finished goods are held by the business. Parts arrive at the manufacturing plant from suppliers, 'just in time' to be placed into the manufacturing process, and as the products are processed along the line they arrive at the next work station just in time, thereby moving through the whole system very quickly.

JIT relies on the management ensuring that manufacturing waste is kept to a minimum and that nothing is made or brought onto the premises that is not immediately required. JIT requires precision, as the right part needs to be in the right place at the right time. Waste is described as being the results of any activity that adds cost without adding value (which includes moving and storing).

JIT is also known as 'lean production' or 'stockless production' and the theory is that it should improve the profits and the returns on investment by the following means:

- reducing inventory levels;
- increasing the inventory turnover rate;
- improving product quality;
- reducing production and delivery lead times;
- reducing other costs (machine set-ups and equipment breakdown).

JIT also recognizes the fact that any under-utilized capacity can be used to build up a small stock of products or components (buffer inventories) in order to ensure that in the event of a problem the production process will not be interrupted.

JIT is primarily used in manufacturing processes which are repetitive in nature and where the same products and components are used and produced in relatively high volumes. Once the flow has been set up, there should be a steady and even flow of materials, components and finished products passing through the facility. Each work station is linked in a similar way to an assembly-line (although the exact layout may be a jobbing or batch process layout). The goal is to eliminate all queuing and to achieve the ideal lot-size per unit of production.

Delbridge, Rick, *Life on the Line in Contemporary Manufacturing: The Workplace Experience of Lean Production and the 'Japanese' Model.* Oxford: Oxford University Press, 2000.

Gross, John M. and McInnis, Kenneth R., *Kanban Made Simple: Demystifying and Applying Toyota's Legendary Manufacturing Process.* New York: Amacom, 2003.

J

Kaizen

Kaizen is a Japanese term which implies the adoption of a concept of aspiring towards gradual, but orderly, continuous improvement. The *kaizen* business strategy seeks to involve individuals from across the organization at any level of the organization.

The goal is to work together in order to achieve these improvements without having to make large capital investments. Each change or improvement collectively complements and moves the process onwards. *Kaizen* requires a culture of sustained continuous improvement, whilst focusing on the elimination of waste in areas, systems and processes of the organization. Above all, the cooperation and involvement of all employees is vital to the overall success of the philosophy.

Colenso, Michael, *Kaizen Strategies for Successful Organizational Change: Enabling Evolution and Revolution in the Organization* (Kaizen Strategies). London: Financial Times, Prentice Hall, 2000.

Imai, Masaaki, *Gemba Kaizen: Collaborating for Change*. San Francisco, CA: Berrett-Koehler Publishers, 2000.

www.kaizen.org

Kanban

Kanban is a Japanese word which means 'signal'; in effect this is exactly what the system does, by sending a signal to employees to perform a particular action related to the process or work station in which they are involved.

The system works on the following set of rules:

- An empty container gives a factory worker permission to work to fill the box.
- If a worker does not have an empty box to fill, the worker is blocked from doing any more work and is reassigned somewhere else where their work is needed.
- The *kanban* control system uses a signalling device to regulate **just-in-time (JIT)** flows.

- The cards or containers make up the *kanban* pull-system.
- The authority to produce or supply additional parts comes from downstream operations.
- A *kanban* is a card that is attached to a storage and transport container. It identifies the part number and container capacity, along with other information.
- A *kanban* system is a pull-system, in which the *kanban* is used to pull parts to the next production stage when they are needed.

The *kanban* system differs from schedule-based systems as these are push-systems. They have a detailed production schedule for each part to be used in order to push parts to the next production stage on schedule. *Kanban* is more flexible as it does not rely on the forecasting of customer demand in order to estimate the production lead times.

The *kanban* system requires the **just-in-time (JIT)** production philosophy to be embraced fully, particularly with regard to rapid set-up times and small lot-sizes.

David, J. L., *'Kanban': Just in Time at Toyota*. Portland, OR: Productivity Press, 1989.

Gross, John M. and McInnis, Kenneth R., *'Kanban' Made Simple: Demystifying and Applying Toyota's Legendary Manufacturing Process*. New York: Amacom, 2003.

Kanter, Rosabeth Moss

Rosabeth Moss Kanter has written a wide variety of books, primarily on management and management techniques. One of her main concepts brought together **empowerment**, organizational **change management** and bureaucracy. Kanter is a strong supporter of participative management and claims that management should use employees in order to achieve **synergy** within the organization. She is also a strong supporter of a **flat structure** in organizations, with less hierarchical controls, which she feels would stifle empowerment and entrepreneurial opportunities.

Kanter, Rosabeth Moss, *Rosabeth Moss Kanter on the Frontiers of Management*. Boston, MA: Harvard Business School Press, 2003.

www.pfdf.org/leaderbooks/kanter

Keiretsu system

The *keiretsu* was formerly a unique Japanese type of corporate organization but, increasingly, other countries have been moving towards this form of organizational arrangement.

The key aspect of a *keiretsu* is that a group or a family of affiliated trans-national organizations operate together (both vertically and horizontally) in an integrated manner. Importantly, the *keiretsu* has its own trading entities and banks, thereby allowing it to control each part of the economic chain in a major industrial or service-based sector.

A *keiretsu*, therefore, can not only research and develop a technology and products, but can also plan the production, secure the finance, cover the insurance implications and then find the resources (wherever they are) in order to process them. The purpose of the exercise is to maintain control and production in Japan, where the finished products will be packaged, before being distributed across the world.

Keiretsu use **just-in-time (JIT)** and specific forms of supply chain management:

- They apply pressure to suppliers to reduce prices.
- They encourage supplier involvement in *kaizen*.
- They involve suppliers at the earliest stage of the development of new products, in as much as they ask for comment on designs and do not merely supply the designs prior to the commencement of production.
- They commit suppliers to the notion that they will only supply quality parts and components.
- They use a two-vendor policy, as a means of ensuring that suppliers remain competitive as they risk losing a portion or all of their contracts to the better supplier.
- They encourage suppliers to use just-in-time.
- They use a monthly master schedule using *kanban* as a signal for the adjustment of this schedule.
- They are committed to a levelled production.

Burt, David, *The American Keiretsu: A Strategic Weapon for Global Competitiveness*. New York: Irwin Professional (USA), 1993.

Miyashita, Kenichi and Russell, David, *Keiretsu: Inside the Hidden Japanese Conglomerates*. New York: McGraw-Hill Trade, 1995.

K

Kepner, Charles (and Hirotsugu Iikubo)

In their book *Managing Beyond the Ordinary*, Charles Kepner and Hirotsugu Iikubo identified what they call the ten critical tasks, in effect a structure which suggests a blueprint for collaborative problem-solving:

1 Understand the situation fully and know what's going on. Listen with an open mind to every person who might have insight into the situation.

2 Clarify your objectives.

3 Determine what information you need, to solve the problem, and the sources of that information.

4   Get a complete and accurate picture of the problem. After the information-gathering in step 3, there should be a shared and factual view of the problem.

5   Find the cause and be able to prove it. Once the cause of the problem has been agreed, this view needs to be analysed in order to proceed having ensured that nothing has been omitted or ignored.

6   Define the ideal solution. There needs to be a permanent, or at least a long-term, solution.

7   Find the best actions possible to achieve your objective. Access all information resources and collect knowledge and experience with similar problems.

8   Create a workable draft solution. The draft solution will highlight difficulties that were not obvious until this point.

9   Fine-tune your plan. If the plan works on paper it still needs to be rechecked to anticipate potential risks and impacts on other areas of operations and activities.

10   Present your plan and gain acceptance. Once the plan has been completed, it is imperative that those that will be affected accept its recommendations. The solution needs to be communicated in terms of both how the problem was solved and why the solution offered has been reached. Above all, those involved should be made to realize that the solution has been arrived at by critical rational analysis, rather than a **top–down** imposition.

Kepner, C. H. and Hirotsugu, Iikubo, *Managing Beyond the Ordinary*. New York: Amacom Books, 1996.

Key factors for success (KFS)

There are of course many interpretations of key factors for success, or KFS. The KFS of different businesses differ radically in accordance with their primary business plans and objectives. In effect, KFS relate to the essential elements of a business's plan, which determine whether or not that plan will be followed through and achieved.

For a retail operation, for example, at least seven key factors for success could be identified, these would include:

- The selling of products or services at a sufficient gross margin to sustain profitability.
- The offering to customers of a convincing and compelling range of products and services.
- Ensuring that customer acquisition costs are in line with average sales.

- Providing customers with a user-friendly environment.
- Attracting significant visitor traffic and managing a high conversion rate.
- Providing and managing cost-effective and efficient product fulfilment.
- Providing significant and quality customer support before, during and after purchase.

Key performance indicators (KPI)

'Key performance indicators' refers to a system which seeks to develop both the organizational and individual skill levels within a business. Typically, the KPI system of development includes the following processes:

- Confirmation of the outcomes required.
- Establishing the goals and tests.
- Development of the KPIs and tests.
- Establishing KPI accountability frameworks.
- Launching of the KPI system.

A more detailed look at the five steps is addressed in Table 23.

Smith, Jeff, *The KPI Book: The Ultimate Guide to Understanding the Key Performance Indicators of your Business*. London: Insight Training and Development, 2001.

Knowledge management

Knowledge management can be seen as one of the key factors of organizational development. Knowledge management recognizes that information and ability are among the most valuable assets an organization possesses. In the past, organizations have not been able to quantify or recognize this aspect as being one of their prime assets, as it is intangible. Knowledge is not just information or data, it needs to have a meaning and a purpose, and in human resources management this means the ability to apply and use information. In other words, knowledge management is all about people and the process of being able to use information. There is no compelling definition of the term 'knowledge management' and it has been variously described as intellectual capital or property, amongst other different attempts to explain its purpose and worth.

The key concern for human resources departments is the retaining of individuals who are able to impart knowledge as an essential function of their relationship with the business. Thus knowledge management is

Table 23 The five key performance indicators

Step	Detail
Confirmation of the outcomes required	The KPIs are based on what the business hopes to achieve, typically customer service improvements, improvement of stakeholder relations or the reduction of operating costs.
Establishing the goals and tests	Each KPI will need a specific goal; the test examines whether the accomplishment of the goal will achieve the outcome required.
Development of KPIs and tests	What are the drivers of the outcomes? How will the performance and move towards performance be measured? How will the KPIs need to be amended to fit in with the existing management information systems?
Establishing KPI accountability and frameworks	Who will ultimately be accountable for each of the KPIs? Some of the KPIs will be achieved by cooperation, but who will monitor this?
Launching of the KPI system	**'Goals down, plans up'** is a term which is associated with the development of key performance indicators (KPI) and change management. When launching KPIs there are four usual stages: • Goals down, plans up – which requires the KPIs to be cascaded down to the operational teams. The KPIs are the goals and the teams develop their relevant KPIs through the plans they develop to achieve these goals. • Individual performance plans – which require management and team leaders to create their own KPIs from the organizational plan. • Documentation development – all KPIs are logged and a process for updating the next planning cycle is organized. • Training – both 'hard' and 'soft' skills are developed in terms of group training, and individual skills training for both technical and functional skills (hard skills) and behavioural performance (soft skills) are included.

a complex process, but includes questions as to how to share knowledge, how to find it, how to use it and how to convert it or transfer it from one individual to another.

Davenport, Thomas H. and Prusak, Laurence, *Working Knowledge: How Organizations Manage What They Know*. Boston, MA: Harvard Business School Press, 2000.

von Krogh, Georg, Ichijo, Kazua and Nonaka, Ikujiro, *Enabling Knowledge Creation.* Oxford: Oxford University Press, 2000.

Kotter, John

John Kotter and L. A. Schlesinger recognized that many employees are inherently resistant to change. There are enormous implications arising out of change which could affect individuals' opportunities for promotion or better pay, or the fact that they may need to travel to an

Table 24 Reasons for resisting change

Reason for resisting change	Description
Parochial self-interest	This category suggests that the individuals are more concerned with the impact of change on themselves and how it might affect their future, rather than considering the continued success of the business. Change for these individuals means losing something which they value and, as such, they will resist the change. There is a danger that if enough individuals feel this way, they will collaborate to block the change.
Misunderstanding	Essentially this is a communication problem. Inadequate information has been passed to the employees by the management and, as a result, much of what the employees know and understand has been derived from **grapevine** communication. At the root of this, the employees do not trust the management and will seek to find alternative justifications as to why the management are instituting the changes.
Different assessment of the situation	Not all employees will see that there are good enough reasons to be instituting the changes. Each will seek to find reasons why the changes are being proposed and they will come to their own conclusions, which may inevitably lead to resistance. It should not be assumed, even with the most complete and open consultation process, that individuals will reach the same conclusions.
Low tolerance to change	These individuals value their security and stability in work. The introduction of new systems or processes will tend to undermine their self-belief. Management will need to recognize that there is fear and reassure the employees, who may otherwise resist the change.

K

alternative location. The theorists attempted to classify why employees may be resistant to change and suggested four broad categories, as listed in Table 24.

Kotter and Schlesinger suggested a number of ways in which management could seek to minimize resistance to change:

- through education and communication;
- through participation and involvement;
- through facilitation and support;
- through negotiation and agreement;
- through manipulation and co-opting;
- through explicit and implicit coercion.

Kotter, J. P. and Schlesinger, L. A., 'Choosing Strategies for Change', *Harvard Business Review*, 57 (1979), pp. 106–14.

www.pfdf.org/leaderbooks./Kotter

Labour process approach

Harry Braverman's *Labor and Monopoly Capital* (1980) put forward the theory that various work processes led to the degradation of work, particularly as a result of the adoption of scientific management (such as that of **F. W. Taylor**) which was at the heart of a capitalist trend towards work design. Braverman felt that employees were becoming little more than machines in themselves as they serviced the manufacturing process and that human resources departments maintained the employees rather like the employees maintained the machinery in their factories.

John Storey has also added to the debate, questioning whether the problems of viewing employees as simply part of the production process could be resolved. After a brief introduction to some of the main early contributions to labour process theory, four processes will be outlined. Braverman had suggested that management exercised complete control over the production process and each step of the labour process had been broken down into its constituent elements. Management then expected the workforce to perform their tasks in the most efficient manner, following the instructions without question. The workforce would have no understanding of the overall process as their contribution would be fragmented. Braverman, adopting a Marxist approach, believed that scientific management represented a class issue transferred to the workplace, with capitalists controlling the labour processes and alienating the workforce from their work.

J. Child (1985) developed his own framework within a labour process model, which highlights the structure of employee–manager relations. Child argued that in situations where the management concentrates on investment in technology it ignores the development of the labour processes. Management imposes changes on the labour processes as a result of having to adapt to new technologies and emerging competitive pressures. He also identified four strategies used by management to incorporate new technology:

- direct labour is eliminated through automation and flexible production;

- the contracting out (**outsourcing**) of the workforce with payment on the basis of labour time;
- the elimination of traditional divisions of labour (demarcations) with the expansion of job roles and responsibilities;
- the **deskilling** of jobs, with the knowledge and skills of the workforce being transferred to management.

Braverman, Harry, 'Labor and Monopoly Capital', *New York Monthly Review Press*, 1974.

Child, J., 'Managerial Strategies, New Technology and the Labour Process', *Job Redesign: Critical Perspectives on the Labour Process*, ed. D. Knights, H. Willmott and D. Collinson. Aldershot: Gower, 1985.

Storey, John, *Developments in the Management of Human Resources*. Oxford: Blackwell, 1992.

Leadership continuum

The leadership continuum model was proposed by R. Tannebaum and W. H. Schmidt in 1973. It suggested that autocratic leaders who have authority to make decisions and control subordinates are more likely to make their own decisions and not engage their subordinates, whereas a more democratic (or *laissez-faire*) manager gives subordinates a greater degree of **delegation** in decision making. The essence of the continuum is summarized in the diagram in Figure 40.

See also **contingency approach.**

Tannebaum, R. and Schmidt, W. H., 'How to Choose a Leadership Pattern', *Harvard Business Review*, May–June 1973.

Leadership strategy

The precise leadership strategy of a business will very much depend on a number of priorities, but it is important to realize that there is a distinct difference between leadership and management. Beginning with the priorities, it is safe to assume that leadership strategy will be based on some, or all, of the following:

- The achievement of optimal performance.
- The acquisition of an overview rather than detail.
- The ability to become involved in detail if necessary.
- Issues including development, continuity and improvement.
- The taking of remedial action.
- Monitoring and evaluating work and those involved in work.
- Ensuring that those with the right skills and capacities are matched to the right jobs.

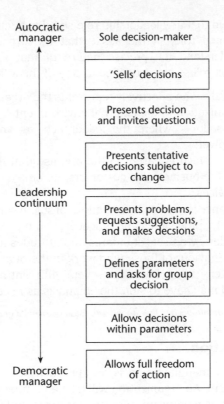

Figure 40   Leadership continuum

- Continuous improvement through systems such as **total quality management**.
- **Motivation** and the promotion of a harmonious workplace.
- General operational management activities.

It is generally thought that leadership requires a number of different and often mutually supporting skills. These include:

- the ability to show measurable results;
- the ability to inspire;
- the actuality, or the illusion, of hard work;
- the receiving and giving of respect;
- the ability to give **added value** to the organization, its processes, products and services;
- a degree of apparent honesty;
- the ability to take and give responsibility, accepting and giving the rewards associated with this responsibility.

It is also believed that any leadership role should effectively represent a specifically named role, in the sense that the organization and its employees understand the precise nature of that leader's function. These leadership roles can be typified as any of the following:

- A figurehead – who effectively represents the organization or a part of the organization to the external environment.
- An ambassador – where the leader acts as an advocate or a problem-solver.
- A servant – which is based on the premise that the manager is a servant of the business, its customers, its employees, its products and its services.
- A maintenance leader – who attends to problem solving, continuous improvement, procedures and practices, and may handle crises.
- A role model – who sets standards and attitudes and tries to influence the behaviour of those who work in the organization.
- A ringmaster – who may adopt several different roles, as outlined above, and may have to shift the emphasis as needs arise.

Pettinger, Richard, *Introduction to Management*. Basingstoke: Palgrave Macmillan, 2002.

Lean production

Lean production/manufacturing is an approach based on the Toyota Production system. An organization will take a number of steps to assist in ensuring that its manufacturing activities focus on five key concepts:

- Value centred on customer needs by creating activities as and when customers demand them.
- Value creation – which occurs along a series of steps and is known as the value stream. This is achieved through a closely synchronized flow of the organization's activities.
- Continually making improvements within the production process in order to maintain customer service and strive for perfection.

Central to an organization adopting the lean production/manufacturing approach is the question of waste reduction and a high level of engagement of all company personnel in implementing and improving the manufacturing process.

The benefits available to an organization adopting the lean production/manufacturing process are high. It is claimed that organizations have achieved an 80% reduction in cycle time, a 50% reduction in lead times, a 50% reduction in the levels of their inventory, and an increase in customer response rates, as well as an increase in quality.

Lean Enterprise Institute: www.lean.org/

Learning effects

'Learning effects' refers to cost savings which are achieved as an international business moves along an **experience curve**. As it continues to operate and learn from its experiences, the business will be able to make considerable cost savings by adjusting its operating procedures.

Legitimate power

Legitimate power derives from the authority which a manager has in a **chain of command**. Legitimate power is used on a daily basis and the manager's legitimate power will increase as his or her responsibilities increase.

> Greenleaf, Robert K., Spears, Larry C. and Covey, Stephen, *Servant Leadership: A Journey into the Nature of Legitimate Power and Greatness*. Mahwah, NJ: Paulist Press, 2002.

Leveraged buy-out

Leveraged buy-outs are an alternative means by which a business can seek to acquire another company. The business which is buying another company borrows money to pay for the majority of the purchase price. The debt which has been incurred is secured against the assets of the business being purchased. Interest payable on the loan will be paid from the acquired company's future **cash flow**.

During the 1980s leveraged buy-outs became very much a trend and businesses were able to raise loans of millions of dollars to purchase other businesses, which were often unwilling to sell. Many of these purchases ended in disaster, with the borrowers being declared bankrupt, as they could not meet the interest demands. However, many other businesses recognized that once they had purchased another business on this basis they would need to run the acquired business far more efficiently than the previous owners in order to ensure that sufficient funds were available to pay the interest.

Theoretically, of course, leveraged buy-outs can be, and are, used by international businesses to acquire overseas companies. In practice the approach is dependent upon the prevailing regulations which apply in different nations.

Lewin, Kurt

Kurt Lewin, in the 1950s, identified three stages which individuals, groups or organizations pass through when dealing with change, as described in Table 25.

Table 25 Dealing with change

Stage	Description
Unfreezing	This stage calls on the management and human resources departments to make it clear to employees that there is a requirement to make a change in the business. Employees are consulted, changes are planned, organized and scheduled and appropriate training is arranged.
Changing	This is the actual implementation of the changes, which rests upon the flexibility of the planning process and the steps which have been taken during the unfreezing stage.
Refreezing	Now that the change has been implemented, an assessment needs to be made of how effective and satisfactory the change has been. Whatever the new systems or procedures that have been put in place, these are effectively the new ways of doing things and should now be fully accepted by the employees and the organization as a whole.

Lewin, Kurt, *Field Theory in Social Science*. Westport, CT: Greenwood Press, 1975.
Lewin, Kurt, *Resolving Social Conflicts*. Washington, DC: American Psychological Association, 1997.

www.psy.vu.nl/kli

Lewison, Daniel

Lewison's 1978 study produced a model of the stages of career evolution; it adds credence to the managerial career stages. He suggested that adult life, rather predictably, involves a series of transitions every 5–7 years. The key points are described in Table 26.

Lewison, Daniel J., Darrow, Charlotte N., Kein, Edward B., Lewison, Maria H. and McKee, Braxton, *The Seasons of a Man's Life*. New York: Alfred A. Knopf, 1978.

Likert, Rensis

The Likert scale is named after Rensis Likert (1903–1981) and is used particularly in questionnaires. The respondents are asked to mark their level of agreement with a series of statements related to an attitude which is being measured. They are usually asked to state their agreement or disagreement on a 5-point scale. Each degree of agreement is

Table 26 Career stages

Age	Stage description	Detail
17–22	Early adult transition	Independence, breaking of family ties.
22–28	Entering the adult world	Education completed, career selection initiated.
28–33	Age 30 transition	Career review, feeling of last chance to change career.
33–40	Settling down	Job and career advancement a major preoccupation.
40–45	Mid-life transition	Review period, perhaps a mid-life crisis of confidence.
45–50	Entering middle adulthood	Consolidation and feelings of fulfilment.
50–55	Age 50 transition	Review of previous periods of transition.
55–60	Combination of middle adulthood	Stability, preparation for retirement.
60–65	Late adulthood transition	Retirement, with a period of review and reflection.
65+	Late adulthood	Evaluation of career.

given a numerical value, usually from 1 to 5, 1 to 7 or 1 to 9. In this way, a numerical value can be calculated for all the responses. Likert scales are usually constructed as shown in Table 27.

Singh, Jagdip, Howell, Roy D. and Rhoads, Gary K., *Adaptive Designs for the Likert-type Data: An Approach for Implementing Marketing Surveys*, Special report no. 90–117. Cambridge, MA: Marketing Science Institute, 1990.

www.acce-team.com/human-relations/hrels_04_likert.html

Line authority

The term 'line authority' is applied to individuals who have a direct management responsibility for a number of subordinates. The concept of line authority is integral to the **chain of command**, in which successive levels of management have line authority (responsibility) for all those individuals who are technically, in the hierarchy, lower than them

Table 27 Constructing and using a Likert scale

Stage of procedure	Description
Gathering statements	The first step in creating a Likert scale-based questionnaire is to develop statements which allow respondents to express their reaction. Statements are usually worded so that respondents can react to them by marking their view towards either one end of the scale or the other.
Formatting statements	Each of the statements is now given a graphic scale of between 5 and 9 (always odd) intervals along a continuum, which ranges typically from *Strongly agree* to *Strongly disagree*.
Scale administration	Clear instructions should be given to the respondents to either circle or mark the number in the scale which corresponds to how close their view is to *Strongly agree* or *Strongly disagree*.
Scoring the scale	Normally, *Strongly disagree* would be valued as a 1 on the continuum, whereas *Strongly agree* would variously be valued as either 5, 7 or 9, dependent upon the length of the continuum. The researchers total the score for each statement and its associated set of responses. The total score is then divided by the number of responses to the statement, producing an average score for each statement.

in the organization. Line authority is distinguished from **staff authority** in the sense that the latter refers to management or supervisors who have a specific responsibility for an aspect of an employee's work. Examples of staff authority would include human resources managers, who, technically, have authority in certain respects towards all employees, regardless of grade or position in the hierarchy. Line managers, however, have line authority and can, on a daily basis, exert their decisions upon those for whom they have responsibility.

Liquidation

Liquidation literally means turning a business's assets into readily available cash. This process normally begins when a business ceases to trade in its current form as a result of insolvency. Liquidation is often described as 'winding-up', usually as a result of a creditor finally taking the business to court for non-payment of debts. In these cases an individual known as a receiver or liquidator will be appointed to raise enough cash to satisfy the creditors. This is achieved by the disposal of the business's assets or the selling of the business to a third party as a going concern.

In many cases businesses will choose to go into voluntary liquidation, deciding to cease trading as they are currently organized. In these cases the business appoints a liquidator, who calls a meeting of creditors to endorse the liquidator's powers. The liquidator then assumes control of the business and collects assets, pays debts and, if there is a surplus, distributes it to the company's members according to their rights.

The liquidation value is equal to the current realistic and realizable amount of money which either an asset or a business is worth if it has to be sold immediately. The liquidation value represents the true market value of any assets or businesses, incorporating an evaluation of the business's liabilities. Technically, should the liquidation value of a business be less than the cumulative value of its shares, then the business should no longer be trading and the share price does not accurately reflect the true value of the business itself.

In the majority of cases the liquidation value is only ever a useful measure if a business is on the verge of collapse. In reality, it is not uncommon for the liquidation value, when compared with the current share price, to reveal that the business is indeed worth less than the cumulative value of all of the shares available.

Liquidity

The liquidity ratio, which is also known as the 'acid test ratio', compares the business's liquid or current assets with its current liabilities. Under the majority of circumstances a business's liquid assets are considered to be cash, trade debts and any other assets which can readily be sold. The ratio is normally configured in the following manner:

$$\frac{Current\ assets}{Current\ liabilities}$$

The liquidity ratio seeks to indicate whether the business is capable of paying its debts without having to make further sales. It is a prime measure of a business's solvency. The majority of accountants recommend that the ratio should produce a figure of around 1.5 and that values below 1.0 indicate that there is a severe problem with the business. Equally, values greater than 2.0 indicate that the business has invested too much money in short-term assets.

A variation, known primarily as the acid test ratio, presents a slightly different version of the liquidity ratio. The acid test ratio is:

$$\frac{Current\ assets - stock}{Current\ liabilities}$$

Again, most accountants would recommend that the figure should be equal to 1, indicating that the business has $1's worth of liquid assets for every $1's short-term debt. If the business has an acid test ratio result of less than 1, then it has a low liquidity and may be unable to find sufficient funds to finance its short-term debt commitments.

Chorafas, Dimitris N., *Liabilities, Liquidity and Cash Management: Balancing Financial Risk.* New York: John Wiley, 2002.

Lissack, Michael

Michael Lissack was formerly an investment banker, is an active angel investor, and has funded and supported a number of internet-based businesses.

Lissack is primarily interested in complexity theory, coherence, networking and models of management. Lissack's primary ideas include the notions:

- that complexity research and theory have applicable uses for management;
- that whilst management control is difficult, control can be achieved without force but with confidence.

Lissack, Michael (ed.), *The Interaction of Complexity and Management.* Westpoint, CT: Greenwood Press, 2002.

www.lissack.com

Locked in

The term 'locked in' can refer to either managers or employees in general. It tends to be used as a term which implies that, despite personal feelings to the contrary with regard to finding alternative employment, the individual is somehow tied financially, or contractually, to the organization. Typically, managers and employees can be locked into an organization in the sense that their future pension benefits, or ongoing share ownership schemes, require them to continue to work for the organization for a considerable number of years. They may also have signed a caveat to their contract of employment in which they undertook to remain with the organization for a specified period, probably following the business's funding of education or training.

Logical incrementalism

James Quinn suggested that real business strategy should develop as a result of consensus. He further suggested that:

- Planning systems should produce strategy.
- Strategy formulation is inherently a political act.
- Strategy formulation is neither behavioural nor formal.
- Strategies should emerge incrementally on an opportunistic basis.
- Incrementalism is the ideal policy for large organizations.
- Incrementalism must be carefully managed.

Strategy is seen as an evolving process between the environment and the intentions of the decision-makers. Strategy is clarified and defined incrementally as events unfold.

Quinn, James Brian, *Strategies for Change: Logical Incrementalism*. Burr Ridge, IL: Richard Irwin, 1980.

Loose–tight principle

'Loose–tight principle' refers to the concept of tight central control of an organization by its headquarters' senior management; simultaneously it allows certain managers and specifically subsidiaries a loose autonomy. This allows these individuals and subsidiaries to have a degree of initiative within clearly defined managerial limitations.

The loose–tight principle is considered to be one of the major contradictions of strategic management and is exemplified by other forms of autonomy, such as:

- **quality circles**;
- flexitime;
- job enrichment.

Whilst the bureaucratic, hierarchical principles remain, responsible autonomy is promoted.

L

Macro-environment

The term 'macro-environment' refers to all of the external activities or influences which may have an impact upon the operations of a business or organization. Some do not have a direct impact, but may influence how the business operates over a period of time. In the vast majority of cases organizations have little or no possibility of affecting these macro-environmental factors. Typically the macro-environment would include society in general, politics, economics, socio-political change, technology, or socio-cultural changes and trends.

Most businesses develop a means by which they can assess, or analyse, the macro-environment and identify strategic issues which may affect their operations. Typically this would include:

- An identification of the principal phenomena that will have an impact on the organization.
- A determination of the trends of each of those phenomena.
- Classification of the phenomena according to whether they are opportunities or threats.
- An evaluation of the phenomena in terms of their importance as opportunities or threats.

Once the opportunities and threats have been prioritized, the organization can then identify the strategic impacts they are likely to have upon the business.

See also **Five Forces model** *and* **micro-environment**.

Mager, Robert

Dr Robert F. Mager is primarily concerned with education and training. He has also written about goal analysis, instruction, trouble-shooting, performance, decision making, returns on investment, organizational change and industrial management.

Mager, Robert F., *What Every Manager Should Know about Training*. Cirencester: Management Books 2000, 2000.

www.cepworldwide.com/Bios/mager.htm

Management audit

A management audit is essentially a review of the operations of an organization and an assessment of the return on investment of those operations. Normally a management audit is carried out as an integral part of a **strategic plan**. In other cases it is carried out when a business is facing a particular crisis or a problem in leadership. However, it is good practice to carry out a management audit when things appear to be running as well as they could be, but when an organizational problem has been identified. The primary purpose of management audits is to increase efficiency, to provide a better means of measuring organizational performance, and to increase morale and commitment to achieving the organization's objectives.

Gray, Iain and Manson, Stuart, *The Audit Process*. London: Thomson Learning, 1999.

Management buy-out

A management buy-out involves the acquisition of a business by its existing management. In many cases the management group will establish a new holding company, which then effectively purchases the shares of the target company. There are variations of management buy-out, notably 'management buy-in', where an external management buys the business, and 'buy-in management buy-out', which is a combination of the two.

Management buy-outs may arise as a result of any of the following:

- A group may decide to sell a business because it has become a non-core activity.
- An organization may find itself in difficulties and need to sell part of its business.
- The owner of a business may choose to retire.
- A receiver or administrator may sell the business as a going concern.

The normal sequence of events in a management buy-out is as follows:

- Agreement of the management team as to who will become the managing director.
- Appointment of financial advisors.
- Assessment of the suitability of the buy-out.
- Attainment of approval to pursue the management buy-out.
- Evaluation of the vendor's asking price.
- Formulation of business plans.
- Selection of suitable equity investors and receipt of written offers.

- Appointment of legal advisors.
- Selection of lead investor.
- Negotiation of the best equity deal obtainable.
- Negotiation of purchase of the business.
- Carrying out of a due diligence test with the aid of an auditor.
- Obtaining finance and other equity investment.
- Preparation of legal documents.
- Achievement of legal ownership.

Andrews, Phildrew, *Management Buy-Out*. New York: Kogan Page, 1999.

Management by exception

This is a form of management which states that efficient managers should concentrate primarily on dealing with situations which significantly deviate from plans. In other words, they focus their attention upon exceptions to the normal procedures, standards and quality and effectively ignore performance that is in accord with normal plans.

Management by objectives (MBO)

The concept of management by objectives was developed by **Peter Drucker** in the 1950s. This management concept relies on defining objectives for each employee and then comparing their performance, and directing that performance, against the objectives which have already been set. MBO requires that clear objectives are set, and that every employee is aware of what is expected of them, a factor which often means that the employees themselves have a considerable input into the setting of the objectives. Also at MBO's heart is **delegation**, as it requires employees to take some responsibility for the achievement of objectives. It is recognized that employees are much more able and willing to seek to achieve their objectives if they have some degree of independence in how those objectives are achieved, rather than being led or directed overtly by management.

MBO has at least one fatal flaw, in as much as the objectives of individuals within different departments can differ. When the employees are required to act together collaboratively, the objectives of one may override those of another, who has different priorities and a different set of objectives. Inevitably, conflict or inertia may occur, which will clearly have an impact on productivity. Provided the business has thought the whole process through, objectives need not be mutually exclusive, but can be compatible. MBO would seek to impel all collaborative projects forward and facilitate inter-disciplinary cooperation.

Management by walking about (MBWA)

The driving force behind this approach to management was the belief that senior managers, in particular, were perceived by employees as being elitist and unwilling to expose themselves to the realities of day-to-day business operations. In effect, the managers sought to isolate themselves in their offices and dispensed orders from a distance, without any real idea of the realities of shop-floor life. The concept probably derives from Japan and was originally applied primarily to manufacturing industries. As the term suggests, managers are encouraged to visit the shop floor and see what was happening, solve problems on the spot and interact with the employees. In Japan, management by walking about is termed *gemci genbutsu*, which literally means 'go and see'.

There are a number of human resource management implications arising out of the adoption of a system of management by walking about. The fact that senior managers are out and about in the factory or offices of an organization means that they may inevitably interfere with normal lines of communication, authority, and supervisory management decisions. Clearly, a senior manager becoming involved in what would normally be a situation that could be handled using day-to-day management and procedures could cause unnecessary friction within the organization. Human resource management would, therefore, need to ensure that a clear notion of cooperation, communication and demarcation is established.

Management career stages

Typically, management careers can be described as proceeding through three distinct stages:

- *Exploration* – the search for suitable jobs.
- *Career path* – the individual (now in the mid-20s to mid-30s) establishes a pattern from the previous stage, and each job sought represents a progression. Promotion is sought internally and externally.
- *Maintenance stage* – the career path is established and nurtured. At this point the manager's career may either grow or stagnate. It may reach a plateau, offering little development opportunity.

The career plateau occurs when the manager becomes 'stuck' in a particular job. Inevitably there are far more potential candidates for higher posts than there are posts themselves. Plateau managers may face redundancy or early retirement, as can be seen in the diagram in Figure 41.

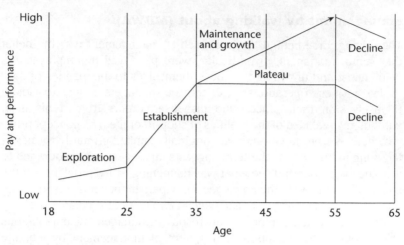

Figure 41   The management career path

Management grid

See **Blake, Robert and Jane Mouton.**

Management gurus

Management gurus are individuals who, for a limited period of time, galvanize management thinking and are the darlings of the lecture circuit. Management gurus do not necessarily offer a complete solution to management thinking, but attempts are always made to apply their theories, or in some cases their business practices (such as Branson, Prahalad and Gates), to a more holistic approach.

While management gurus come and go, their promotion, exposure and study is variable. One such attempt to categorize and quantify their impact is made by www.thinkers50.com. The website ranks the top fifty living management gurus – hence many of the management gurus from the past (such as **F. W. Taylor** and **Elton Mayo**) and recently deceased gurus (such as **Igor Ansoff**) are not included. The latest list available covers 2003:

1 **Peter Drucker** was born in Austria, worked as a journalist in London and then moved to America. His first book, *Concept of the Corporation* (1946), was a major study of General Motors. He has written 29 books, notably *The Practice of Management* (1954) and *Management: Tasks, Responsibilities, Practices* (1973). His latest works include *Management Challenges for the 21st Century* (1999) and *Peter Drucker on the Profession of Management* (1998).

2 **Michael Porter** (born in 1947) became Harvard's youngest professor. His 'Five Forces theory' remains a solid part of all under-graduate and graduate business courses. Porter's main books include *Competitive Strategy: Techniques for Analyzing Industries and Competitors* (1980), *Competitive Advantage* (1985), *The Competitive Advantage of Nations* (1990), and *Can Japan Compete?* (2000).

3 **Tom Peters** (born in 1942) is considered to be the first of the modern gurus, primarily through his two books *In Search of Excellence* (1982) and *Liberation Management* (1992). Critics claim his theories are simply rhetoric because as a businessman Peters has failed to make his mark.

4 **Gary Hamel** (born in 1954) is the co-author (with **C. K. Prahalad**) of *Competing for the Future* (1996) and *Leading the Revolution* (2000). He is Visiting Professor at Harvard Business School and London Business School and runs a multi-disciplinary management consultancy.

5 **Charles Handy** (born 1932): his first book was *Understanding Organizations* (1976), which developed the concept of the sham-rock organization. His latest book is *The New Alchemists: How Visionary People Make Something Out of Nothing* (1999).

6 Philip Kotler (born in 1931) is the lead writer on the classic marketing textbook *Marketing Management: Analysis, Planning, Implementation, and Control* (eleven editions). In his latest book, *Marketing Moves: A New Approach to Profits, Growth and Renewal* (2002), he explores 'holistic marketing'.

7 **Henry Mintzberg**'s first book was *The Nature of Managerial Work* (1973), which examined the nature of managerial work. In later books Mintzberg has set the agenda as far as the study and prac-tice of strategic management is concerned.

8 Jack Welch (born in 1935) is the former CEO and Chairman of General Electric and was instrumental in making the business the second-most profitable in the world. He is a consultant.

9 **Rosabeth Moss Kanter** is a Harvard Business School Professor with a sociology background. Kanter takes a more humanistic view of business than many other gurus. Her latest books include *Common Interest, Common Good: Creating Value Through Business and Social Sector Partnerships* (1999) and *E-volve!* (2001).

10 Jim Collins is perhaps best known for his influential book *Built to Last: Successful Habits of Visionary Companies* (1994), and his most recent bestseller is *Good to Great: Why Some Companies Make the Leap . . . And Others Don't* (2001).

11 Sumantra Ghoshal is Founding Dean of the new Indian School of

Business. Working with Christopher Bartlett, he has written *Managing Across Borders: The Transnational Solution* (1988), *Transnational Management* (1990), *Organization Theory and the Multinational Corporation* (1993), and *The Individualized Corporation* (1997).

12 **C. K. Prahalad** (born in 1941) writes extensively with Gary Hamel for the *Harvard Business Review* as well as writing best-sellers including *Competing for the Future: Breakthrough Strategies for Seizing Control of Your Industry and Creating the Markets of Tomorrow* (1994). He is primarily interested in strategic management.

13 **Warren Bennis** (born in 1925) was a protégé of **Douglas McGregor**, leading to his first major book *The Temporary Society* (1968). In a number of subsequent titles he has written extensively on the nature of leadership.

14 **Peter Senge** (born in 1947) is best known for his work on the Fifth Discipline (learning). *The Fifth Discipline* (1990) was his first major success, and since then he has written *The Fifth Discipline Fieldbook: Strategies and Tools for Building a Learning Organization* (1994), *Schools That Learn* (2000) and *The Dance of Change* (1999).

15 Robert Kaplan and David Norton: this writing team created the '**balanced scorecard**'. They have since extended and applied its use in their latest book *The Strategy-Focused Organization: How Balanced Scorecard Companies Thrive in the New Business Environment* (2000).

16 **Stephen Covey**'s book *The Seven Habits of Highly Effective People* (1989) has been an international bestseller for more than five years. Covey runs a highly successful and influential training company.

17 **Edgar H. Schein** (born in 1928) is another protégé of Douglas McGregor. His initial work culminated in the publication of *Organizational Culture and Leadership* (1985). He returned to the subject of organizational culture in 1999 with *The Corporate Culture Survival Guide: Sense and Nonsense about Corporate Culture*.

18 **Chris Argyris** is highly influential in the area of the 'learning organization'. His key titles include *Personality and Organization* (1957) and *Organizational Learning* (1978). His latest book is *Management Trap: How Managers Can Know When They're Getting Good Advice and When They're Not* (1999).

19 **Kenichi Ohmae** (born 1943) is a highly respected Japanese guru. He is a strategic thinker and has written, amongst others,

The Invisible Continent: 4 Strategic Imperatives of the New Economy (2000) and *The Emergence of the United States of Chunghwa* (2003).

20 Bill Gates (born in 1955), Harvard drop-out, is arguably the most successful businessman alive. He runs the Microsoft computer software giant.

Other notables in the listing are: Kjell Nordstrom and Jonas Ridderstrale; Clayton Christensen; **John Kotter**; Nicholas Negroponte; **James Champy**; Andy Grove; Scott Adams; Richard Pascale; Daniel Goleman; Naomi Klein; Chan Kim and Renée Mauborgne; Don Tapscott; Michael Dell; Richard Branson; Edward De Bono; Ricardo Semler; Thomas A. Stewart; Geoffrey Moore; Jeff Bezos; Paul Krugman; Lynda Gratton; Alan Greenspan; Manfred Kets De Vries; **Robert Waterman**; Watts Wacker; Patrick Dixon; **Geert Hofstede**; Don Peppers; Stan Davis and Fons Trompenaars.

Clearly, any attempt to rank management gurus only offers a snap-shot of the range and scope of the thinkers. The 'Thinkers50' ranking adopts a pragmatic approach, grading the management gurus on the basis of the following criteria:

- the originality of their ideas;
- the practical use of their ideas;
- presentation of the ideas;
- their writing ability;
- their following, in terms of those applying the ideas in the real world;
- whether the gurus put their own ideas into practice;
- the international flavour of their ideas;
- how well researched their ideas are;
- the impact their ideas have had on business.

The 'Thinkers50' website is www.thinkers50.com

Other links to management guru coverage include:

www.pfdf.org (the Peter Drucker Foundation for Non-profit Management – which has a range of notes and articles).

www.business2.com (covers 30 or so management gurus and rates them by the Star Power and Big Ideas).

www.derekstockley.com.au/guru.html (an Australian-based link and resource site for 50 management gurus).

www.sosig.ac.uk (a useful general search site known as the Social Science Information Gateway).

www.gurusonline.tv/uk/index_uk.asp (a large guru interview and link site also available in Portuguese and Spanish).

M

Management information systems

A management information system, or MIS, is a computer application which is used to record, store and process information which can be used to assist management decision making. Generally a business will have a single integrated MIS, into which data from various functional areas of the business is fed and to which, senior management has access.

There are two additional sub-types of MIS. These are decision support systems and executive information systems. Decision support systems also collect, store and process information accessible by management. They contain data on the business's operational activities and allow managers to manipulate and retrieve data, using modelling techniques to examine the results of various different courses of action. An executive information system (EIS) provides similar facilities for senior management, combining internal information along with external data. It is used to support strategic decision making and presents the information in a variety of formats, primarily aimed at enabling the users to identify trends.

Laudon, Kenneth C. and Laudon, Jane P., *Management Information Systems*. New York: Prentice Hall, 2003.

Managerial culture

'Managerial culture' refers to the organization and professional stance which the managerial structure of a business represents. Typical managerial cultures may be based on innovation, the value of human resources, quality, or a number of other different issues. These managerial cultures determine the climate in which all interpersonal and group interactions take place.

Whilst there may be an overriding, organization-wide managerial culture, the exact nature of each individual manager's own stance, or ways of carrying out work, and, indeed, how he or she deals with employees, makes decisions and solves problems, will vary.

Watson, Tony J., *In Search of Management: Culture, Chaos and Control in Managerial Work*. London: Thomson Learning, 2000.

Manifest conflict

See conflict management.

Market concentration strategy

See concentrated marketing.

Market development

Market development is a marketing strategy which aims to increase sales by selling existing products into a new market.

Raymond, Martin, *The Tomorrow People*. London: Financial Times, Prentice Hall, 2003.

Market penetration

This is a marketing strategy adopted by businesses in order to increase their sales of existing products in markets in which they already operate. Market penetration is usually achieved by an aggressive use of the **marketing mix**, which uses a balance of price-cutting, sales promotions and advertising, enhanced distribution and new product development.

Market segmentation

Market segmentation involves the identification of specific target markets for broader-based products and services, in order to enable a business to develop a suitable **marketing mix** for each of the target segments.

Market segmentation probably came into existence in the 1950s when **product differentiation** was a primary **marketing strategy**. By the 1970s, however, market segmentation had begun to be seen as a means of increasing sales and obtaining a **competitive advantage**. In recent years, more sophisticated techniques are being developed to reach potential buyers in ever more specific target markets.

Businesses will tend to segment the market for the following reasons:

- to make marketing easier in the sense that segmentation allows the business to address the needs of smaller groups of customers who have the same characteristics;
- to find niches, typically unserved or under-served markets, and to be able to target these buyers in a less competitive environment;
- to increase efficiency in being able to apply resources directly towards the best segments, which have been identified by the business.

There are some common rules regarding market segmentation which determine whether the identified segments are significant enough or measurable. These are described in Table 28.

In effect, there are two ways of segmenting a market. These are

Table 28 Market segmentation

Segmentation criteria	Description
Size	The market itself needs to be large enough to warrant segmentation. Once a market has been segmented, it may be revealed that each of the segments is too small to consider.
Differentiation	There must be measurable differences between the members of the segments and the market in general.
Responsiveness	With the market segmented, marketing communications need to be developed to address the needs of each segment. If a business cannot develop marketing communications which can contact a segment and have an impact upon it, there is little value in knowing about the segment in the first place.
Reachability	Marketing communications need to be able to get through to the segment in order to be effective. There may well be a single best advertising medium or promotional device which can reach the segments and tell them the business's message.
Interest	Having established what benefits the segment is looking for, the business needs to be assured that this is precisely what the potential customers require and that the product or service matches these requirements.
Profitability	A decision needs to be reached as to whether it is cost-effective to reach these segments, considering the cost which may be incurred in running multiple marketing programmes alongside one another. Existing products or services may need to be redesigned in order to match the specific needs of each segment.

known as either *a priori* or *post hoc*. These two approaches are typified in the following manner:

- *A priori* segmentation is effectively based on a mixture of intuition, use of secondary data, and analysis of existing customer database information. *A priori* segmentation takes place without the benefit of primary market research and may well produce relatively simplistic segmentation, such as male or female, young or old, regional segments, or buyers and non-buyers.
- *Post hoc* segmentation uses primary market research to classify and

describe individuals within the target market, but segments are not defined themselves until after the data collection and analysis has been carried out. The definition of each segment requires the placing of all members of the target market into specific segments.

There are a number of different types of information which are used extensively in market segmentation. These can be best described by category as in Table 29.

Table 29   Categories of information used in market segmentation

Measured variable	Description
Classification	Broadly speaking, classification actually encompasses demographic, geographic, psychographic and behavioural features. It requires a system of classifying individuals and placing them into segments by using a mixture of these variables.
Demographic	Demographic features are those such as age, gender, income, ethnicity, marital status, education, occupation, household size, type of residence and length of time of residence, amongst many other demographically based measures.
Geographic	This broad range of variables includes population density, climate, zip or postcode, city, state or county, region, or metropolitan/rural district.
Psychographic	Another broad range of variables which includes attitudes, hobbies, leadership traits, lifestyle, magazines and newspapers read, personality traits, risk aversion, and television or radio programmes watched or listened to.
Behavioural	These variables encompass the current ways in which the target market views, buys and responds to products, services and marketing. The category includes brand loyalty, benefits sought, distribution channels used, and level of usage.
Descriptor	Descriptor variables actually describe each segment in order to distinguish it from other groups. The descriptors need to be measurable and are usually derived solely from primary research, rather than secondary sources of information. Descriptors will typically explain in shorthand the key characteristics of each segment and the members of that segment, so that these characteristics can more readily be exploited by subtle changes in the marketing mix. A descriptor variable may include such features as: under 30, single, urban dweller, rented accommodation, medium to high income, etc.

McDonald, Malcolm and Dunbar, Ian, *Market Segmentation*. Basingstoke: Palgrave Macmillan, 1998.
Wedel, Michel and Kamakura, Wagner A., *Market Segmentation: Conceptual and Methodological Foundations*. New York: Kluwer Academic, 1999.

Market to book value

The 'market to book value' ratio is considered to be a solid indicator of a business's ability to create value above and beyond its physical and financial assets. The term is usually used to describe the difference in value between the actual total value of all the assets of a business and the prevailing stock or share price.

It is therefore possible to calculate the market to book value by expressing it as a measure of business performance in terms of value creation. Any capital investment should create value for an investor, which results in the valuation of the business being higher than the book value of its assets. The book value itself is the amount of investment capital recorded on a balance sheet (or of stockholders' equity, as reported as historical value). The market value, therefore, is the bid price for a share, based on current stock market exchanges. Typically, the following ratio or formula is used:

$$\text{Market to book value} = \frac{\text{Stock price per share}}{\text{Book value per share}}$$

Marketing mix

Major marketing management decisions can be classified according to the following four categories:

- product;
- price;
- place (distribution);
- promotion.

These variables are known as the marketing mix, or the '4 Ps of marketing'. They are the variables that marketing managers can control in order to best satisfy customers in the target market. The marketing mix is portrayed in Figure 42.

The business attempts to generate a positive response in the target market by blending these four marketing-mix variables in an optimal manner.

- *Product* – The product is the physical product or service offered to the consumer. In the case of physical products, it also refers to any

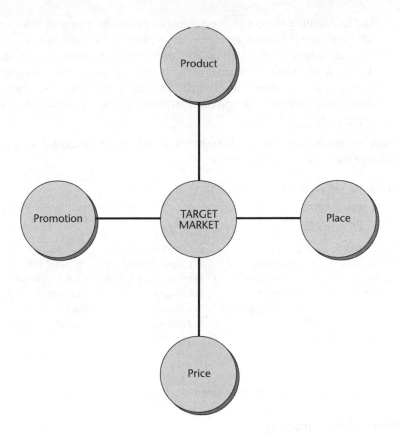

Figure 42   The 4Ps of maketing

services or conveniences that arc part of the offering. Product decisions include aspects such as function, appearance, packaging,
service, warranty, etc.

- *Price* – Pricing decisions should take into account profit margins
  and the probable pricing response of competitors. Pricing includes
  not only the list price, but also discounts, financing, and other
  options such as leasing.
- *Place* – Place (or placement) decisions are those associated with
  channels of distribution that serve as the means for getting the
  product to the target customers. The distribution system performs
  transactional, logistical, and facilitating functions. Distribution
  decisions include market coverage, channel member selection,
  logistics, and levels of service.
- *Promotion* – Promotion decisions are those related to communicat-

ing and selling to potential consumers. Since the costs of this can be large in proportion to the product price, a breakeven analysis should be performed when making promotion decisions. It is useful to know the value of a customer, in order to determine whether additional customers are worth the cost of acquiring them. Promotion decisions involve advertising, public relations, media types, etc.

Table 30 summarizes the marketing mix decisions, and includes a list of some of the aspects of each of the 4Ps.

Table 30   Marketing mix decisions

Product	Price	Place	Promotion
Functionality	List price	Channel members	Advertising
Appearance	Discounts	Channel motivation	Personal selling
Quality	Allowances	Market coverage	Public relations
Packaging	Financing	Locations	Message
Brand	Leasing options	Logistics	Media
Warranty		Service levels	Budget
Service/Support			

See also **Seven Ps** *and* **Booms and Bitner.**

Marketing strategy

The term 'marketing strategy' refers to specific processes adopted by the marketing function of a business in order to achieve specific goals or objectives. Marketing strategy also encompasses the deployment of a business's resources in order to develop and maintain the business's market opportunities. At its core, the marketing strategy seeks to deploy a **marketing mix** in the most effective manner, not only to achieve the business's goals and objectives, but also to satisfy the customers' needs and wants.

Fill, Chris, *Marketing Communications: Contexts, Strategies and Applications.* London: Financial Times, Prentice-Hall, 2001.

Maslow, Abraham

Abraham Maslow (1908–70) categorized human needs into five groups, which he arranged as a hierarchy (see Figure 43). Whilst Maslow's theory has been systematically applied in the field of human resource management, marketing has much to learn from the concept.

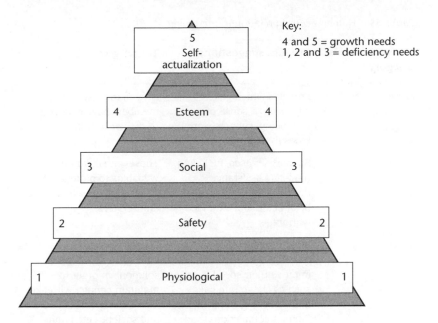

Figure 43   The human needs hierarchy

Maslow's theory can be directly adapted to marketing, as can be seen in Table 31.

Maslow, Abraham H. and Frager, Robert (ed.), *Motivation and Personality*. London: Longman, 1987.

www.ship.edu/~cgboeree/maslow.html

Mass customization

Mass customization is an increasing trend and of considerable importance to marketeers. Mass customization involves the production of mass-produced, standard products, with slight variations or customizations for particular market or customer segments. As the manufacturing process has developed technologically, and become more flexible, it is possible to produce these personalized products without having a detrimental effect on profit margins. Indeed, these customized products can often warrant a premium price, providing a margin in excess of what had previously been enjoyed by the manufacturer. Manufacturers have therefore realized that mass customization is a means by which they can improve their profitability without the attendant loss of production or productivity.

See also **customization**.

Table 31 Human needs in relation to marketing

Maslow's needs category	Product suggestions	Target groups
Physiological	Products which give customers a sense of well-being, such as warming foods in winter.	Grey market, whose members have concerns over their health.
Safety	Support services, including road-side assistance, insurance cover, private health care and extended warranties.	Those with children or valuables to protect, who need safety-based products and services.
Social	Products which allow customers to maintain and improve their social lives, such as cheap rate calls in the evening, reduced rate internet connections, and membership privileges to clubs, allowing customers to bring friends free.	People moving to new areas, who need networking solutions in order to maintain contact with like-minded individuals (clubs and societies etc.) and groups set up for single people or single-parent families.
Esteem	Products which give customers the feeling of being successful, such as luxury cars, electrical products and jewellery items.	New high-income earners and higher-status groups with a need to show outward signs of conspicuous consumption.
Self-actualization	Higher, further or additional education aimed at self-improvement in the job market.	Higher-educated individuals seeking vocational skills and learning, or adolescents looking for opportunities to conform to perceived ideals in terms of fashion and looks.

Materials management

Materials management involves the planning, organization and control of all aspects of a business's physical inventory, including shipping, distribution, warehousing, and dealing with work in progress. For international businesses the essential problem is to minimize the total costs involved and to maximize savings where those savings can be identified. For international businesses this requires an integrated materials management or logistics organization, which takes full responsibility for supply, production and distribution. Clearly any reduction in cost can contribute to profit.

Arnold, J. R. and Chapman, Stephen, *Introduction to Materials Management*. New York: Prentice-Hall, 2003.

Matrix in the mind

A 'matrix in the mind' is an internal information network which allows a business to capitalize, on a global basis, the skills and capabilities of its management and employees. Matrix in the mind is a logical development of the **matrix structure**. It is radically different, but only in the sense that the interdependencies and support functions of various parts of the organization are virtual, by means of integrating electronic devices, including connections via the Internet, video-conferencing and other interactive and cooperative two-way communications.

The matrix in the mind allows the key personnel in the organization to have access to information, managers and employees at a local level. All information, knowledge and experience can be transferred, either geographically or between divisions or subsidiaries of the business. The matrix in the mind also allows the business's norms and values to be transmitted to geographically remote parts of the organization.

Matrix structure

The use of a matrix organizational structure allows the opportunity for teams to be developed in order that particular tasks can be undertaken. Matrix structures often develop in stages, with the first being the establishment of temporary teams, who, having studied a particular problem and suggested recommendations, might be considered significant enough to be retained on a more permanent basis. These teams will consist of a number of different individuals from the different functions of the organization, see Figure 44.

As can be seen in Table 32, a matrix structure has some advantages and disadvantages.

Sutherland, Jon and Canwell, Diane, *Organisation Structures and Processes*. London: Pitman Publishing, 1997.

M

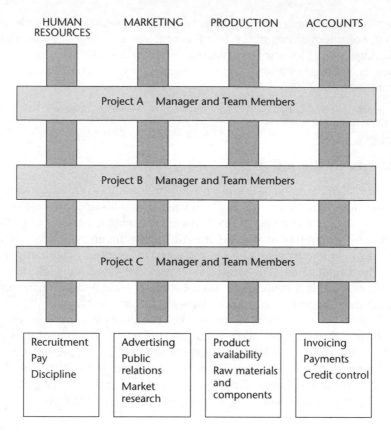

Figure 44 Example of a matrix structure

Mayo, Elton

Elton Mayo was employed by the Hawthorne Works during the 1920s and 1930s to attempt to improve the electrical company's productivity. As a result of this work he developed a theory which has since become known as the Hawthorne Effect.

Initially Mayo adopted the scientific management theory of **F. W. Taylor**, in his attempt to discover what environmental features of the workplace were affecting productivity. He made amendments to the lighting, the heating and the availability of refreshments, then went on to make changes to the length of the working day and week. Each time he made a change the rate of productivity increased. Puzzled by his findings, Mayo reversed his actions by removing tea-breaks and reducing the level of lighting, but productivity continued to increase. Mayo's

Table 32 Evaluation of the matrix structure

Advantages of a matrix structure	Disadvantages of a matrix structure
Good use can be made of specialist and functional knowledge from within the organization.	Because there is not a clear line of command and authority, this may affect a manager's ability to understand requirements and make changes.
Enhanced communication can be facilitated between departments, providing a greater level of consistency and efficiency of policies.	There is often a higher level of stress and a feeling of constant competition, with added responsibility.
The availability of multiple sources of power allows the establishment of recognized mechanisms to deal with different forms of culture.	Demand on individuals and departments may be inconsistent, resulting in a high demand in some areas and only a limited demand in others.
The structure enables the organization to adapt to environmental changes by moving the main emphasis from a functional one to a project-based one.	There may also be inconsistency between individuals with the ability to flourish and those who are more technically-minded. This could cause exclusion for some employees by those who are competitive enough to wish to manage the project teams.

conclusion was that the changes had been made in consultation with the employees, and that this factor had been the determining influence on productivity, together with the fact that the employees had a good working relationship with their supervisors. It was this research that led to what became known as Mayo's Hawthorne Effect.

Further research was then undertaken in another department of the organization. Two different groups of employees were working on complex equipment; one group considered that their status was high because of the complexity of the job role. The second group considered themselves to be lower in status, and this resulted in a degree of competition between the two groups. Both groups had established their own sets of rules and code of behaviour and each had established the pace of work and degree of output. Individuals within the group who did not comply with these standards were put under pressure from the other members of the group.

Each group was given a target output for the day by the management of the organization. On some days these targets were exceeded but the groups would simply report that they had reached the target figures, and

M

include the excess in the target figure for the following day. Mayo's conclusions from this were that:

- The groups had been given a **benchmark**. Their benchmark had been the employer's output target and they had been able to compare this with their own output totals.
- They had established for themselves a concept of a fair day's output and did not feel they needed to exceed this target.

Mayo felt that lessons could be learned from this research in that a group's needs have to be in accord with organizational rules. Consultation was the key to achieving this, together with close monitoring of day-to-day organizational activities.

Mayo made three interesting discoveries from his research, which form the basis of this 'solidarity theory':

- output and motivation improved when employees were being observed;
- peer pressure contributed to the level of support by the individuals within the group;
- the group had strong feelings about what was possible and reasonable – this was as important to the group as their reaction to the demands of their managers.

Bratton, John and Gold, Jeffrey, *Human Resource Management: Theory and Practice.* Basingstoke: Palgrave Macmillan, 2003.
Mayo, Elton, *The Social Problems of an Industrial Civilization*. London: Routledge, 1975.

www.accel-team.com/human_relations/hrels_01_mayo.html

McClelland, David

As a behavioural scientist for over 20 years at Harvard, David McClelland studied the human need for achievement. McClelland is best known for his research on achievement **motivation**, distinguishing between three types of motivation:

- A need for achievement (n-ach), where individuals seek personal responsibility, attainable but challenging goals, and feedback on performance.
- A need for affiliation (n-affil), where individuals have a desire for friendly relationships, sensitivity to the feelings of others, and a preference for roles with human interaction.
- A need for power (n-pow), where individuals have a desire to make an impact, and to be influential and effective.

Power need (n-pow) takes the form of a high need for power, expressed as 'personalized power' or 'socialized power'. The key characteristics are:

- A high level of personalized power with little inhibition or self-control, and the impulsive exercise of that power. There are tendencies for these individuals to be rude, to use alcohol, to sexually harass, and to collect symbols of power (such as big offices, big desks, fancy cars, etc.).
- When these people give advice or support, it is with the intent to bolster their own status.
- They demand loyalty to themselves rather than to the organization.
- When such a leader leaves the organization there is likely to be disorder and a breakdown of team morale and direction.

Achievement need (n-ach) is reflected in attaining challenging goals, setting new records, successful completion of difficult tasks, and doing something not done before. Key characteristics are:

- A preference for a job in which success depends on effort and ability rather than on chance and factors beyond their control.
- A preference for tasks that enable them to exercise their skills and initiation in problem-solving.
- A need for frequent and specific feedback about performance so they can enjoy the experience of making progress toward objectives.
- For managers in large organizations, moderate to high achievement is secondary to higher power needs. If achievement is dominant, the manager may try to achieve objectives alone rather than through team development.
- Typical jobs include sales representatives, real estate agents and owner-managers of small businesses.

Affiliation need (n-affil) revolves around establishing or restoring close and friendly relationships, joining groups, participating in social activities, and enjoying shared activities. Key characteristics are:

- cooperative, supportive, and friendly behaviour;
- the valuing of belonging and conformity to a group;
- satisfaction from being liked and accepted by others;
- a preference for work with others, with group harmony and cohesion;
- a person low in affiliation tends to be a loner, and may lack the motivation or energy to maintain good social contacts in networking, group presentations and building close personal relations with peers and subordinates;

- a person with a high affiliation tends to be reluctant to let work interfere with harmonious relationships;
- moderate affiliation is related to effective management, since strong needs often lead to the avoidance of unpopular decisions, permitting exceptions to rules, and showing favouritism to friends. However, this can lead to subordinates feeling confused about rules and playing to the manager's preferences.

McClelland argues that, on the basis of his research, n-affil (a desire to be liked) handicaps managers, who are led to make exceptions when they should not. He describes the n-pow manager as being dedicated to the organization, committed to the work ethic with energy and devotion. The best leader, he argues, is the n-ach individual. The ideal combinations of these three needs are shown in Figure 45.

Large organizations	Entrepreneurial small organizations or autonomous subsidiaries of large organizations
n-pow (high) n-ach (moderate) n-affil (moderate)	n-ach (high) n-pow (moderate) n-affil (low)

Figure 45 Recommended combinations of motional needs

McClelland, D. C., *Power: The Inner Experience*. New York: Irvington, 1979.

www.accel-team.com/human_relations/hrels_06_mcclelland.html

McGregor, Douglas

Douglas McGregor was a management consultant theorist and a social psychologist. In 1954 he became Professor of Management at the Massachusetts Institute of Technology, and later he taught at Harvard where he helped establish the Industrial Relations section. Douglas McGregor's book *The Human Side of Enterprise* was published in 1960, examining the behaviour of individuals at work. He formulated two models, which he called Theory X and Theory Y.

Theory X assumes that the average human has an inherent dislike of work and will do all that is necessary to avoid it. This assumes the following:

- Because people dislike work they have to be controlled by management and often threatened, in order to work hard.
- Most people avoid responsibility, need to be directed by management, but seek security within work as a primary concern.
- Managers who adhere to the Theory X approach rarely give their subordinates any opportunity to show traits other than those associated with Theory X.

Theory X has given rise to what is often known as tough or **hard management**, typified by tight control and punishment. **Soft management** adopts the opposite view, aiming to create a degree of harmony in the workplace.

Theory Y, on the other hand, assumes the following:

- Most people expend the same amount of energy or effort at work as in other spheres of their lives.
- Providing that individuals are committed, or made to be committed, to the aims of the organization in which they work, they will be self-directing.
- Job satisfaction is the key to involving and engaging the individual employees and ensuring their commitment.
- An average individual, given the opportunity and encouragement, will naturally seek responsibility.
- If they have commitment and responsibility, employees will be able to use their imagination, ingenuity and creativity to solve work problems with less direct supervision.

Managements which follow Theory Y are often considered to be soft management systems, which recognize that the intellectual potential of their employees is vital to the success of the business. In many cases, it is argued, businesses ignore the Theory Y benefits and under-utilize their employees.

McGregor saw his two theories as being very separate attitudes. He believed that it was difficult to use Theory Y for large-scale operations, particularly those involved in mass production. It was an ideal choice for the management of professionals. For McGregor, Theory Y was essential in helping to encourage participative problem solving and the development of effective management.

McGregor, Douglas, *The Human Side of Enterprise*. New York: McGraw-Hill Education, 1995.

www.accel-team.com/human_relations/hrels_03_mcgregor.html

Meyerson, Debra

Debra Meyerson is an active writer and researcher on organizational change, gender and race, equity, organizational culture, and stress. In her article 'Everyday Leaders' she identified that many managers and employees are at variance with the dominant culture of their organizations and live by their own values, identities and ideals. She identified a particular group, which she called 'tempered radicals', who seek to challenge the normal assumptions and push organizations into adaptive change.

Meyerson, Debra, 'Everyday Leaders: The Power of Difference', *Leader to Leader*, 23 (2002), pp. 29–34.

www.stanford.edu/group/WTO/people/visiting/meyerson.shtml

Micro-environment

'Micro-environment' refers to that of a business's external **stakeholders** who are in direct contact with the organization. These are the groups which significantly influence the action of the organization, and may include partners, providers of finance, regulators, government and competitors. Some of the micro-environmental external stakeholders will have a positive effect on the business, such as creating demand or supplying the business with resources. Others, such as regulators or government, may impose constraints on the business which can affect its development. Typically a business will attempt to analyse its micro-environment and may carry out the following steps:

- an identification of the key stakeholders as far as the organization is concerned;
- an assessment of the influence of each of these key stakeholders;
- a classification of the stakeholders in terms of opportunities or threats (in some cases a stakeholder may be classified as both an opportunity and a threat);
- an evaluation of the importance of each of these opportunities and threats.

On the basis of the opportunities and threats identified, the organization can now establish its strategic objectives.

See also **macro-environment**.

Micro-leadership

'Micro-leadership' is a means of describing self-directed work. Micro-leadership involves the balancing of innumerable counter demands on an individual's time, efforts and energy. Micro-leadership is the ability to manage these often contradictory demands and to place emphasis and priority upon job tasks and duties, notwithstanding any priorities which have been set by a more senior individual.

Minimum efficient scale

The minimum efficient scale is taken to be the level of output at which a manufacturer's economies, achieved by an optimum level of production, have been eliminated by a scaling down of the output. The minimum efficient scale is the lowest output level which is economically viable for the business to sustain, albeit for a short period of time.

Mintzberg, Henry

Henry Mintzberg is a much respected and well published management consultant who has written on many different aspects of management, **organizational culture** and **organizational design**. Mintzberg, amongst other theorists, identified a number of key design parameters which needed to be addressed, regarding organizational design. These are:

- Job roles – relating to the position within the organization, the number of tasks involved in the job and the amount of control individuals have over their own work.
- Behaviour formalization and training – by ensuring that behaviour is regulated and adequate training takes place.
- Horizontal and vertical job specialization – to ensure that the work load is spread in the most productive manner.
- Training and induction – training and induction are vital in the establishment of specifications and behaviour formalization.
- Unit grouping and size – groups or clusters would need to follow a logic related to the organization's objectives.
- Planning and control systems – to ensure that the business's objectives are being addressed.
- Liaison devices – with senior management and between groupings.
- Centralization or decentralization? – determining the right level of freedom to give each department or group and putting in place set procedures to ensure coordination.

Mintzberg, Henry, *The Nature of Managerial Work*. London: Longman, 1990.
Mintzberg, Henry, *The Structuring of Organizations*. New York: Prentice-Hall, 1990.

www.henrymintzberg.com

Mission statement

In many cases indications of a human resource management's fundamental policy will be contained within a mission statement. A mission statement essentially describes, as succinctly as possible, the organization's business vision. This would include the fundamental values and the essential purpose of the organization. It will also make allusions as to its future, or its pursuit for the future, as mission statements tend to be a statement of where a businesses wishes to be rather than a description of where it is at the current time. In this respect, mission statements, although the fundamental ethos may remain the same, are subject to periodic change. A business may choose to incorporate within its mission statement a vision of how it wishes its employees and systems to respond to, react to and fulfil the needs of its customers or clients. Human resources departments will, therefore, seek to match these aspirations by instituting employee development programmes and associated training, in order to fulfil the espoused desires and commitments made in the mission statement.

Morgan, Gareth

Gareth Morgan suggests, through his analysis of power-play, that valuable insights are possible into understanding the power structures of organizations. He links **organizational culture** with his analysis of power and he suggests that power incorporates the following elements:

- **group think**;
- know-how;
- symbolism;
- decision control;
- technological dependence;
- boundary management;
- resource-based control and management;
- bureaucracy-based control and management.

Morgan, Gareth, *Images of Organization*. Newbury Park, CA: Sage Publications, 1998.
Morgan, Gareth, *Creative Organization Theory*. Newbury Park, CA: Sage Publications, 1989.

www.imaginiz.com

MOST analysis

MOST analysis is a tool used in strategic planning which aims to help businesses to clarify their policy direction. MOST is an acronym which means:

- where the business intends to go (**M**ission);
- the key goals which will help to achieve this (**O**bjectives);
- analysis of the options available for proceeding forward (**S**trategies);
- how these strategies are going to be put into action (**T**actics).

The key is for this whole process to hang together from top to bottom and also in reverse (see Figure 46). From the top, clarifying the mission drives the objectives, which creates strategic options, which forces tactical actions to be taken. From the bottom, every action at tactical level should help to make the strategies work; all strategies should help to achieve the objectives; and all the objectives should take the business towards the mission.

Businesses fall into many traps by attempting to tackle strategy internally:

- Allowing distractions from moving the business forward, caused by day-to-day actions, or demands from customers, suppliers and competitors.
- Failing to clarify where the business wants to get to and what timescale is involved.
- Omitting to obtain agreement to the mission from the board and management of the business.
- Not clarifying the key objectives that need to be reached (and the timescale) for the mission to be successful.
- Not obtaining external and objective assistance in analysing the strategic options available to satisfy the key objectives.
- Missing out the strategy stage altogether and going straight from objectives to tactics, which can lead to dead ends.
- Not ensuring that everything achieved at tactical level ensures the success of the strategies.

Figure 46 MOST analysis

- Failing to define accurately the timescales, responsibilities and monitoring and control procedures needed to move forward at the necessary pace.

Motivation

Motivation involves the instilling in employees of a drive to take action. In human resource terms this means providing an incentive to employees to perform to the best of their abilities. The subject of motivation has been at the heart of a large number of theories over a number of years, including those of **Abraham Maslow** and **Frederick Herzberg**. Both theorists recognized that there were a series of actions or circumstances which could be initiated by an employer in order to achieve a degree of motivation. Both recognized too that simply providing pay and a degree of security were insufficient in the long term to motivate employees. Motivation needed to be longer lasting and reinforced by concrete rewards and praise. At its most basic, motivation needs to be sustained by employers in order not only to ensure continued high performance and productivity, but also to create a situation where employees have a positive attitude towards work, a commitment to the organization and, above all, a belief that their individual roles are not only valued but of crucial interest to the organization.

Motivational needs model

A motivational needs model can be typified as the flow of factors and the impact of various influences that affect the motivation of employees and managers.

As Figure 47 suggests, at the core of the job itself is an individual's

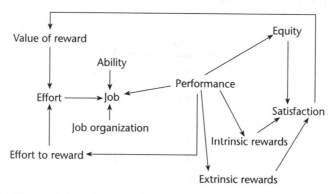

Figure 47   Influences affecting motivation

effort, ability and performance within the confines of the way the job was originally (or subsequently) organized.

Performance is affected by equity (fairness), intrinsic rewards (rewards deriving from the job itself) and extrinsic rewards (deriving from factors outside the job itself). Equally, satisfaction itself is affected by these factors, which in turn have an impact on the individual's assessment of whether the reward is of value. Both performance and the value of reward have a direct impact on the effort expended. Any motivational needs model will be purely conjecture as the precise ways in which motivation is achieved, or indeed viewed by an individual, will often differ.

Multi-domestic strategy

A multi-domestic strategy tends to lead a business with international operations to allow the operations in one country to be relatively independent of those in other countries. In essence, a multi-domestic strategy emphasizes the unique conditions which apply to each country in which the multinational organization operates. This may involve separate design, production and sales operations.

In using multi-domestic strategy the business focuses upon local responsiveness to specific strategies wholly designed to suit that nation's market.

Multinational enterprise

A multinational enterprise is a business which owns separate operations in at least two countries. Businesses become multinational enterprises and develop their foreign markets for a number of different reasons, which are either proactive or reactive in nature. The key proactive, or pull, factors include:

- the desire to increase global market share;
- the need to satisfy demand for a unique product or service in a foreign market;
- the wish to generate greater profits by reducing costs or acquiring new resources;
- the need to achieve greater **economies of scale**;
- the advantage of spreading risks by diversifying the sources of sales and inputs;
- the need to satisfy managerial targets;
- the wish to take advantage of potential tax benefits.

The key reactive, or push, factors are:

- the need to offer an alternative to the competitive pressures present in a domestic market;
- the search for an alternative to declining domestic sales;
- as a response to increasing costs of production in the domestic market;
- the need to seek alternatives to a saturated domestic market;
- the wish to provide a market for unused managerial or production capacity;
- the desire to seek a market to sell excess stock due to over-production in a domestic market;
- the aim of prolonging the product life cycle of products which are reaching the end of their life cycle in the domestic market;
- the wish to copy key competitors, for strategic reasons.

Multi-skilling

The term 'multi-skilling' relates to incorporating a higher level of flexibility into job roles across the organization, usually in those activities requiring unskilled to skilled, or technical expertise. This flexibility often crosses boundaries which have historically or traditionally been set, and it requires the willingness of employees if it is to succeed. The newly multi-skilled employees would also have to be prepared to work at their newly acquired skills and follow training or retraining programmes. Commonly, trained employees will assist with the retraining of those going through the multi-skilling process.

There are some advantages and disadvantages to multi-skilling, including those shown in Table 33.

The introduction of multi-skilling can affect employees in more than their work situation and may spill over into their domestic life, particularly if their extended role involves irregular work hours. However, employees could find that their job satisfaction is increased, because they are no longer so strictly supervised or controlled.

Mutual dependence

The term 'mutual dependence' can refer either to internal relationships and needs within the organization or to the dependencies which may develop over time between businesses.

Mutual dependence implies a symbiotic relationship in as much as both parties need, require and desire something from the relationship. Mutual dependence goes somewhat further than simple needs for

Table 33 An evaluation of multi-skilling

Advantages	Disadvantages
An organization can introduce new equipment and working methods quickly.	Labour turnover can increase as employees become more skilled.
The employees improve their overall level of skills and knowledge	The costs of training and retraining programmes can be high.
All of the organization's resources are used to their full potential.	Because individuals can move from one group to another, there could be resultant shortages in particular groups. This can affect the way the group performs in the longer term as there is a constant risk that a member of the group or team will be missing.
The employees can contribute more effectively, and to their full potential, to meeting the organization's objectives.	Managers tend not to be involved in the multi-skilling process and often remain rigid in their views of the tasks they should perform.
	Employees do not always enjoy job satisfaction, particularly if they are not involved in tasks they were initially trained to do.

support, and may well suggest that the two parties in question are reliant upon each other to be able to carry out specific tasks, roles or operations.

Myers–Briggs Type Indicator

The Myers–Briggs Type Indicator®, or MBTI®, is based on the teachings of Carl Gustav Jung, and identifies four behaviour preferences:

- extroversion (E) versus introversion (I);
- sensing (S) versus intuition (I);
- thinking (T) versus feeling (F);
- judgement (J) versus perception (P).

The combination of these four preferences produces a personality type, such as ESFP or ISTJ. The model can be used for a variety of different applications, including interpersonal skills development, self-aware-ness, career counselling and team building.

The MTR-I (Management Team Roles–Indicator) system is an exten-sion to the Myers–Briggs Type Indicator, as it can assign team roles based on a questionnaire. The Myers–Briggs system is amongst a wide variety of different psychometric tests, including the Keirsey Temperament Sorter and the Careers Values Inventory.

www.mtr-i.com

M

Nanus, Burt

In 1986, Burt Nanus and Warren Bennis wrote *Leaders*. They maintained that the subject of leadership remained the most studied and least understood of all the social sciences. They claimed that whilst management as a function and reality were obvious, it was difficult to state precisely what management was or to replicate the management function itself. They stated that:

> Leaders articulate and define what has previously remained implicit or unsaid; they invent images, metaphors and models that provide a focus for new attention. By so doing, they consolidate a challenge provoking wisdom. In short, an essential factor in leadership is the capacity to influence and organise meaning for the members of the organisation.

Bennis, Warren and Nanus, Burt, *Leaders*. New York: HarperCollins, 1997.

See also **Bennis, Warren.**

Negative sum game

A negative sum game occurs when two parties engage in actions which ultimately are to the detriment of both sides. There are many examples of negative sum games which are actively pursued, both within an organization and between organizations. Primarily, negative sum games occur when both sides assume that their own overall gain will be greater if they continue to pursue the current lines of action. Equally, they believe that the losses the other side will suffer will be greater if they continue to pursue that action. In the final analysis, however, both sides risk losing more and both lose, comparatively speaking, as a result of their joint actions and inability to change their course of direction. A negative sum game is, therefore, a lose–lose situation and is the opposite of a **positive sum game**.

Net cash flow

A business's net cash flow is equal to all of its cash receipts minus its cash payments during a given period of time. In effect, net cash flow is equal to a business's net profit, less of course any depreciation, depletion or amortization. Net cash flow is more commonly known simply as **cash flow**.

Net profit margin

The net profit margin is often referred to as the 'net margin' and is calculated by deploying the net profit margin ratio. This divides a business's net profit by its net revenues and then expresses this relationship as a percentage. A business's net profit margin serves as a means by which the cost control functions can be assessed. If a business has a high net profit margin then it is seen to be able to convert revenue into profit. Net profit margins are often used to compare businesses in the same industries, since they are under the same pressures and have similar opportunities.

Net profit margins are also useful in the comparison of unlike businesses in unlike markets, as the net profit margin reveals to potential investors the comparative profitability of different types of businesses.

The net profit margin ratio differs from the **gross profit margin** ratio in as much as it expresses the net profit as a percentage of the sales generated. In effect, it measures the percentage return on sales after expenses such as tax have been taken into account. The ratio is:

$$Net\ profit\ margin = \frac{Net\ profit\ after\ tax}{Sales} \times 100$$

Therefore a business with a total sales revenue of some £3,200,000 has a net profit after tax of £200,000. The calculation is:

$$\frac{200,000}{3,200,000} \times 100 = 6.25\%$$

Typically, the business would then compare this figure with the industry standard to assess its overall ability to produce a net profit from its generated sales.

Network analysis

Network analysis involves the mapping and measuring of relationships and flows between individuals, groups, organizations and information technology. On a network analysis diagram each individual, group or organization will be represented by a node, and lines link these nodes, illustrating the interrelationships on the network between the nodes.

Network analysis can be important within a team, department, division or organization, in as much as the construction of the network map indicates the relative importance of each of the nodes or individuals. In this respect the centrality of a node can be measured in order to determine its importance or prominence within the network.

Scott, John, *Social Network Analysis: A Handbook*. New York: Sage Publications, 2000.

Network structure

Although a network structure can be examined and identified by **network analysis**, the term 'network structure' is a broader one which refers to the overall structure in terms of relationships and hierarchy in an organization. Traditional organizations will adopt a network which is task-structured in order to achieve predictable performances. Increasingly, however, network structures have become more complex, notably as a result of organizations adopting decentralized, team-based or distributed structures. Others have taken the concept of network structures further and have adopted virtual networks or cluster organizations. The network structure, however it may be configured, is designed to provide a supportive coordination between individuals who work in different locations.

The network structure should also reflect both the formal and the informal communications within the organization. In this respect the network structure reflects formal rules, procedures, reporting, norms and, increasingly, the various forms of informal communication which occur without reference to the normal network procedures. Most network structures reflect the hierarchy, however, and provide a means by which the legitimate power and authority vested in individuals within the organization are exemplified in the business's organizational chart.

Many network structures actually fail to recognize the importance of informal communication. Much of this is at a personal level, and is interactive and peer-orientated. When researchers investigate the patterns of communication within an organization they often refer to it as the network structure, and suggest that these network structures explain organizational behaviour in a far more precise manner than any organizational chart or formal structure could hope to achieve.

In the case of **virtual corporations**, which tend to be non-hierarchical and decentralized, the network structure is, perhaps, the only true means by which the interrelationships of the individuals involved can possibly be explained.

Birkinshaw, Julian and Hagsrom, Peter (eds), *The Flexible Firm: Capability Management in Network Organisations*. Oxford: Oxford University Press, 2002.

Networking

In the business sense, networking has a number of different associations. Internally it refers to managers and employees of a business forming working relationships with other members of the organization in order to achieve greater understanding and mutual dependence.

Externally, networking can refer to either individuals or organizations collaborating with one another with no real formal guidelines to their relationship.

Niche strategy

Businesses using niche-strategy approaches seek to concentrate their attention on a narrow piece of the total market. Having achieved this, they seek to provide niche buyers more effectively than their rivals. The key success factors involved in dealing with niche markets are:

- choosing a market niche where buyers can be distinctively identified by their preferences, special requirements or unique needs;
- developing unique capabilities to serve those needs of the segment.

There are two ways in which businesses seek to achieve this:

- by achieving lower costs than competitors serving that market niche (low-cost strategy);
- by offering something different to the buyers in that market (differentiation strategy).

Niches are attractive to businesses for the following reasons:

- They are big enough to produce a profit and may offer growth potential.
- They are often overlooked by the industry leaders.
- Competitors involved in a more multi-segment approach may consider them too expensive in terms of meeting the buyers' needs.
- Few competitors will be specializing in the same niche.
- The business may be able to deploy most of its resources into that niche.
- Once established, superior service can effectively defend the niche from rivals.

See also **Porter, Michael**.

Non-price competition

Non-price competition, as the term implies, is competition that is based on factors other than price. The primary task is, initially, to establish differentiating criteria which mark the product or service as being sufficiently unlike those offered by competitors. Normally, non-price competition would involve factors such as convenience, taste, or a degree of prestige. Businesses have recognized that price-based competition in the medium to long term does little to benefit either organization. Competition based on pricing can temporarily increase market share, but in the longer term, customers begin to expect lower prices, and alternative measures need to be sought in order to maintain market share. Price-cutting merely achieves a cut in the contribution of each unit, and may detrimentally affect profitability.

Non-price competition has, therefore, become an important battlefield for many markets. It is typified by the concept of adding a degree of value to whatever the business is offering its customers. Typically this would include some or all of the following:

- customer loyalty cards;
- additional services;
- home delivery systems;
- discounts in allied product areas;
- extended opening hours;
- customer self-scanning of products;
- incentives for purchasing off-peak or out of season;
- Internet shopping.

Metwally, M. M., *Price and Non-price Competition: Dynamics of Marketing*. Bombay: Asia Publishing House, 1975.

Nonverbal communication

Various studies have shown that during interpersonal communication only 7% of the message is communicated verbally. The remaining 93% is transmitted through nonverbal communication. Arguably, nonverbal communication is purely related to actions, gestures, expressions and other body movements which do not have a vocal root. Increasingly, however, nonverbal communication has included vocal tones, and as a result of the 93% of nonverbal communication in standard interpersonal communications this accounts for 38%; the remaining 55% is via facial expression.

Variations in voice tone, facial expressions and even foot movements are all forms of nonverbal communication. Many individuals will consider that body language is the most important aspect of nonverbal communication, as it can often display a discrepancy between what individuals are actually saying and their physical reactions.

What remains is the fact that words can be manipulated, but gestures and other forms of nonverbal communication are harder to control and often betray the true intentions of the individual.

Knapp, Mark L., *Essentials of Non Verbal Communication*. Orlando, FL: Harcourt School, 1995.

Objectives

The objectives of an organization often derive from, or are the catalyst which creates, a business's **mission statement**. Objectives are broad goals or strategies which the organization seeks to adopt in order to achieve its primary aims. Objectives, by their very nature, are broad and often somewhat ill-defined. They merely represent an outline, or guideline, which suggests the direction in which the organization intends to move. Broad objectives could include a considerable increase in output, the desire to launch new products, or a determination to provide better customer service. As with many issues, there may be little time spent initially on identifying precisely how the objectives themselves will be achieved.

Occupational psychology

Occupational psychology is essentially a UK or European term which is a broad descriptor for the study of the behaviour of individuals at work. As occupational psychology clearly takes a psychological perspective, it attempts to provide insights and perspectives in various areas of behaviour in the workplace. Typically, occupational psychology includes the following:

- the selection process;
- counselling;
- training and development;
- work design;
- work environment;
- motivation;
- performance management;
- linkages between employees and the organization;
- employee well-being;
- quality of working life;
- impacts on the individual from change and transition,

Arnold, John, Cooper, Cary and Robertson, Ivan, *Work Psychology: Understanding Human Behaviour in the Workplace*. London: Financial Times, Prentice Hall, 1998.

Fincham, Robin and Rhodes, Peter, *Principles of Organizational Behaviour*. Oxford: Oxford University Press, 1999.

Ohmae, Kenichi

In his book published in 1995, *The End of the Nation State: The Rise of Regional Economies*, Ohmae put forward three key theories:

- World markets, particularly services, will continue to become highly globalized.
- The modern nation state has developed too many rigid rules and practices to be able to cope with the perpetual change in the international economic environment.
- New region states, consisting of between 5 million and 20 million people, which quite possibly could cross national boundaries, represent a new natural unit for economic growth. They would enjoy **economies of scale** in terms of services, but would not be self-sufficient in any other products.

Ohmae suggested that these regional clusters are the future of international trade, and that successful clusters would spread their economic benefits to neighbouring regions. Whilst the first two ideas are fairly common, the third is somewhat novel. In principle these region states are not unlike some of the smaller European countries.

Ohmae suggested that areas such as Hong Kong are ideal examples of this form of region state. Its gross national product per capita stands at around $12,000. When it was brought into China as part of the Shenzhen Province, it boosted the province's GNP per capita to $5,695, compared with an average of $317 for the rest of China.

Ohmae, Kenichi, *The End of the Nation State: The Rise of Regional Economies*. London: HarperCollins, 1996.

www.pfdf.org/leaderbooks/ohmae

On-the-job consumption

'On-the-job consumption' refers to management participation in activities which effectively diminish shareholder value. The term refers to time and resources that may be expended by a manager in order to pursue his or her own goals at the expense of the overall profitability or efficiency of the business itself. More generally, on-the-job consumption involves the behaviour of managers who choose to use their authority and control over the financial resources of the business in order to secure their own job security, income, power or status. This is often exemplified by individuals at director level who create elaborate or expensive perks for themselves which are not necessarily linked to performance.

Operating budget

A business's operating budget is, essentially, a forecast of its future financial needs. The operating budget may cover a range of different time periods, but typically will cover the forthcoming years.

The operating budget will include estimates not only of the financial requirements, but also of the expected revenue streaming into the business, which will (ultimately) fund the operations. The operating budget will, therefore, incorporate sales, production and **cash flow**.

It is the function of managers and accountancy personnel to monitor the relationship between the operating budget and the actual figures being produced, as they occur. Changes or divergent figures are monitored, assessed and adjusted as required.

Operations management

Formerly, operations management was known as 'production management', and applied almost exclusively to the manufacturing sector. For many organizations, the term 'production management' is still preferred. However, the management function related to manufacturing has broadened to incorporate many aspects related to the supply chain. It has therefore become common to use the term 'operations management' to describe activities related both to manufacturing and, increasingly, to the service sector.

At its heart, operations management deals with the design of products and services, the buying of components or services from suppliers, the processing of those products and services and the selling of the finished goods. Across all of these disparate areas of business, operations management can be seen as an overarching discipline which seeks to quantify and organize the whole process. None the less, there is still a considerable emphasis placed on issues directly related to manufacturing, stock control and, to a lesser extent, the management of the distribution systems. As Figure 48 illustrates, a large manufacturing organization will include aspects of operations management under a wide variety of different, but closely related, managerial disciplines. Primarily, human resources, marketing, administration and finance,

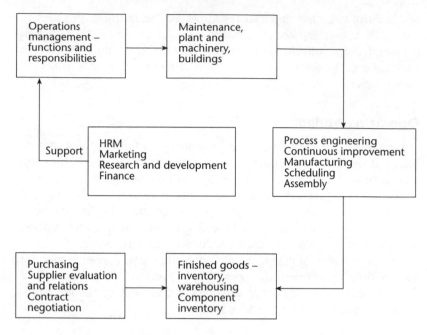

Figure 48 The functions of operations management

and, of course, the research and development department of an organization, support and are mutually dependent upon the operations division.

Given the wide spread of different job roles and tasks within operations management, it is notoriously difficult to give a perfect definition of what an operations manager would actually do. Certainly they would be responsible for a wide range of different functions, but the functions themselves will often be determined by the nature of the business itself and on whether it is a service-based industry or an organization primarily concerned with manufacturing.

Hill, Terry, *Operations Management: Strategic Context and Managerial Analysis*. Basingstoke: Palgrave Macmillan, 2000.

Operations research

Operations research is concerned with the development and application of various quantitative techniques which can be used to solve problems. Methodologies and theories which are used primarily in mathematics and statistics are adapted and used to identify, formulate, solve, validate, implement and control decision making. Effectively it is a scientific approach to the analysis and solving of problems. Operations research aims to provide rational foundations for the understanding of decision making, particularly in complex situations and thereby provide a predictable system of behaviour and performance. Typically, operations research utilizes analytical or numerical techniques, which have often been derived from either computer or mathematical models of systems.

Operations research has its foundations in the pre-World War Two years, when it was known as operational research. The UK used operational research to prepare for an anticipated air war and the impact that radar would have on tracking incoming streams of enemy aircraft. Arguably, operational research was one of the key elements which helped the UK win the Battle of Britain in 1940.

The field has evolved and is now primarily concerned with the development of mathematical models which can be used to optimize systems.

The Institute for Operations Research and Management Sciences is at www.informs.org

Taha, Hamdy A., *Operations Research: An Introduction*. New York: Prentice Hall, 2002.

Operations strategy

Essentially, an organization's operations strategy aims to deploy the organization's resources in order to gain a **competitive advantage**. The operations strategies are usually defined in very broad terms and imply aspirations in respect of levels of service, quality, flexibility and cost control. In many cases an organization will identify a key objective which will give it a competitive advantage, but this may mean that other objectives may need to be sacrificed in order to achieve the primary goal.

Organizational conflict

See **conflict management.**

Organizational culture

There are a number of ways in which an organization's culture can be classified. The main classifications were suggested by a number of researchers, including Roger Harrison, Charles Handy, Terence Deal and Allan Kennedy, and R. E. Quinn and M. R. McGrath. As years have passed, so these classifications have become more developed, making it possible only to approach them in generally broad terms.

In 1972 Harrison suggested four main categories of organizational culture – power, role, task and person. Charles Handy reworked Harrison's theory and identified them as described in Table 34.

During the 1980s Deal and Kennedy developed their own set of theories about organizational culture and the way in which it affected how management made decisions and formed their strategies. Their conclusions are shown in Table 35.

Table 34   Categories of organizational culture according to Handy

Culture	Description
Power	This type of culture is based on trust and good personal communication. There is little need for rigid bureaucratic procedures since power and authority rest with only a few individuals. The power culture is dynamic in that change can take place quickly but is dependent on a small number of key, powerful individuals. This culture tends to be tough on employees because the key focus is the success of the organization, often resulting in a high labour turnover.
Role	This type of culture tends to be bureaucratic in nature, thus requiring logical, coordinated and rational processes with a heavy emphasis on rules and procedures. Control lies with a small number of employees who have high degrees of authority. These tend to be stable organizations, operating in a predictable environment with products and services that have a long lifespan. Not considered to be innovative organizations, they can adapt to gradual, minor change, but not to radical ones.
Task	This type of organizational culture relies on employees' expertise. The **matrix structure** tends to prevail in these organizations, with teams of individuals specializing. They need, and tend, to be flexible organizations with individual employees working with autonomy, allowing fast reaction to changes in the external environment and having set procedures in place to address this aspect.
Person	This type of culture relies on collective decision making, often associated with partnerships. Compromise is important and individuals will tend to work within their own specialist area, coordinating all aspects and working with autonomy without the need to report to other employees.

Table 35   Organizational culture according to Deal and Kennedy

Culture	Description
Macho	These types of organization have to make decisions quickly and adopt a tough attitude towards their employees and fellow managers. There is a high degree of internal competition and the operations tend to be high risk. The majority of these organizations do not form strategies or plan for the long term but are considered short-termist, with a low level of cooperation within the organization itself. There is a high labour turnover, resulting in a weak organizational culture.
Work hard/ play hard	This type of culture tends to be associated with sales. The majority of individual employees are sales orientated but the level of risk is low. It is the employees' ability to accumulate sales that is important and the culture tends to encourage team-building and social activities for employees. The organization encourages competition and offers rewards for success, but does not necessarily value quality as highly as volume.
Company	These types of organization are often in high-risk areas and operate on the basis that decisions take a long time to come to fruition. Decision making takes place at the top of this hierarchical organization and the overall approach can often be old-fashioned. Each new invention or technical breakthrough will pose a threat to the business.
Process	This type of culture operates in a low-risk, slow-feedback environment where employees are encouraged to focus on how they do things rather than what they do. They tend to be systems- and procedures-based, requiring employees to work in an orderly and detailed fashion, attending meetings and work groups. There will be rigid levels of management in the hierarchical structure, but because the organization operates in a predictable environment, reactions from management are often slow.

Quinn and McGrath also identified four different organizational cultures, as shown in Table 36.

It should be remembered that no one organization fits neatly into any one of the categories mentioned, and the majority are too complex to be

Table 36 Organizational culture according to Quinn and McGrath

Culture	Description
Rational	The rational culture is firmly based on the needs of a market. The organization places emphasis on productivity and efficiency and encourages management to be goal-orientated and decisive. All activities are focused on tangible performance and employees are rewarded on achievement.
Adhocracy	This type of culture is an adaptive, creative and autonomous one where authority is largely based on the abilities and charismatic nature of leaders. These organizations tend to be risk-orientated and emphasis is placed on employees' adherence to the values of the organization itself.
Consensual	These types of organization are often concerned with equality, integrity and fairness and much of the authority is based on informal acceptance of power. Decisions are made by collective agreements or consensus and dominant leaders are not often present. Morale is important, as is cooperation and support between employees in order to reach organizational objectives. Employee loyalty is high.
Hierarchical	This type of culture relies on stability and control through the setting of rigid regulations and procedures. Decisions are made logically on facts alone with the management tending to be cautious and conservative. The employees are strictly controlled, with management expecting obedience.

categorized generally. The classifications should be regarded only as a reference point for comparison of extremes.

Handy, C. B., *Understanding Organizations*. London: Penguin Books, 1993.
Quinn, R. E. and McGrath, M. R., *The Transformation of Organisational Cultures: A Competing Values Perspective in Organisational Culture*, ed. C. C. Lundberg, and J. Martin. Newbury Park, CA: Sage Publications, 1985.
Schein, E. H., *Organizational Culture and Leadership*. New York: Jossey-Bass, 1997.

Organizational design

The way in which an organization decides to configure its activities can be depicted in terms of organizational design. The primary objective of any organizational design is to ensure that the structure conforms to the following:

- the business objectives;

- the business resources;
- the environment in which the business operates.

It is the structure, or the design, of the organization that dictates the relationship between the different parts of the organization and those who work within it. The design also specifies the following:

- the divisions of work;
- the hierarchical structure;
- the authority structure;
- formal links within the organization.

Organizational design, therefore, is the process of actually configuring the organization in relation to its strategies to attain optimum performance. Organizational design has to be reactive and flexible in the sense that changes may have to be made if discontinuity occurs. The net effect of not changing the design is to create a gap between the way in which the organization works and the strategy objectives. It is therefore imperative that the organizational design does not have an adverse effect on the performance of the business. The following problems may be encountered, and strategies adopted:

- As the organization grows, the design is amended to decentralize decision making, making it easier for experts in certain areas to take control.
- Changes in strategy must be matched with changes in design.
- Changes in priorities must be matched with changes in design.
- Technological changes may mean changes in information, communication and decision making; all need to be reflected in the organizational design.

Harvey-Jones, John, *Managing to Survive*. London: Mandarin, 1994.

Organizational development

Organizational development (OD) is a planned process of change. This form of development is about performance improvement, in which a business will seek to align more closely to the environment and markets in which it operates in order to achieve its strategies efficiently and effectively. OD can involve developing organizations in terms of culture, values, people, structures, processes and resources.

OD is a complex issue and often specific regarding process, timing, and those involved. There are, however, some overarching processes and elements that can be identified as being common to many OD situations. OD tends to begin with research into the current situation to assess all the issues. This research will inevitably involve the following aspects:

- clarifying the impact of any obligations which have to be honoured;
- the availability of appropriate resources such as skills, facilities and finances;
- the desires and career aspirations of those who will be affected;
- the proposed plan's overall fit with future business strategy.

Once the research process is completed, the organization should have a better view of how the OD will work in practice. This begins with planning the change programme, which may involve the design of a new organizational structure, job descriptions and evaluation, salary and benefits provision, physical resources, the phasing in of the overall project, and the management of its impacts on existing employees.

Throughout the process, the organization needs to ensure that it conducts communication, development and counselling events to assist the establishment of the new organizational structure. It may also be necessary to reshape or re-profile certain areas of the organization with the intention of improving employee retention and making the best use of skills and expertise in order to achieve the intended developments in efficiency.

Hamlin, Bob, Keep, Jane and Ash, Ken (eds), *Organisational Change and Development: A Reflective Guide for Managers, Trainers and Developers*. Financial Times, Prentice Hall, 2000.

Mello, Jeffrey, *Strategic Human Resource Management*. Mason, OH: South Western College Publishing, 2001.

Organizational mapping

Organizational mapping seeks to identify the tasks and functions carried out by each individual employee, to act as a means by which under- or over-commitment of individuals can be identified. The process begins with assigning a number to each task which needs to be performed. It also requires the name of the responsible individual and the projected time required to perform the task, usually expressed as either hours or weeks. Once this has been carried out, it is possible to total up the projected time for the completion of all necessary tasks for each individual, which will produce either a negative or a positive number in relation to the time available. The process should then reveal where key employees are over- or under-committed. Typically, the organizational mapping is displayed as a traditional organizational chart, which details the over- or under-commitment.

http://dev.skyrme.com/updates/u59_f1.htm

Organizational norms

Organizational norms reinforce the socialization process of individuals within a business. The organizational norms and the socialization process work together in order to instil in the management and employees the goals of the organization as a whole. Organizational norms seek to identify the ways in which individuals spend their time, manage information, communicate, take responsibility and make decisions. In other words, organizational norms involve the moulding of attitudes and behaviours in order to achieve collaboration and performance.

Organizational politics

Organizations are essentially political systems and power is used on a day-to-day basis to determine organizational relationships. Within the organizational context, politics is a means of recognizing and ultimately reconciling various competing interests. Whilst, in the past, business organizations were controlled rigidly by management, they have increasingly developed into various forms of democratic working environments that are no longer based on coercion. Clearly, in their politics, organizations can range from the autocratic to the democratic. Within these two extremes there are bureaucratic organizations, which run their politics on a very formalized basis, or technocratic systems in which the politics are based on skills and abilities.

Politics involves what can often be non-rational influences on decision making. It is widely believed, however, that successful organizational politics can lead its practitioners to higher levels of power, and ultimately result in a more reasoned organization, which can adapt and change, as well as being more effective in its decision making. In order to understand organizational political behaviour, Table 37 may prove to be a useful starting point in as much as it identifies three key dimensions:

- Where the political activity takes place – whether internal (inside) or external (outside the organization).
- The direction of the influence – either vertical or lateral.
- The legitimacy of the political action.

Organizational socialization

Organizational socialization is said to begin at the very point when an individual starts his or her career in an organization. Individuals need to understand and analyse the particular **organizational culture** in

Table 37 Defining organizational politics

Dimensions		
Internal/external	Internal examples: Exchange of favours, reprisals, obstruction, symbolic protests.	External examples: Whistle-blowing, legal action, information leaks.
Vertical/lateral	Vertical examples: By-passing chains of command, complaining to managers, interaction between peers.	Lateral examples: Exchanges of favours, formation of coalitions or groups.
Legitimate/illegitimate	Legitimate examples: Any actions taken in accordance with the overall organizational procedures and policies	Illegitimate threats.

which they are now placed. Whilst formal training programmes are important in developing technical knowledge or skills, a more discrete and subconscious form of socialization begins to take place in order to bring the new individual into the organization, both physically and mentally. Individuals may need to be re-socialized, as they may bring with them views and ways of carrying out work which are not expressly acceptable to their new employers.

Organizational strategy

'Organizational strategy' can refer to either a functional-level, business-level or corporate-level strategy. The organizational strategy is the specific pattern of any decisions or actions which managers will undertake in order to use the business's **core competences** in obtaining a **competitive advantage**. Organizational strategy, therefore, means that the business will seek to mobilize its resources in the form of the functional skills of employees and management and/or the attributes of the organization itself in order to achieve specific goals. Clearly, organizational strategy involves a coordination of both the functional and the organizational resources in order to achieve any objectives.

Normally, organizational strategy is formulated at three distinct levels. These are:

- *Functional level* – which is carried out by functional managers with the aim of strengthening the business's functional and organizational resources, to coordinate, and to create and maintain, core competences.
- *Business level* – which is carried out by the senior management and aims to mobilize functional core competences in order to gain a competitive advantage.
- *Corporate level* – which may be derived from the key **stakeholders** in the business, notably the senior executives, and will seek to ensure that the business finds ways in which to create value and to compete, perhaps through **diversification** or some form of integration, acquisition, or merger with another organization.

Stacey, Ralph D., *Strategic Management and Organisational Dynamics: The Challenge of Complexity*. London: Financial Times, Prentice-Hall, 2002.

Organizational structure

Organizational structure is a crucial consideration for all businesses. Efficient organizational structure requires three main criteria:

- The way in which the organization is divided into sub-units. This is known as horizontal differentiation.
- The location of the decision-making responsibilities within the structure. This is known as vertical differentiation.
- How the business has established integrating mechanisms.

Arguably, there is a fourth consideration, which is known as 'control systems'. This is taken to mean how the performance of sub-units within the organization is assessed and how well the managers of those sub-units control the activities within their area of responsibility.

It is essential for organizations which are pursuing a variety of different strategies as part of their international business activities to choose and then adopt appropriate organizational **architecture**, which is responsive enough to implement the identified strategies. The organizational structure or architecture of a multinational business organization will very much depend on whether it is a multi-domestic business, global, or trans-national. As multinationals spread their interests across the globe they inherently become more complex. In addition to this, they also become less able to change. None the less, the move towards increased globalization of industry has meant that businesses trading internationally must be able to adapt or amend their organizational structure to incorporate new strategies and operations in new markets.

Organizational values

An organization's values are standards which the business regards highly and holds as its ideal. Values may be ethical standards, but essentially they guide the organization as to how to carry out business. Organizational values can derive from senior management, line management or even teams and employees. Often, organizational values are incorporated into the business's **mission statement**. In effect, the organization seeks to establish role models for these values.

Ouchi, William

William Ouchi suggested an approach to human resource management that has been adopted in Japan. Ouchi's Theory Z began with the development of three management strategies:

- The development of a commitment to life-long employment.
- Encouraging employees to feel a sense of belonging to the organization by projecting to them its philosophy and objectives.
- Attention to detail in the selection and recruitment process and ensuring that new recruits accept the organization's values and are accepted into its social environment.

As can be seen in Table 38, Ouchi came up with six techniques which would assist in the implementation of the strategies.

www.pfdf.org/leaderbooks/ouchi

Output controls

The term 'output controls' has a specific reference to international businesses in as much as it suggests the inherent difficulties in setting goals for subsidiaries and then expressing those goals in terms of objective criteria. The more complex an international business becomes, perhaps with a series of subsidiaries in different nations, the more difficult it will be for the parent company to judge the performance of those subsidiaries. There is no simple solution, yet output controls seek to provide an objective means by which the goals can be expressed. The objectivity needs to be applied equally to all subsidiary organizations; only then can it be used as a true performance measurement and a means by which the subsidiaries' ability to meet those goals can be judged.

Table 38   Implementation of management strategies

Technique	Implementation method
Seniority-based promotion systems	Make new recruits feel they can spend the rest of their career with the organization by allowing them to gain experience through job rotation. Make progress through management levels steady and slow so that the employees gain generalist as opposed to specialist skills.
Continuous development	Ensure that employees are continuously updated by means of training and appraisal. Encourage long-term career plans to allow a sense of job security.
Groups and teams	Encourage group-based tasks rather than individual-based tasks to help develop the socialization process.
Communication	Communication has to be open and easily accessible through all levels of the workforce. There is no distinction in dress code between managers and employees and these use the same facilities, such as canteens.
Employee participation	Encourage discussion and participation, particularly regarding areas of anticipated change.
Production-centred systems	The focus is on productivity, although a high level of concern for employee welfare and satisfaction is always shown.

Outsourcing

The outsourcing of human resources is gradually gaining ground as a primary means by which businesses handle the functions relating to employees. There have been significant changes in policy where a shift has been in progress from providing human resources in-house to using external organizations. In effect, outsourcing is the use of another organization or an agency for some, or all, of the business's human resource functions.

Outsourcing is not merely restricted to the smaller business. Notably, businesses which have grown significantly over recent years have a greater tendency to consider outsourcing, largely as they prefer to focus on the operations of the core business, and there is a culture of outsourcing which has enhanced this growth.

In the USA, where there is a strong tradition of outsourcing human resources activities, the industry was worth an estimated $13.9 billion in 1999 and, according to research businesses such as Dataquest, it is expected to have reached $37.7 billion in 2004.

Outsourcing of human resources falls into four broad categories:

- Professional Employer Organizations (PEO) take on all of the responsibilities of the human resource administration for a business, including the legal responsibilities, the hiring of staff and termination of employment. Typically, the relationship is cooperative, with the PEO handling human resources and the business itself dealing with all other aspects of operations. Not all PEOs take the full responsibility for human resources, with some merely handling payroll and benefits systems.
- Business Process Outsourcing (BPO), although a general term used to describe outsourcing in the broadest sense, refers to human resources in respect of supporting the human resource functions with technology and software (including data warehousing and other services).
- Application Service Providers (ASPs) restrict their relationship with a business to providing either web-based or customized software to help manage human resource functions such as payroll and benefits.
- E-services can either be ASPs or BPOs, which again are restricted to web-based services such as recruitment, software and data warehousing or other forms of data storage and access provision for human resources.

Incomes Data Services, *Outsourcing HR Administration*. London: Incomes Data Services, 2000.

Vanson, Sally, *The Challenge of Outsourcing Human Resources*. Oxford: Chandos Publishing, 2001.

Perceived conflict

See conflict management.

Performance appraisal

Performance appraisals are the most common form of performance management, but the concept also incorporates employee feedback, development and compensation. Overwhelmingly, however, the majority of employees are dissatisfied with performance management systems (the Society of Human Resource Management quotes a 90% figure).

Framing an effective performance management system can be fraught with difficulties; however, the following aspects are seen to be integral in the creation of such a scheme:

- A clear definition and measurement of performance is vital.
- Content and measurement should derive from internal and external customers.
- There should be a formal process for investigating and correcting situational influences and constraints on performance.

Above all, accurate and fair performance management needs to assess employees in relation to the factors listed in Table 39.

A 360-degree appraisal has rapidly become an integral part of performance management. A standard 360-degree appraisal system requires face-to-face feedback sessions, where an employee is given an opportunity both to ask questions and to listen to feedback.

Many businesses have instituted a more sophisticated system in which employees are evaluated by a number of individuals, including senior staff and colleagues. The quality of the data collected is high and becomes the primary focus and driving force behind training programmes. In order to ensure that the system works to its best potential, there are six steps which need to be considered. These are summarized in Table 40.

After these six steps, a development plan needs to be agreed in order to identify specific improvements and intended outcomes. There also

Table 39 Factors in performance assessment

Communication, coordination and support	Equipment and environment
Amount and relevance of training received.	Equipment and tools necessary to do the job.
Information, instructions, and specifications needed to do the job.	Process for obtaining and retaining raw materials, parts, supplies.
Coordination of work activities.	Dependability of equipment.
Cooperation, communication, and relations between co-workers.	Conditions in which job is performed.
Financial resources available and time allowed to produce quality and quantity of work.	

needs to be a genuine commitment by the business to provide resources and other support in order for these outcomes to be met.

Appraisals are, in effect, a way of judging an employee's performance in a given job. The performance appraisal considers more than productivity, but is often used as the basis upon which increases in wages or salaries are considered. Whilst managers and colleagues constantly form and re-form opinions of those who work for them or with them, a formal appraisal meeting puts these considerations into a more formal context.

The basic functions of an appraisal system are:

- to determine the short-, medium- and long-term future of the employee;
- to identify possible training needs;
- to motivate the employee;
- to assist management in deciding what levels of pay increases will be accorded to that individual.

Typically, appraisals will take the form of a performance review, a review of potential or a rewards review. There are, of course, a number of different ways in which appraisal schemes are organized, which include the ranking method, the 360-degree performance appraisal, the rating scale, and behaviourally anchored rating scales (BARS).

Appraisals rely on being able to provide positive criticism to individuals, and the setting of realistic standards which require the employee to give maximum effort in order to achieve the set goals. Appraisal systems

Table 40   Requirements in evaluating employees

Steps	Description
Open mind	Those undergoing the appraisal need to have commitment, vision and often the courage to face how they are viewed, as well as a willingness to implement any suggestions. As drawbacks are highlighted, an objective and open-minded view needs to be taken towards criticism.
Self-evaluation	A clear and honest listing of current competences is essential. The gaps in competence should be highlighted and prioritized, as this gives a clear message to those providing feedback that the individual is prepared to discuss critical areas of his or her abilities.
Plan of action	There needs to be a clearly established set of performance categories. Normally feedback will be provided by managers and peers, both direct and indirect colleagues. The ideal number should not exceed 6–8 individuals.
Mental preparation	Self-evaluation techniques require an individual not to be defensive, and to be prepared to receive feedback. Whatever is said needs to be listened to and accepted.
Action	During the interviews those providing feedback are delivering the information for a positive purpose. Advice, suggestions and assistance should be sought, as well as clarification. The interview should be frank and honest.
Analysis	In essence, the feedback needs to be analysed in terms of strengths and weaknesses that have been identified. The strengths and weaknesses need to be categorized in order to identify areas needing improvement or, perhaps, clarification. Specific areas may need specific actions.

need to have clearly defined rules and expectations and, above all, the appraiser (the individual delivering the appraisal) and the appraisee (the individual being appraised) need to be speaking the same language. This implies, therefore, that a degree of training for both parties needs to be instituted prior to the running of an appraisal system. This not only sets the pattern and nature of the appraisal, but also allows for the unscheduled reviewing of factors which have been brought up during the appraisal interviews. Clear documentation needs to be drawn up, as well as a log to note performance deficiencies and performance improvements.

DeNisi, A. S. and Kluger, A. N., 'Feedback Effectiveness: Can 360-degree Appraisals be Improved?' *Academy of Management Executive*, 14(1) (2000), pp. 129–39.

Ghorpade, J., 'Managing Five Paradoxes of 360-degree Feedback', *Academy of Management Executive*, 14(1), (2000), pp. 140–50.

Maddux, Robert B., *Effective Performance Appraisals*. Eldridge, US: Crisp Publications, 2000.

Neal, James E., *The no. 1 Guide to Performance Appraisals: Doing it Right!* Perrysburg, OH: Neal Publications, 2001.

Neal, James E., *Effective Phrases for Performance Appraisals: A Guide to Successful Evaluations*. Perrysburg, OH: Neal Publications, 2003.

Soltani, Ebrahim, Gennard, John, van der Meer, Robert and Williams, Terry, *Content Issues of HR-Related Performance Measurement: A Total Quality Management Approach*. Paper, University of Strathclyde, 2002.

Performance/importance grid

A performance/importance grid can be used by an organization in order to identify its priorities, as well as its current strengths and weaknesses. In effect the performance/importance grid is a variant form of a **SWOT analysis.** Its direct application is to identify current priorities and current success in specific areas of a business's operations. The grid enables the organization to identify the ideal strategies in relation to these two criteria, which are categorized as being either high or low (see Figure 49).

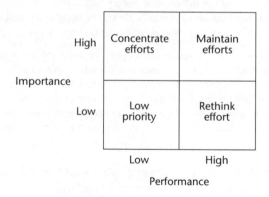

Figure 49 The performance/importance grid

Performance management

Performance management can be seen as a systematic and data-orientated approach to managing employees, based on positive reinforcement as the primary driver to maximize their performance, on the assumption that there is a disparity between what employees are currently achieving (on the basis that they have to do the work and perform to this standard) and the possibility that they desire to perform better (based on the assumption that they have desires to perform more effectively if given the opportunity and the encouragement). In many respects, the concept behind performance management is a recognition of this potential gap between actual performance and desired performance. This can be illustrated in the graph in Figure 50, which identifies the discretionary effort of an individual. This discretionary effort is applied according to circumstances and is variable. Performance management seeks to identify the gap between 'having to' and 'wanting to', and to push the performance up to the 'want to' level.

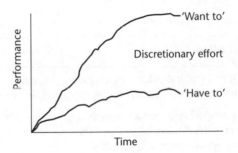

Figure 50 The gap between actual and desired performance

Performance management has been used in its various forms since the mid-1970s and it is believed to be applicable to almost every area of a business. Its primary focus is, of course, employees. The first major step in implementing a performance management system is to move away from the negative reinforcement of standards, which seeks to punish individuals for not achieving (often) unspoken levels of performance. Performance management uses positive reinforcement to generate effort beyond what is normally (minimally) exhibited by the employees. In this way, the discretionary effort is encouraged and the organization as a whole can move towards a maximization of performance.

Kotter, John P. and Heskett, James L., *Corporate Culture and Performance*. London: Free Press, 1992.
Porter, Michael, *The Competitive Advantage: Creating and Sustaining Superior Performance*. London: Simon & Schuster, 1998.

PEST analysis

This concept originally began with just four criteria, with the acronym

PEST (Political, Economic, Social and Technological). These forces are seen as being the principal external determinants of the environment in which a business operates. In later years the four forces became five under the acronym SLEPT (Social, Legal, Economic, Political and Technological). The concept has now been extended to include seven forces, using the acronym STEEPLE (Social, Technological, Economic, Educational, Political, Legal and Environmental protection).

The purpose of the Five Forces model, or its variants, is to examine or audit where threats originate and where opportunities can be found. In other words, the broader STEEPLE acronym applies to the macro-environment (factors outside the organization). The main areas of interest within each letter are listed in Table 41.

Table 41 The STEEPLE acronym

Letter	Description
S	Social and cultural influences, including language, culture, attitudes and behaviour which affect future strategies and markets.
T	Technological and product innovation, which suggests how the market is developing, as well as future developments in research and arising opportunities.
E (E1)	Economic and market competition, which considers factors such as the business cycle, inflation, energy costs and investments. An assessment is made as to how they will affect the level of economic activity in each market.
E (E2)	Education, training and employment, primarily the trends in these areas which may affect the availability of trained labour as well as the potential demands of new generations and probable expectations.
P	Political, which focuses on current and proposed policies which will have an impact on the business and the workforce.
L	Legal, which focuses on current and proposed legislation, of equal importance is the business's adherence to current laws and regulations.
E (E3)	Environmental protection, which addresses the business's current and future impact on the environment, working on the basis that environmental protection will continue to be a major issue in restricting and amending the ways in which a business operates.

Porter, Michael, *Competitive Advantage*. New York: Free Press, 1985.

See also **Porter, Michael.**

Peters, Tom

Although Tom Peters has written extensively on broader issues regarding the success of businesses, his central message concerns the use of leadership, or rather the habits of leaders. He prefers to use the term 'leadership' rather than 'management' as he suggests that managers should focus on leadership qualities, specifically motivating and facilitating their employees. He therefore places leadership, as can be seen in Figure 51, at the centre of all aspects of the business, including creating new ideas through innovation, satisfying customers, and above all, deploying people (employees) in the most effective manner.

Although Tom Peters is probably best known for his theories on customer orientation, he has identified twelve attributes or traits of the most successful US businesses, many of which have human resource implications, as can be seen in Table 42.

Figure 51   The central position of leadership

Peters, Tom and Waterman, Robert H., *In Search of Excellence: Lessons from America's Best-running Companies*. London: Profile Business, 1995.

www.tompeters.com

Piece-work

Piece-work means that employees are not paid for the hours that they work; instead they are paid for the number of items produced. A worker should, theoretically, not get less than the minimum wage if paid on a piece-work basis.

Many factories pay staff a flat rate per hour plus 'piece'-work (so much extra per piece of work), which allows experienced staff the opportunity to increase their wages.

Pioneering costs

The term 'pioneering costs' is associated with the costs and risks facing an international business entering a new overseas market for the first time. In many respects they are trail-blazing organizations, and do not have the benefits of knowing how to deal with that overseas country,

Table 42 Attributes of successful US businesses

Trait or quality	Description
Quality obsession	Given the assumption that quality is of paramount importance, leaders should tackle quality issues the moment they arise.
Passionate systems	The drive for quality should not just be a system; it should be an ideology with a system.
Measurement of quality	Everyone in the organization should understand how quality is measured.
Quality rewards	Incentives should be given to those who consistently provide quality.
Quality training	All employees should receive quality training on quality.
Multi-function teams	**Quality circles** should be established, with the power to drive change.
Small improvements	Any quality improvement, however small, should be celebrated and rewarded.
Continuous Hawthorne Effect	Employees should always be given new goals, and leaders should be seen to be seen.
Quality teams and structures	A structure of quality teams should be established to examine closely all aspects and processes of the business.
Total involvement	Suppliers and distributors should be included in any quality drive or vision.
Quality and cost	There is a direct relationship between quality (which reduces wastage, etc.) and profitability. All employees should be aware of this.
Quality utopia	When specific quality goals have been achieved, new ones should be set for employees to strive towards.

either from experience or by learning lessons from other international businesses that have come before. Pioneering costs include the time and effort required to learn how the market operates and how the country's government, rules and regulations can have an impact upon the business's ability to succeed. Pioneering costs are borne alone by the first entrant into the market. Later entrants can benefit from lessons and mistakes learned by the pioneer. However, assuming the pioneer has been successful, later arrivals may find it as difficult, if not more so, to establish themselves in the new marketplace.

Porter, Michael

Michael E. Porter is currently a professor at the Harvard Business School and is considered to be the leading authority on competitive strategy and competitiveness. He graduated with an MBA from Harvard in 1971 and a PhD in 1973. He has written some 16 books and 75 articles, including *Competitive Strategy: Techniques for Analyzing Industries and Competitors* (1980), *Competitive Advantage: Creating and Sustaining Superior Performance* (1985), *The Competitive Advantage of Nations* (1990) and *On Competition* (in 1998).

Over the years he has received a number of awards, including the Adam Smith Award from the National Association of Business Economists. Porter serves as an advisor to several different countries and has led major economic studies into countries as diverse as New Zealand and Peru.

Michael Porter's classic **Five Forces model** appeared in his 1980s book *Competitive Strategy: Techniques for Analysing Industries and Competitors*. It has become the standard analysing tool for many businesses.

The Five Forces shape every market and industry and help a business to analyse the intensity of competition, as well as the profitability and attractiveness of the market and industry. The Five Forces can be best explained as in Table 43.

Table 43 The Five Forces in marketing competition

Five Forces	Description	Implications
Threat of new entrants	The easier it is for new businesses to enter the industry, the more intense the competition. There may be factors which may limit the number of new entrants, which are known as **barriers to entry**.	Customers may already be loyal to major brands. Incentives may be offered to customers in order to retain them. Fixed costs will be high and there may be a scarcity of resources. Businesses and customers may find it expensive to switch suppliers and take the attendant risks.
Power of suppliers	This measures how much pressure suppliers can place on businesses within the industry. The larger the supplier and the more dominant the more it can squeeze a business's margins and profits.	In some markets there are few suppliers of particular products as there are no available substitutes. Switching to other suppliers may prove difficult, costly and risky. If the product is extremely important to the buyers they will continue to purchase it. In many cases the

⇒

Table 43 The Five Forces in marketing competition (*continued*)

Five Forces	Description	Implications
		supplying industry has a higher profitability than the buying industry.
Power of buyers	This is a measure as to how powerful customers are and what pressures they can apply to a business. The larger and more reliant customers are, the more likely they are to be able to affect the margins and volumes of businesses.	There may be a small number of buyers who purchase large quantities of products and services. Buyers may be tempted to switch to an alternative supplier. If a product is not at the core of their business or requirements, buyers may choose not to purchase for a period of time. The more competitive the market, the more price-sensitive the customers may be.
Threat of substitute products	This is a measure of how likely it is for buyers to switch to a competing product or service. If the cost of switching is low, then this will be a serious threat.	Businesses should be aware that similar products, if not exact substitutes, may tempt the buyer to switch, temporarily at least, to another supplier. If, for example, a supermarket chain is offered considerably cheaper alternatives to plastic shopping bags, they may be tempted to move over to cardboard boxes or paper sacks.
Competitive rivalry	This measures the degree of competition between existing businesses in an industry. It is usually the case that the higher the level of competition, the lower the return on investment. Margins are pared down to the lowest levels.	Assuming there is no dominant business, then many of the competitors will be of a similar size. There will also be little differentiation between competitors' products and services. The more stagnant the industry, in terms of market growth, the higher the possibility that competitors will focus on taking customers away from other businesses, rather than attempting to develop the market themselves.

Porter, Michael E., *Competitive Strategy: Techniques for Analyzing Industries and Competitors.* New York: Free Press, 1980.

Porter, Michael E., *Competitive Advantage: Creating and Sustaining Superior Performance*. New York: Free Press, 1985.

Porter, Michael E., *The Competitive Advantage of Nations*. New York: Free Press, 1990.

Porter, Michael E., *On Competition*. Boston, MA: Harvard Business School Press, 1998.

www.isc.hbs.edu/index.html/

Porter's diamond

Michael Porter's theory on the **competitive advantage** of nations was published in 1990. He suggested that there are four attributes of a nation which shape the environment in which businesses compete, and that these attributes either promote or impede the creation of competitive advantage. He arranged his four attributes in the form of a diamond, arguing that the diamond is a mutually reinforcing system. In other words, the effect of one attribute affects the state of the others. His four attributes are:

- **Factor endowments**, which constitute a nation's position in factors of production, such as skilled labour, or infrastructure.
- Demand conditions – the nature of the home country's demand for products and services.
- Relating and supporting industries – whether supplier industries and related industries exist and whether they are internationally competitive.
- Business strategy, structure and rivalry – concerning how businesses are created, organized and managed, as well as the nature of domestic rivalry.

Porter went on to suggest that there may be two other variables which could influence the diamond; these were:

- Chance – including innovations or major events which could reshape the structure of the industry and provide opportunities for one nation's businesses to overtake another's.
- Government – through its adoption of policies such as regulation, anti-trust laws or investments, the government can have an impact for good or ill on the nation's advantages.

Portfolio analysis

Product portfolio analysis is probably most closely associated with attempts to assess the market growth rate and a product's relative market share. Product portfolio analysis is a key marketing activity in determining the direction and intensity of **marketing strategy**.

See also **portfolio planning**.

Portfolio planning

'Product portfolio' is, essentially, a very similar term to 'product mix'. However, it is something of an extension of this concept, as not only does it describe the products and product lines owned by the business, but it also describes the business's desire to satisfy the needs of target markets, as well as its goals in terms of profitability and other objectives. Product **portfolio analysis** and planning are probably most closely associated with attempts to assess the market growth rate and a product's relative market share. Product portfolio analysis and planning are key marketing activities in determining the direction and intensity of **marketing strategy**.

Portfolio planning can be a broader issue than simply referring to products or product lines. It may indeed be the way in which an organization seeks to configure business strategy, investment strategy, the business's infrastructure and its current projects. The relationships between these four elements and the business's portfolio can be exemplified in the diagram in Figure 52.

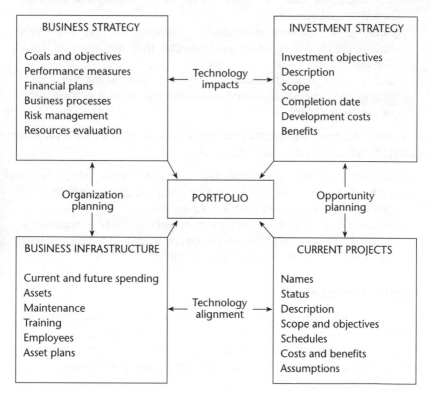

Figure 52   Dimensions of portfolio planning

Cooper, Robert G., Edgett, Scott J. and Kleinschmidt, Elko J., *Portfolio Management for New Products*. New York: Perseus Books, 2001.

Positive sum game

The term 'positive sum game' suggests that, in international trade, all countries involved benefit, even though some may benefit more than others. Indeed, international trade only occurs because both parties benefit from the exchange. International trade is considered to enhance world prosperity, therefore economic integration, or globalization, is a positive sum game and not, as some suggest, a process of exclusion and marginalization. Adopting the positive-sum-game viewpoint, the inference is that all countries, both the developed and the lesser developed nations, achieve material gains from international trade, regardless of whether the trade is imbalanced. By the removal of any restrictions to international trade, resources can be to a greater or lesser extent more fairly distributed throughout the world. Any increase in the transfer of technology, skills or competition increases productivity, which in every nation should bring about economic growth and a rise in real incomes. This is a positive sum game for all countries.

See also **negative sum game.**

Prahalad, C. K.

In two *Harvard Business Review* articles, C. K. Prahalad and Gary Hamel looked at a business's fitness for global strategy and the tasks or role of senior managers. In their first study, they discovered the following:

- It was the mental models of strategy which distinguished the successful businesses from the least successful ones.
- Less successful businesses followed a conventional approach to strategic fit.
- Less successful businesses were primarily concerned with products or markets rather than **core competences**.
- Conformity of focus and behaviour ensured any drive towards financial objectives in less successful organizations.
- More successful businesses leveraged their resources.
- These successful businesses used innovation to reach their goals.
- They were concerned with challenging their resources to build up core competences.

In their second study, they turned their attention to the links between an organization's leader's vision and the organizational success. They suggested the following:

P

- Organizational learning is based on the knowledge that any **competitive advantage** will ultimately be eroded by the competitors.
- The organization therefore succeeds not by long-term planning but in the development of core competences.
- The primary difference between large organizations and smaller developing businesses is their available resource base, but it is not the relative size that matters; it is the difference between what the developing business would ideally want in terms of resources and what they do have available.
- They suggest that in fact the resource gap is not the main significant factor. It is a question of ambition, or of lack of ability to stretch what they do have to achieve what they desire.

Hamel, Gary and Prahalad, C. K., 'Do you Really have a Global Strategy'. *Harvard Business Review*, July–August 1989.

Hamel, Gary and Prahalad, C. K., 'Strategy as Stretch and Leverage'. *Harvard Business Review*, March–April 1993.

www.fastcompany.com/online/49/prahalad.html

Price to earnings ratio

The price to earnings ratio has the following structure:

$$\frac{\textit{Current market price of shares}}{\textit{Earnings per share}}$$

The price to earnings ratio is usually calculated on an annual basis and expresses the relationship between the actual share prices, as a multiple of the earnings which each share provides in the form of a dividend. In the following example, a business has a share price of some £10 and has paid a dividend of £0.50. Therefore:

$$\frac{10}{0.50} = 20$$

This reveals that the current market price for the share is 20 times its earnings. Technically, this means that on current earnings performance it would take 20 years to justify the current value of the share price. In actual fact, however, a high multiple suggests that the business is growing at a fast rate as low yields are most closely associated with high multiples. Other investors may take the opposite view and consider that high multiples simply reflect the fact that the business's share price is grossly over-inflated.

The price to earnings ratio, therefore, is used as a fundamental invest-ment appraisal tool when making a judgement as to whether the shares of a business represent good value when compared with the market as a whole.

Prior hypothesis bias

'Prior hypothesis bias' refers to decision-making situations where a cognitive bias occurs. In these situations, managers tend to base their decisions on prior beliefs which are strongly held, despite the fact that empirical evidence suggests that those prior beliefs are wrong or unfounded. In these cases, the manager believes that the relationship between certain disparate variables is already known, when in fact there may be no relationship or the interaction between those variables is misunderstood. Decisions are therefore made on an ambiguous basis rather than through logical processes.

Problem child/question mark/wild cat

One of the four **Boston growth matrix** categories, variously named problem child, question mark or wild cat. Almost all new products start life by being launched into high-growth rather than low-growth markets, as the perception is that high-growth markets will eventually generate a greater return. However, the drain on resources at this stage can be enormous. Initially the volume of products sold will be low and significant marketing expenditure will be required to raise market awareness and stimulate sales.

If a problem child product's sales can be made to grow faster than other competing products, then it will move into the **star** category. If the product is not supported and for a time has a static market position, it will eventually lose sales to competing products and fall into the **dog** category.

Problem solving

Problem solving is at the core of all managerial activities, and clearly problems may arise on innumerable occasions even in the course of one day. The exact way in which managers handle problems will depend on their proactivity (in the sense that they will seek to anticipate problems), their responsiveness (in the sense of how quickly they will deal with the problem) and their management style (relating to whether they deal with the problem themselves or delegate others to deal with it on their behalf, and whether they involve anyone else in the decision-making process to solve the problem). There is no definite problem-solving model which has the capacity to work in all given situations and with all management styles. However, the diagram in Figure 53 illustrates the basic decision-making processes involved in problem solving.

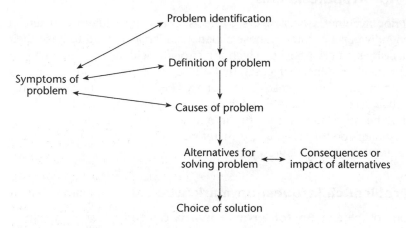

Figure 53   Decision making and problem solving

The key areas require managers to collect as much information as possible regarding the problem, once they have been alerted to the fact that the problem exists. Information can be gathered from a variety of different sources, but there is always a danger of receiving either too much, or contradictory information, which may conspire to make the problem solving all the more difficult. The manager must therefore assess, analyse and evaluate any information related to the problem before attempting to solve it in any meaningful manner.

Pettinger, Richard, *Mastering Management Skills*. Basingstoke: Palgrave Macmillan, 2001.

Procedural justice

Procedural justice represents both managers' and employees' access to legitimate channels within the organization in order to deal with problems and disputes. Procedural justice means that there is a detailed mechanism in place which the organization applies, either through management or through the human resources department, to deal with specific problems which may arise from the interaction between different managers and employees. Procedural justice also means that there is a standard procedure, a set of standards and ethics, which is applied to the handling of any such situations. Procedural justice should not be confused with any form of civil or criminal procedure, and it may not be precisely in accordance with governmental rules or regulations regarding the handling of disputes, complaints, arbitration or grievances.

Product development

Product development is a complex procedure which involves considerable interaction between different elements of an organization. Product development begins with an idea for producing a new product or service, in line with the possibility of it offering the potential for success and furthering the overall objectives of the business.

The process involved in developing products from an idea to the fulfilment stage (where the product or service reaches the end-user or consumer) involves four connected sequences of events. Planning for new products begins at the strategic level, where perhaps an opportunity has been identified, but this must now be translated into reality in the form of a product design and specified requirements. Clearly this needs to be in line with the organization's business plans or product strategies. Having successfully negotiated this area of product planning the product now moves into the development stage, where it is transformed from a concept needing to identify the solutions it will provide and the functions it will require, to a detailed design which will act as a precursor to any manufacturing or processing of the product or service in the future.

Assuming that the product is still a viable concern, it can then move into manufacturing and processing, where further teething problems are ironed out before the product goes into full production.

As the product reaches this stage, the marketing department of the business will roll into action and begin obtaining as much pre-publicity as possible for the new product or service. As soon as the product or service is available, deals that have been struck with distributors and re-sellers will be fulfilled. Normally this fulfilment process will coincide with advertising in selected media in order to raise awareness of the product or service on the part of the end-user. Once the products or services are available through the business, distributors or re-sellers, it can then be delivered directly to the consumer or end-user. Figure 54 illustrates the processes through which product development takes place.

Fitzsimmons, James and Fitzsimmons, Mona J. (eds), *New Service Development*. New York: Sage Publications, 1999.

Ulrich, Karl T. and Eppinger, Steven D., *Product Design and Development*. New York: McGraw Hill, 2003.

P

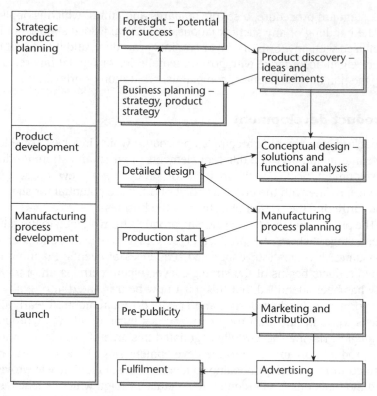

Figure 54   The process of product development

Product differentiation

Product differentiation is also known as brand differentiation. Product differentiation involves the identification of tangible and intangible benefits or features that can be used to differentiate a brand from competing products or services.

Tangible features or benefits tend to be conscious and rational benefits such as the precise function of the brand and what it achieves or provides for the customer. The intangible benefits tend to be emotional or subconscious features that the business wishes to attach to the brand, such as providing warmth or nourishing food to 'the family', safety, or other physiological needs.

Differentiation strategies include featuring low prices, larger selections, convenient, efficient and rapid service, the latest or most trendy product, prestige or best value overall, and reliability.

Product proliferation

Product proliferation is a description given to the vast numbers of new products and services released by businesses. It is also a name describing the variety of products and services.

Businesses continue to pursue policies of product proliferation on the following series of assumptions:

- that a broader product line adds to the general demand for products offered by the business;
- that broader product lines do add to the supply costs;
- that broader product lines can act as a deterrent to competitors (effectively a **barrier to entry**).

Clearly, product proliferation has both supply and demand implications. The strategy does not tend to deter competitors, whilst the costs associated with supporting a broad product line are a significant concern.

Bayus, Barry L. and Putsis, William J. Jr, *Product Proliferation: An Empirical Analysis of Product Line Determinants and Market Outcomes*. Gainesville, FL: *Marketing Science*, vol. 18, no. 2 (1999).

Product stewardship

Businesses increasingly recognize the wider responsibilities they have with regard to the whole life cycle of their products. This has led to the development of the concept of product stewardship. It involves the following:

- The examination of the design of products to assess their efficiency.
- The consideration of raw materials, energy (and sources), and components used in the manufacture of the product.
- The identification of alternative sources of raw materials, energy and components which are more environmentally friendly.
- An examination of the disposal methods for the product at the end of its useful life.
- The examination of waste caused by the production methods.
- Clear policies and strategies on recycling and re-use of materials.
- Providing enhanced packaging information with after-sales service details and guidance on safe disposal and use of the product.

Welford, R. J., *Corporate Environmental Management: Systems and Strategies*. London: Earthscan, 1996.

P

Product team structure

In product team structures, tasks are divided along product (or project) lines. The team will be supported by functional specialists, who are an integral part of cross-functional teams. In essence, product team structures (see Figure 55) are similar to **matrix structures** but are easier to control and less costly to operate.

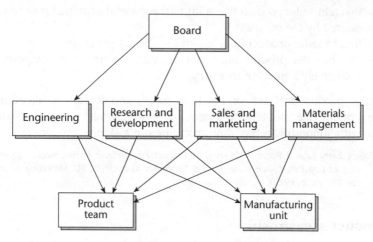

Figure 55 Example of a product team structure

Profit ratio

At its simplest, profit can be described as the difference, or excess, between the selling price of raw materials, products or services and the costs associated with providing these to a third party. Profit can be expressed as being either gross (before tax, expenses, etc.) or net (after taxes and expenses, etc.). Profits can, therefore, be calculated using the following simple formula:

Revenue – costs (before or after tax and expenses) = profit

The term 'profit' equally applies to a surplus of net assets at the end of a trading period, compared with the net assets which were available to the business at the start of the trading period. The profit figure, clearly, has to be adjusted to take into account the fact that capital may have been added or taken out of the business during that period.

Given profit's importance, it remains one of the most difficult figures to calculate objectively. A business's true profits can be measured in a variety of ways; it is not just a simple task of identifying the figure which is ultimately taxed and then, perhaps, distributed in the form of dividends to shareholders. Profit can be, of course, and often is, reinvested in the business in order to produce greater profits in the future. Profit, as recorded by the business in whatever form, can be found most clearly in the profit and loss statement (account).

Profit sharing

This is a term which is applied to a number of schemes offered by employers which aim to give the employees a stake in the business; many were prompted in the UK by the Finance Acts (1978, 1980 and 1984).

Around 20% of UK businesses have some form of employee share ownership and the move is seen as a form of employee participation and industrial democracy. In reality, however, the level of share ownership is low and the employees have little or no real control over the business (mainly as the shares tend not to have voting rights).

The three most common forms of profit sharing are:

- Employee Share Ownership Plans (ESOP), which were brought to the UK from the US and provide a means by which employees can gain equity in the business. A trust is formed and the dividends on the preference shares pay off the loans used to purchase the shares on behalf of the employees. The shares are held in trust, but employees have the right to sell them.
- Profit sharing schemes (PSS) usually take the form of Approved Profit Sharing (APS) schemes, which involve the distribution of shares to employees free of charge. Shares are purchased through a trust, which is financed from the profits of the business. Alternatively, employees can become involved in SAYE (save-as-you-earn), whereby employees sign a savings contract with the option to purchase shares at the end of the contract period, at a predetermined price. Both of these methods are more popular as they have tax benefits attached to them.
- Profit related pay (PRP) schemes are present in around 20 per cent of private sector businesses and are, essentially, an element in the total employee pay package. Profit related pay varies according to the profits made by the business, making a direct link between the activities of the employees and their productivity, and the extra pay that they ultimately receive in the form of PRP.

Profit sharing is seen as an effective means by which a business can encourage individual performance and motivation. Employees have a direct interest in the success of the business and therefore greater commitment and profit-consciousness.

The obvious downside as far as employees are concerned is that they are tying both their jobs and their savings to the success or failure of the business. As far as the business is concerned, there is also a worry that increasing staff involvement (particularly in share ownership) may mean that the staff will make increasing demands that the business give them a greater role in the decision making. Management may be unwilling to make concessions in the area of strategic decision making which could affect profitability and the level of employees' pay, as they may be considering longer-term issues.

Profit strategy

A business's profit strategy is, to a large extent, wholly dependent upon many external factors related to the demand generated as a result of the growth or distribution of national, and increasingly international, income. The profit potential is determined by the demand for products and services, the availability of funding and the extent to which the business can attract suitable employees. The relationship between these factors and a business's profit strategy can be seen in the diagram in Figure 56.

Figure 56 Factors affecting profit strategy

These, then, are the external factors which affect the formulation of the business's profit strategy. However, internally there are other factors to take into consideration. A business must configure its offerings in line with the demands for which products and services and also, to a large extent, the availability of supplies, which determines its ability to offer these products or services. The profit strategy is also influenced by the strategies regarding each individual product and service, the way in which these are manufactured, the human relations strategies and the way the business itself is run and what motives it may have.

Gundling, Ernest, *The 3M Way to Innovation: Balancing People and Profit*. London: Kodansha Europe, 2000.

Project management

Project management involves the planning, organizing, controlling and directing of what are usually one-off activities. Typically, a team will be assigned to manage a specific project and will use the project evaluation and review technique (PERT) or **critical path analysis (CPM)** in order to structure the management of the activities related to the project.

Project planning is the process that is concerned with organizing the implementation of a project so that it meets its objectives in terms of costs, functionality, quality, reliability and scheduling. A project plan serves five main functions:

- It defines the scope of the project and states the end products that will be delivered, taking into account any assumptions or constraints.
- It details the project activities and how they will be performed.
- It details the interdependence between the activities and a schedule of when these activities will be accomplished.
- It identifies the resources required in order to develop the project to achieve the desired results.
- It describes all the procedures and processes which will be managed during the project from the point of view of scheduling, cost, procurement, risk and quality.

Figure 57 illustrates the inter-relationship between these activities. The core processes are those required to implement the project, whilst the facilitating processes ensure that the project meets its goals and will be managed successfully.

A project portfolio is simply a collection of projects. The projects will be at various stages in their progress and, at different times, some will need more attention than others. The art of project portfolio

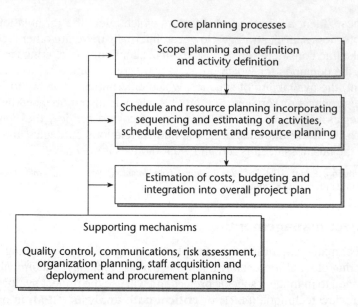

Figure 57 The interrelationship between planning processes

management is to balance the needs of each of the projects throughout their life cycle and ensure that each of them remains consistent with the project management process; it also provides progress reports and ensures that systems are consistently applied across the organization. This will enable the business to better allocate resources, with a clearer understanding of forthcoming requirements.

Lester, Albert, *Project Planning and Control.* Oxford: Butterworth-Heinemann, 2003.

P

Quality assurance

Quality assurance is the attempt by a business to make sure that agreed quality standards are met throughout the organization, primarily to ensure customer satisfaction. There has been a degree of international agreement about quality, consistency and satisfaction, which are enshrined in the International Standards Organization (ISO) 9000 series of quality systems standards. Businesses that meet these standards are normally assumed to have achieved quality assurance.

Quality circle

A quality circle is a discussion group which meets on a regular basis to identify problems concerning quality, investigate solutions and make recommendations as to the most suitable solution. The members of quality circles are employees, and they may include individuals with specific skills or expertise, such as engineers, quality inspectors or salespersons. Quality circles were first created in the 1950s in the Toyota motor company. In the 1980s this Japanese form of employee participation and consultation was adopted on a large scale in both Europe and the US. Quality circles aim to use untapped knowledge from the employees, as well as providing them with the opportunity to show their knowledge and talents through their problem-solving skills.

Quantum innovation

A quantum innovation is far more than a simple improvement. It is a considerable change and transformation of either a product, a service or a manufacturing or service-delivery procedure.

In the past, organizations have gone through a four-stage process with regard to innovation:

- They have concentrated on problem solving related to crises, as they arise.
- They moved towards being more proactive and attempted to engage in cost-cutting exercises.

- They adapted to **total quality management (TQM)** or other quality improvement programmes.
- They then realized that TQM is simply not enough.

Quantum innovation requires businesses to look beyond **benchmarking** and even beyond their most successful competitors and the top performers in their industry. Quantum innovation requires a radically different way of doing things; in effect, it intends to break the mould.

Potentially, of course, a quantum innovation can provide significantly better returns on investment, but it is risky. It has been estimated that whilst incremental growth or **incremental innovation** provides a year-on-year 10–20% increase in returns, a quantum innovation has the potential of returning a growth of 60–70% per annum.

Question mark

See **problem child.**

Quick ratio

This is a fundamental business-health test or formula. The quick ratio, or the acid-test ratio, measures current assets, less stock, against current liabilities. This ratio shows how well a business is able to cover its short-term obligations, in other words, its **liquidity**. It is considered to be one of the most stringent tests as it simply considers those current assets which can be turned into cash immediately, and does not consider stock as being immediately convertible into cash. The ratio shows creditors or potential investors what proportion of the business's short-term debts can be met by selling liquid assets.

Current assets – stock = current liabilities

An alternative way of working out a business's ability to turn assets into cash, in order that sufficient money will be available to pay creditors, is:

Debtors + cash balances = current liabilities

Quinn, R. E.

Quinn has written extensively, with a number of other authors, on strategic processes and on **organizational culture** and **organizational structure**. Together with M. A. McGrath he wrote about mechanic versus organic systems of **organizational design**, but it was his work with J. Rohrbaugh in 1981 which provided a useful model to describe competing values within an organization. The general thrust of their theory is illustrated in Figure 58.

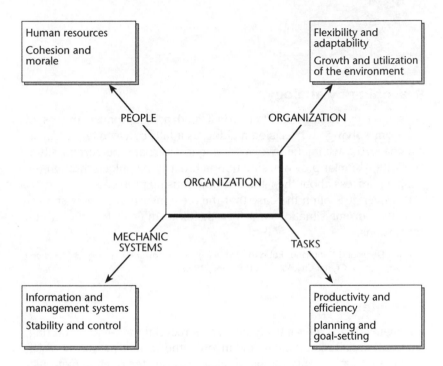

Figure 58   Competing values within organizations

The theorists suggested that the primary thrust of an organization, be it people orientated, task orientated, or by virtue of the fact that it is inherently an organic or mechanic system, will determine the ways in which it can seek to balance what appear to be four radically different and competing sets of values.

Quinn, R. E. and Rohrbaugh, J., 'Competing Values Approach to Organizational Effectiveness', *Public Productivity Review*, 5 (1981), pp. 122–40.

Quinn, R. E. and McGrath, M. A., 'Moving Beyond the Single-Solution Perspective: the Competing Values as a Diagnostic Tool', *Journal of Applied Behavioral Science*, 18 (1982), pp. 463–82.

Rr

Reasoning by analogy

Reasoning by analogy is often considered a compromise means of **problem solving** and decision making, as it falls between two conflicting goals. The technique involves trying to associate the current situation with a similar previous situation in order to be guided through the thinking process about the situation now causing problems.

However, it is often the case that the previous situation was simpler than the current situation and it is therefore difficult to draw useful conclusions.

Long, Derek and Garigliano, Roberto, *Reasoning by Analogy and Causality: A Model and Application.* Crystal City, VA: Ellis Horwood, 1993.

Re-engineering

Re-engineering is alternatively known as recycling, de-manufacturing, reclamation and remarketing, and involves the various means by which products or components can be re-used, either by the original manufacturer, or by an organization specifically set up to deal with this material.

Re-engineering is an integral part of an increasing trend towards sustainable product design and sustainable manufacturing, as it not only accommodates demands that the lowest possible percentage of a product is discarded, once it has reached the end of its useful life, but also recognizes that many parts or components of products can, in fact, have secondary value.

See also **change managment** *and* **Hammer, Michael.**

Related diversification

Related **diversification** takes place when a business diversifies and achieves a **strategic fit**, thus complementing its existing **value chain**. Related diversification allows the business to build shareholder value by capturing cross-business fits, which include:

- the transference of skills and capabilities from one business to another;
- the sharing of resources or facilities in order to reduce costs;
- the achievement of leverage through the use of common brand names;
- the combination and deployment of resources to create new competitive strengths and related capabilities.

Relationship marketing

Relationship marketing attempts to develop a long-term relationship with customers on the premise that it is far cheaper to retain existing customers than to attract new ones. There are a number of factors involved in relationship marketing which tend to frame the exact nature of how it works within a given organization, these are:

- a primary focus on customer attention;
- an orientation towards product benefits rather than product features;
- an emphasis on commitment, and on contact with customers;
- the adoption of a total quality approach;
- the development of ongoing relationships with customers;
- the deployment of staff at various levels, to maintain contact;
- the cultivation of key customers;
- an emphasis on trust, honesty and promise keeping.

Egan, John, *Relationship Marketing*. London: Financial Times, Prentice-Hall, 2001.
Payne, Adrian, Christopher, Martin, Peck, Helen and Clark, Moira, *Relationship Marketing for Competitive Advantage: Winning and Keeping Customers*. Oxford: Butterworth-Heinemann, 1998.

Research and development

New product development and the bright ideas associated with such an endeavour must be tempered with the practicalities of production. Whilst many good ideas appear to be workable on paper, the realities of the situation may mean that the product cannot be produced in a cost-effective and efficient manner.

An organization has to assess whether it is looking for a new product which its current production process is capable of producing. It would serve no purpose for an organization to develop an idea for a new product only to discover that the actual production process has to be carried out elsewhere, possibly by subcontractors or business partners. After all, one of the key considerations in developing new products, regardless of their design, is that the organization should make full use of its production facilities.

The design of new products is often changed gradually as the organization becomes aware that the design is presenting problems. This process, although not enjoyable for the designer, needs to be considered from the point of view of efficiency and overall benefit to the organization. Whether the design is undertaken by the organization itself or by external organizations, the business must ensure that it performs feasibility studies. These are carried out at the earliest possible stage to ensure that resources are not wasted in the development of a new product when there is no likelihood of its production being cost-effective. This screening process needs to be rigorously enforced to make sure that the business does not invest funds in product designs that are impractical and will never come to fruition.

The development of new products can be not only time-consuming but expensive. The desire to develop new products should be tempered by an awareness that many small businesses fail as a result of over-investing in new product development. However, the introduction of new products is central to the long-term success and growth of an organization. It should be noted that only a small percentage of new products are ever successful. It is imperative for an organization to plan its new product development using the following steps:

- allow an initial screening period, in which an investigation is carried out to assess how the product fits in with current products and services;
- investigate whether the new product could be produced using current production methods;
- test the production process;
- fully cost the production process;
- carry out the necessary market research;
- produce a test batch of new products and test market them.

Resource strengths and weaknesses

Clearly a business's resource strengths are the cornerstones of the organization's strategy and important to the building of **competitive advantage**. In order to assess a business's resource strengths and weaknesses, normally a strategic balance sheet is constructed, in which the resource strengths represent competitive assets and the weaknesses represent competitive liabilities. This process is known as VRIO (value, rarity, imitability and exploitation) analysis.

Restructuring

Simply a mention of the word 'restructuring' brings enormous dread to both an organization and its employees. Restructuring is a recognition of the fact that as the organization is currently structured there are severe deficiencies in its operations. Inevitably, for employees and human resources managers, any restructuring exercise will involve an enormous degree of upheaval. Restructuring tends to occur either when a business is teetering on the brink of disaster, or as a pre-requisite demanded by a financial institution before funds will be released to the organization.

For human resources, restructuring can mean not only dealing with a potentially large percentage of the employees as casualties of the process, but also that those that remain may have their jobs entirely redesigned or re-aligned, to match a new structure which aims to be more efficient and productive.

Retained profits

Retained profits are also known as 'ploughed back profits' and as the term implies, they are a proportion of a business's profits which have not been distributed in the form of dividends to the shareholders.

The retained profits are usually earmarked for reinvestment in assets. This is common practice for businesses, since it is considerably cheaper to use retained profits rather than borrow money in the form of loans, which would require interest payments as well as repayment of the principle.

Retrenchment

A retrenchment strategy is exemplified by moves which businesses may seek to make in difficult times, or when the markets or the external environment are unpredictable. Such businesses may opt for a scaling down of operations, perhaps identifying the current areas of business activity that are most under threat. They will partially or completely remove themselves from weaker parts of the market, or divest themselves of some business operations in order to refocus on stronger areas. Retrenchment often involves a considerable regrouping through both cost and asset reduction, as a result of a reverse trend, or declining sales and profits. Retrenchment is often referred to as a turnaround, or a reorganization strategy. In essence it seeks to strengthen the business and force it to return to its distinctive **core competences**. Retrenchment can involve the sale of land or buildings, the reduction of production lines, the closing of marginally profitable businesses, the closure of obsolete manufacturing units or automated processes, a reduction in the number of employees, and the institution of stringent expense-control systems.

David, Fred, *Strategic Management: Concepts*. New York: Prentice-Hall, 2001.

Return on investment (ROI)

This is the US equivalent of 'return on capital employed (ROCE)'. Whilst management may use this formula – assessing profit before tax and interest as a percentage of total assets – shareholders are more interested in the estimation of profit after interest, and comparing this with the figure for the assets less the liabilities.

An assessment of the return on investment seeks to identify the net profit (after tax) as a percentage of the total assets of the business. The ratio is:

$$Return\ on\ investment\ = \frac{Net\ profit\ (after\ tax)}{Total\ assets} \times 100$$

This ratio is extremely important as it measures the profits available after all charges have been deducted, compared with the assets owned by the business. Typically, the total assets figures are the year-end figures, but they can be an average of the opening and closing figures.

A business with a net profit of £250,000 (after tax) and total assets to the value of £3,200,000 would calculate as follows:

$$\frac{250,000}{3,200,000} \times 100 = 7.81\%$$

This figure would then be compared with the industry standard. A complication might be the age and depreciation of the fixed assets of the business. If depreciation is a factor then the business will reveal a higher ROI. Conversely, if the business has relatively new fixed assets, valued at or near the purchase price, then the ROI will be significantly lower.

Troy, Leo, *Almanac of Business and Industrial Financial Ratios*. New York: Aspen Publishers, 2003.

Walsh, Ciaran, *Key Management Ratios: Master the Management Metrics that Drive and Control Your Business*. London: Financial Times, Prentice-Hall, 2003.

Return on total assets

Return on Total Assets (ROTA), as the term implies, is a measurement of whether or not a business is effectively using the assets which it owns. Typically, the equation takes the following form:

$$\frac{Income\ before\ interest\ and\ tax}{Fixed\ assets\ +\ current\ assets}$$

Troy, Leo, *Almanac of Business and Industrial Financial Ratios.* New York: Prentice Hall, 2003.

Walsh, Ciaran, *Key Management Ratios: Master the Management Metrics that Drive and Control your Business.* London: Financial Times, Prentice-Hall, 2003.

Risk assessment

Risk assessment is the process of identifying potential loss exposures and measuring the degree of loss that could result from them. Risk assessment or analysis also involves an estimation of the probability that losses may occur, and evaluation of the potential actions which could be undertaken in order to meet risk management objectives.

See also **risk management.**

Risk management

Risk management is an integral part of managerial responsibility. Risk management does not just apply to managers in senior positions, as it takes place on a daily basis at various levels of risk. There are no tried and trusted methodologies of risk management, but there have been several attempts to create a standard model. An example can be seen in Figure 59.

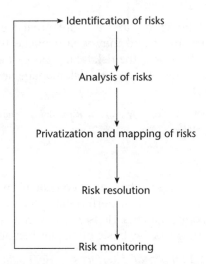

Figure 59   Standard risk management model

This is, however, a rather simplistic means of assessing risks and dealing with the risk management procedure, since it suggests that risks can be addressed one-by-one; in fact risk management often involves dealing with several risks simultaneously. Therefore a more complex risk management model, such as that in Figure 60, may be employed.

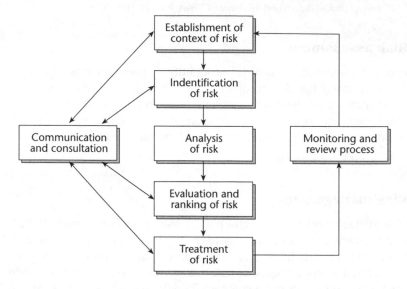

Figure 60   Complex risk management model

Other businesses prefer to take a more proactive approach with regard to risk management and may well evaluate the probability of risks and their impacts prior to the risk taking place or even threatening to take place. These forms of proactive risk management can be exemplified as in Figure 61.

Smith, Preston G. and Merritt, Guy M., *Proactive Risk Management*. Shelton, CT: Productivity Press, 2002.

Rummler, Geary

Rummler is a writer, researcher and consultant who is primarily concerned with instructional and performance technologies and how they operate within organizations. He is also associated with **organizational design** and suggests five basic principles behind this:

- *Minimizing the number of interfaces* – He suggests that as the number of individuals who handle a transaction increases, there is

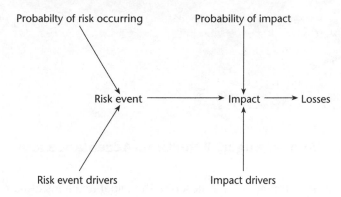

Figure 61   Proactive risk management model

an increase in the probability of delay or error. He therefore recommends minimizing the number of steps in a process, and perhaps minimizing the number of signatures, reviews or authorizations required.

- *Maximizing the proximity of customers and suppliers* – Ensuring that the business is up to date with what suppliers can provide will enable it to specifically state to the customers what is available in order to match their requirements.
- *Optimizing the **span of control*** – Rummler believes that the span of control could be wide or narrow, depending upon the type of work involved. He suggests that businesses need to find the optimum level, rather than impose a standardized span of control.
- *Minimizing the number of management layers* – Rummler believes that too many managers inhibit employee performance. Organizations with too many management layers will also have problems in making quick decisions.
- *Maximizing clarity* – He believes that one of the greatest problems managements face, particularly in bureaucratic organizations, is what he refers to as 'fuzzy boundaries'. In effect, in these bureaucracies, too many managers have a say in the running of particular functional operations, or in the outcome of particular problems or decision-making tasks. Rummler believes that the boundaries need to be clarified in order to ensure smooth decision making and problem solving.

Rummler, Geary and Brache, Alan, *Improving Performance: How to Manage the White Space on the Organization Chart.* San Francisco, CA: Jossey-Bass, 1995.

SARAH (Shock, Anger, Rejection, Acceptance and Help)

SARAH is an acronym used to describe the usual reactions of management, or employees, when they face considerable change in the organization, or have perhaps received an adverse **performance appraisal**. The acronym reflects the general series of reactions which culminate in the individual being offered, or requesting, assistance to deal with the situation.

Satisfysing

The concept of 'satisfysing' implies the acceptance of the satisfactory, rather than the optimum. Given that most strategies are based on compromise, particularly when considering objectives, it is often prudent for a business to identify the acceptable, rather than just the ideal. Equally, achievements such as complete efficiency are unlikely, therefore the satisfactory is a good compromise.

SBU (strategic business unit)

A strategic business unit is a separate part of a business organization with distinct missions and objectives of its own. An SBU can therefore plan independently from the rest of the business. Typically, an SBU can be either a division, a product line or, in some cases, a brand.

Table 44   Financial and accounting functions in a traditional structure and in an SBU

Traditional structure		Strategic business unit structure	
Decision support	10%	Decision support	50%
Control	30%	Control	10%
Reporting	20%	Reporting	20%
Transaction processing	40%	Transaction processing	20%

Organizations recognize that the establishment of SBUs can lead to significant efficiency and cost savings, as can be seen in Table 44, which focuses on the finance and accounting aspects, comparing traditional structures with SBUs.

Scenario planning

Scenario planning can provide a structured framework which can be used at all levels of an organization. Scenario planning allows different parts of the organization to contribute to the strategic planning process and to central planning. Scenario planning involves the evaluation of **critical success factors** which are required to deliver particular goals. Key actions can be identified, consistent with the most likely scenario, in order to develop the organization's abilities to deliver these goals. Scenario planning involves the definition of corporate visions and values which will ultimately underpin exactly how the organization will go about achieving its objectives.

Although there is no clear model for scenario planning, a typical scenario plan is outlined in Figure 62.

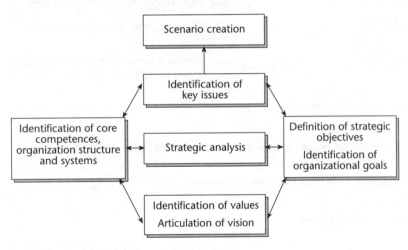

Figure 62   A example of scenario planning

Lindgren, Mats and Bandhold, Hans, *Scenario Planning: The Link between Future and Strategy*. Basingstoke: Palgrave Macmillan, 2002.

Schein, Edgar

Edgar Schein created a questionnaire-based system by which individuals could identify their Career Motivators or Career Anchors. Schein believed that there were eight such anchors and that each individual would have a distinct preference towards one of them. A summary of the 8 career anchors can be found in Table 45.

Table 45 Eight career anchors

Career anchor/competence	Description
Technical/functional	Individuals who define their career through challenges and the work they are undertaking.
Managerial	Problem-solvers who like to lead and control.
Independence	Individuals who value freedom above all.
Security	Those who desire stability.
Entrepreneurial creativity	Those with innovative ideas and practical skills.
Service	Those who value being able to help others.
Challenge	Those who seek solutions or ways around problems.
Lifestyle	Those for whom work is subservient to domestic and social life and just a means to fund it.

Schein, Edgar H., *Career Anchors: Discovering your Real Values*. New York: Pfeiffer Wiley, 1996.

http://web.mit.edu/scheine/www/home.html

Self-regulation

Self-regulation is either a private agreement or a set of standards which have been agreed by members of an industrial sector. These self-regulating standards may be either substantive or procedural. Although it is not always the case, self-regulation may mean the absence of government regulation. However, many governments enter into an agreement with the industry and may provide a safety net.

Theoretically, self-regulation reduces, but perhaps does not eliminate, the need for government regulation or involvement. Self-regulation can be more flexible than government regulation as it can be changed to reflect the impact of new technologies. Self-regulation is also valuable in establishing a dialogue between customers and the industry and establishing trust between them.

Self-regulation, however, is less transparent and potentially subject to manipulation or collusion. Equally, it may be that both customers and the government will lack the means to enforce industry compliance.

Self-regulation is appropriate in some circumstances, but not in cases where there is a monopoly provider.

Senge, Peter

Peter Senge has suggested several different aspects of learning organizations in a series of books written since 1990. Senge describes the learning organization as:

> Organizations where people continually expand their capacity to create the results they truly desire, where new and expansive patterns of thinking are nurtured, where collective inspiration is set free, and where people are continually learning to see the whole together.

Senge argued that many organizational strategies are not conducive to this, and that many lack the necessary tools or guiding ideas to help them. Senge recognized that people can learn to survive situations – he calls this adaptive learning – but that learning organizations need to promote 'generative learning', which enhances an individual's ability to create.

He identified five basic disciplines which distinguish learning organizations from more traditional organizations (see Table 46). These five disciplines can adapt a business and make it into a learning organization.

Senge, Peter, *The Fifth Discipline: The Art and Practice of the Learning Organization*. New York: Random House Business Books, 1993.
Senge, Peter, *Learning Organizations*. Cambridge: Gilmour Drummond Publishing, 1995.

www.infed.org/thinkers/senge.htm

Seven Ps

The Seven Ps are a development from the original Four Ps (product, place, price, promotion). Generally, the Seven Ps are taken to be:

- product;
- place;

Table 46 Five disciplines of learning organizations

Discipline	Description
Systems thinking	Seeing the whole rather than a series of component parts, otherwise there is a risk that the move towards being a learning organization will not be seen as a dynamic process.
Personal mastery	Senge suggests that this discipline involves continually clarifying personal visions and the focusing of energy, patience and objectivity.
Mental models	This involves learning to transcend internal politics, fostering openness, distributing business responsibility and retaining coordination and control.
Building a shared vision	Encouraging experimentation and innovation. Visions spread by reinforcement, which increases clarity, enthusiasm and commitment.
Team learning	Aligning and developing the capacities of members of a team, to enable them to act together. Teams need to learn together to speed up change.

- price;
- promotion;
- process – the steps needed to fulfil the **marketing mix**, including evaluation, modification and supervision;
- physical evidence – the tangible results or benefits of the marketing mix, as predicted in any forecasts made;
- people – taken to mean either the individuals involved in the marketing mix implementation (personnel/agencies/freelancers) or the net impact on changes made to the target audiences (compared with their views/status, etc., Prior to the implementation).

Davies, Peter and Pardey, David, *Making Sense of Marketing: Workbook 3, Determining the Marketing Mix*. Basingstoke: Palgrave Macmillan, 1990.

See also **Booms and Bitner** *and* **marketing mix**.

Seven S Framework

The Seven S Framework is a tool used to describe the inter-relationships between seven key factors which determine the way in which a business operates. It is exemplified as in Figure 63 and Table 47.

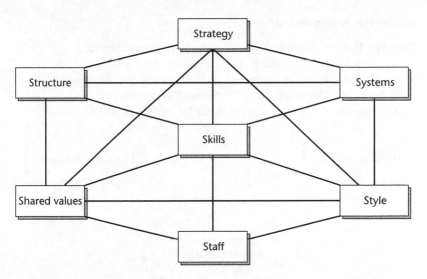

Figure 63   The Seven S Basic Framework

Table 47   Features of the Seven S Framework

S Factor	Description
Strategy	The environment, competition, customers.
Structure	Organizational chart, inter-relationships, authority, power and control.
Systems	Procedures and processes.
Staff	Employees, in terms of functionality, education and background.
Style	Behavioural patterns and common traits (of both managers and employees).
Shared values	Central beliefs and attitudes towards quality, objectives and other factors.
Skills	The core competences of the organization.

Pascale, Richard Tanner, Gioja, Linda and Milleman, Mark, *Surfing the Edge of Chaos*. New York: Three Rivers Press, 2001.

Shamrock organization

Charles Handy suggested the 'shamrock' organization (see Figure 64), which has three interlocking 'leaves' representing different groups of workers, namely flexible workers, core workers and contract workers. Optionally, the shamrock has a fourth leaf, customers.

Handy's four leaves are further described in Table 48.

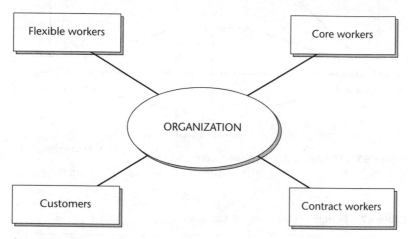

Figure 64   The 'shamrock' organization

Table 48   The 'leaves' of the shamrock organization

Leaf	description
Core workers	These are the small group of specialists at the centre of the organization. They effectively run the organization and control any technology which is used.
Contract workers	Individuals paid on a fee basis linked to performance rather than time. Contractors are used when needed.
Flexible workers	A pool of part-timers, who have the relevant skills. These individuals do not seek, or cannot find, full-time employment.
Customers	The tendency to get customers to do some of the work which would have been carried out by employees. Examples include self-service, supermarkets, cash-points, self-assembly furniture. The self-service aspect is marketed to customers as a benefit, but in fact saves on the wage bill.

Handy, Charles, *The Age of Unreason*. London: Century, 1989.

www.pfdf.org/leaderbooks/121/summer97/handy.html

Simple structure

Simple organizational structures are primarily geared to optimize administrative procedures and streamline coordination and communication. In such structures, there is a clear distinction between managerial roles and managerial levels. In essence, they seek to optimize all aspects of operations and control by simplifying the steps needed to maintain, or attain, organizational objectives. Simple structures tend to be **flat structures**, in organizations with few levels of management or hierarchy.

Situational analysis

Situational analysis focuses primarily upon two different considerations:

- The business's external or **macro-environment**, which incorporates the industrial and competitive conditions.
- The business's internal or **micro-environment**, which addresses its **core competences**, **resource strengths and weaknesses**, and capabilities.

Typically, an assessment of the industrial or competitive conditions would include the following:

- the economic traits of the industry;
- the strengths and weaknesses, and nature, of the competition;
- what causes industry change;
- the competitive position of other businesses;
- the strategic plans of competitors;
- key success factors;
- industry attractiveness.

With regard to the internal business situation, the following would be considered:

- present strategy;
- **SWOT analysis**;
- cost comparisons with competitors;
- current strength of the business's competitive position.

Having carried out this strategic analysis, the business is now able to identify its strategic options and then choose the best strategy for the future.

Situational leadership

See **Blanchard, Ken.**

SMART

SMART is an acronym for Specific, Measurable, Achievable, Results-orientated and Time-constrained. It is a term which can equally be applied to marketing or to many other areas of business activity. Its use seeks to ensure that any activity is quantifiable and objective-related.

Soft management

Soft management, as the term suggests, places an emphasis on employees and motivation as a means by which productivity and performance may be achieved. The system relies on the proactive use of human resources departments to develop, encourage and support employees.

See also **hard management.**

Span of control

The span of control is the number of subordinates for whom a manager has direct responsibility. The ideal number frequently quoted is between five and nine individuals under the control of one manager. Beyond this it becomes increasingly difficult to react or respond to their specific needs. Therefore, additional levels of hierarchy need to be inserted, both above and below each manager, in order to reduce the span of control to a manageable level.

Staff authority

Staff authority is distinguished from **line authority** in that those with staff authority have the power to advise, but not to direct employees. Typically, human resources managers would be considered to have staff authority towards all members of staff, but only line authority within the human resources department itself.

Stakeholder

A stakeholder is an individual or a group that is either affected by, or has a vested interest in, a particular business. Stakeholders can include customers, managers, employees, suppliers, and the community, as well as the organization itself. Each business attaches a degree of importance to each stakeholder and will attempt to understand what its stakeholders require of it. The business will take these views into account when making decisions.

Rahman, Sandra Sutherland, Andriof, Jorg, Waddock, Sandra and Husted, Bryan, *Unfolding Stakeholder Thinking: Relationships, Communication, Reporting and Performance*. Sheffield: Greenleaf Publishing, 2003.

Standardization

The term 'standardization' refers to an organization's efforts to ensure that all the workers are performing their tasks or activities in a consistent manner. An organization striving for standardization would do so to assist in ensuring consistent levels of safety, productivity and quality. The term 'standardization' may also refer to an organization's desire to standardize the parts and components which it uses.

In international business, standardization very much relies upon the specific arrangements required by overseas nations in their moves towards standardized procedures and classifications.

Star

'Star' is one of the categories of product or service which can be found on the Boston Consulting Group's **Boston growth matrix**. Stars are successful products which enjoy a significant level of market demand. Invariably, stars were former **question marks** and, like **cash cows**, they enjoy leading market positions. Stars are typified by products or services which are continuing to grow at a rapid rate (this enables them to maintain their position in the market). Stars provide a business with a significant amount of income, but they also require significant investment in the form of marketing and advertising in order to support their continued success.

Stars have the potential to penetrate other existing markets. They are usually the targets for improved distribution, product extensions and other marketing techniques in order to sustain their continued appeal.

Ultimately, when the growth in the market in which a star is placed slows down, the product or service becomes a 'cash cow'.

Statistical process control

Organizations using a statistical process control (SPC) system would apply a series of statistical methods and procedures that relate to a given process or series of given processes. They would do this to analyse and control the process, and often work to a given set of standards or statistical techniques, by the use, primarily, of control charts.

Strategic alliance

Strategic alliances are either short-term or long-term alliances between two businesses with the purpose of sharing resources. Strategic alliances may include **joint ventures**, but in general they are business relationships in which the two businesses pool their strengths, share risks and try to integrate their business functions for mutual benefits. Unlike in other forms of close cooperation, both business entities remain independent throughout the arrangement. Strategic alliances are an important way of being able to break into new markets, acquire new technical skills and improve on the business's competitive position. A strategic alliance may be created in one of the following ways:

- through internal growth;
- through merger and acquisition;
- through spin-offs.

The alliance strategy is particularly attractive to international businesses wishing to operate in foreign markets which are, relatively, politically stable, or in developing countries which have free market systems (and are not usually suffering from high inflation or a high level of private-sector debt). Strategic alliances can be used to offset many of the risks associated with **pioneering costs**, as the risks are spread.

There are, in effect, six different ways in which a strategic alliance could assist international businesses in entering a foreign market. These include:

- *Exporting* – which has all the advantages of avoiding the set-up costs of manufacturing in an overseas market, but may have the disadvantage of higher transport costs and potential trade barriers. A strategic alliance could be used to form an association with a marketing subsidiary in the host country.
- *Turnkey projects* – this allows an international business to become involved in an overseas market where there may be prohibitions related to foreign direct investment. In essence, the international business exports only the process abilities and understanding, but this may inadvertently create a competitor in the longer run.
- *Licensing* – this involves framing a strategic alliance on the basis that a host country's industry undertakes to manufacture products in accordance with the trademarks and patents of the international

business. The international business may risk losing control over its licences and will be passing on technological know-how to a potential long-term competitor.

- *Franchising* – this involves a strategic alliance with a host country business which will bear the risks and the costs of opening up a new market. There are often problems over control issues with distant franchisees.
- **Joint ventures** – this involves establishing a strategic alliance based on the sharing of costs and risks and the gaining of local knowledge and perhaps political influence. Again the international business may lose a degree of control, and protection, of its technologies.
- **Wholly-owned subsidiaries** – whilst the international business will have to bear all of the costs and risks in opening up the overseas market, a wholly-owned subsidiary offers tighter control over technology and other aspects of the business operation.

In order to make strategic alliances work, both businesses need to have sophisticated formal and informal communication networks, and take steps to build trust between one another. Both parties need to take proactive steps in order to learn as much as they can from the operations of their partner.

Doz, Yves and Hamel, Gary, *Alliance Advantage: The Art of Creating Value through Partnering*. Boston, MA: Harvard Business School Press, 1998.

Strategic business unit

See **SBU (strategic business unit)**.

Strategic fit

Strategic fit involves the matching of strategy and **organizational structure**. It is widely accepted that there are five main stages in developing a strong strategic fit:

- A description of the business need and its contribution to the organization's overall business strategy.
- The objectives of the project in question.
- Why is the action required now?
- What are the key benefits which will be realized?
- What are the **critical success factors** and how will they be measured?

Strategic plan

A strategic plan is an overarching series of activities which aim to implement and develop a new concept, deal with a problem, or establish the foundation of the business's objectives in the coming period. As Figure 65 shows, there is a close relationship between the implementation and the strategic development process.

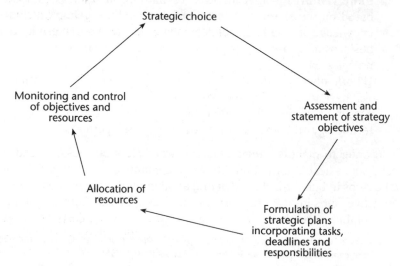

Figure 65   Basic structure of a strategic plan

Strategic planning should, as the diagram illustrates, be a continual process, with the monitoring and control procedures providing the information for the development of this and future strategic plans.

Sustainability

Sustainability is the measure of a business's ability to continue operating in the way in which it is currently operating, for some unspecified period of time in the future. Sustainability can therefore refer to the medium- to long-term demands for products and services, the availability of materials or components, and any other factor which could adversely affect the business's opportunities to continue to operate broadly under the current terms.

Sustainable competitive advantage

A sustainable **competitive advantage** can be typified as being a competitive advantage which either an international business or a specific country has, which cannot easily be imitated and will be difficult to erode over a period of time. In order to have a sustainable competitive advantage a business or a nation needs to have a unique **core competence** which is difficult to copy, unique in itself, sustainable, superior to the competition and, above all, applicable in a number of different situations. Typical forms of sustainable competitive advantage include:

- A vastly superior product in terms of quality.
- Well established and extensive distribution channels.
- A positive reputation and a strong brand equity.
- Low-cost production techniques and processes.
- The ownership of patents or copyrights.
- A monopoly in the form of government protection.
- A superior management team and/or employees.

Switching costs

Switching costs are either the physical or the perceived costs of changing from one brand to another, or from one supplier to another. Indeed, switching costs may be associated with any form of transference from a prior supplier to a new supplier.

SWOT analysis

SWOT analysis is a very useful technique in looking at the overall future of an organization, as well as considering the launch of a new marketing activity. SWOT analysis covers the following aspects, of which the first two considerations look at the internal workings of the organization.

- Strengths – What is the organization or business good at? What are its key advantages over the competition, in terms of its products and services as well as its facilities, customer service and the expertise of its employees?
- Weaknesses – What is the organization not good at? Where does the business fall down in the ways it does things? Are the products and services good enough? Is the marketing good enough?
- Opportunities – What is happening outside the organization that offers it some opportunities? Has the transport system in the area been improved? Has a major competitor closed down?

S

- Threats – What is happening outside the organization that could threaten it? Are there more competitors?

Figure 66 is a common SWOT analysis grid, which helps to place all of the considerations in the right position. The marketing function would need to consider all of these strengths, weaknesses, opportunities and threats before making any major decisions.

Strengths	Weaknesses
Opportunities	Threats

SWOT analysis

Figure 66   SWOT analysis

Dealtry, Richard, *Dynamic SWOT Analysis – The Developer's Guide*. Birmingham: Dynamic SWOT Associates, 1994.

Synergies

Synergies are the benefits which can result from combining different aspects of an organization, rather than allowing them to act separately. In other words, organizations will seek to group complementary activities in situations where there is a strong possibility of collaboration. This means that a mutual benefit can be enjoyed, particularly when common work or activity form the basis of the alliance.

Synergies can also be enjoyed between organizations where complementary skills or production processes, or indeed knowledge of a specific market, can be brought together in order to achieve far more than the two organizations could possibly have hoped for individually. Either synergies can bring about short-term project-based alliances between businesses, or they may well prove to be the foundation of a longer term relationship.

'Business synergy' is a term often applied to franchise operations, in as much as when individuals purchase a franchise they become part of a larger 'family'. All of the members of the family work together and the most effective ideas are shared.

Taguchi, Genichi

Genichi Taguchi carried out a series of experiments in Japan, which were developed to improve the implementation of total quality control (TQC). Taguchi's conclusions and recommendations are used in manufacturing industries within Japan and the US to improve processes and products. It is claimed that Japan has experienced an 80 per cent increase in quality. In the US, the Taguchi method is also known as 'robust design'.

The Taguchi method makes quality decisions about cost effectiveness by the use of key words, which are explained in more detail in Table 49.

Table 49 Key words used in the Taguchi method

Taguchi method	Description
Loss function	The organization has to identify and recognize the importance of quality and realize that poor quality is associated with financial loss.
Orthogonal arrays	The organization has to design efficient experiments and analyse the conclusions of the experimental data, for example, with the use of, linear graphs.
Robustness	The organization has to specify the cost-effective combination of factors which affect variations in the levels of quality and are feasible and practical to control. This will help to minimize the influence of the previously uncontrollable factors.

According to the followers of the Taguchi method, research is the key, as is testing products on a trial-and-error basis. This will give the organization a completely full picture of the product, and provided they focus on all aspects of this methodology, they stand a good chance of gaining a **competitive advantage**.

Peace, Glen Stuart, *Taguchi Methods: A Hands-on Approach*. Boston, MA: Addison-Wesley Publishing, 1993.

Tall structure

A tall structure is an organizational structure which has multiple layers of management and supervision overlaying the productive or employee elements of the organization. Typically, in organization charts, tall structures are shown as very tall, thin pyramids which do not have large numbers of individuals at any one level of the hierarchy.

Tangible resource

Tangible resources, or tangible assets, are items which have a physical substance, and may well be used in the production or supply of products and services. In accounting terms, tangible assets also include leases or company shares. They are, in effect, the fixed assets of the organization and can be differentiated from **intangible resources**, such as goodwill, trademarks or patents, which do not have a physical substance but are still valuable concepts.

Damodaran, Aswath, *Investment Valuation: Tools and Techniques for Determining the Value of Any Asset*. New York: John Wiley, 2002.

Gardner, Mona, Mills, Dixie and Cooperman, Elizabeth, *Managing Financial Institutions: An Asset/Liability Approach*. London: Thomson Learning, 1999.

Taylor, Frederick Winslow

During his research Taylor began with the assumption that employees only work for money. He developed a series of work study techniques which he considered would enable a reduction in the amount of time it would take for employees to carry out different tasks, leaving the planning and organization of tasks for the managers and supervisors. He believed that encouragement and the promise of additional benefits, such as money, as a reward, would make employees sufficiently motivated to work harder.

Taylor, however, was proved wrong. He discovered that employees would only work harder when they were being supervised, but would return to their normal pace of work once the supervision was removed.

Since Taylor's writing on 'scientific management', much emphasis has been placed on job design. Henry Ford developed Taylor's principles into what has become known as Fordism.

Bratton, John and Gold, Jeffrey, *Human Resource Management: Theory and Practice*. Basingstoke: Palgrave Macmillan, 2003.

Kanigel, Robert, *The One Best Way: Frederick Winslow Taylor and the Enigma of Efficiency*. New York: Little Brown, 1997.

Taylor, Frederick Winslow, *Principles of Scientific Management*. New York: W. W. Norton, 1967.

www.accel-team.com/scientific/scientific_02.html

Teamwork

Many organizations have gradually come to the realization that teams represent a proven means by which productivity and performance can be assured. Various industry surveys, particularly in the manufacturing sector, seem to suggest that over two-thirds of all organizations actively encourage teams. The actual nature of the teams is of prime importance and their creation is of particular relevance to human resources management. Essentially, there are three different types of team, all of which have a degree of **authority**, autonomy or **empowerment**.

Empowered teams are usually given the authority to plan and implement improvements. Self-directed teams are virtually autonomous and are mainly responsible for supervisory issues. Cross-functional teams are more complex as they involve various individuals from different departments, who are working towards a common end.

Training needs to be provided to teams both before and during their creation in order to assist the members in establishing relationships with one another and understanding their new responsibilities. It is also essential that teams are given clear instructions and, above all, support from management in order to carry out their tasks. Once a team has been established, with a degree of authority delegated to it, management and human resources departments need to step back and allow the team to develop and learn how the new working practices will operate.

The management and the human resources departments retain the responsibility of monitoring and motivating the teams and their members. This requires effective communication skills and a feedback system to enable teams to request additional assistance should it be required.

Technological myopia

Technological myopia is often described as a business's inability to understand, appreciate or utilize the potential benefits of technology. Technological myopia has been exemplified in recent years by the failure of many businesses' intranets. Whilst the businesses had secured the technical expertise to install and set up the infrastructure for the intranet, they had failed to train managers and employees sufficiently and had also failed to fully utilize the benefits of the new system.

Wyman, J., 'Technological Myopia: the Need to Think Strategically about Technology', *Sloan Management Review*, 26(4) (1985), pp. 59–65.

Theory X and Theory Y

See **McGregor, Douglas.**

Theory Z

See **Ouchi, William.**

Tichy, Noel

Noel Tichy is a writer, researcher and consultant who is primarily concerned with leadership and team building. He believes that leadership is exemplified by individuals who have integrity and are skilled in establishing the direction in which an organization should move. They are also able to gain commitment from other managers and employees and motivate them to achieve specific outcomes. Tichy believes that leadership style is essential and that it begins with self-awareness, and an understanding of how the social style of the managers affects not only their relationship with others in the organization, but also their ability to solve problems and influence others.

In terms of team building, Tichy is concerned with the ways in which teams are actually created. He is firmly of the opinion that all teams need goal clarity. This means that they need to have an understanding and a commitment towards a specific goal. He also cites the fact that team roles are vital, not only in structuring the team but also in establishing any roles and responsibilities. This ultimately allows the team members to work, both together and independently, in a more efficient manner.

Figure 67 A team effectiveness model

With regard to the team dynamics, they must be able to resolve conflict, make decisions and share information. Above all, Tichy believes that teams are effectively communities, in which interpersonal skills, team spirit and well-being dominate and influence the team's effectiveness. A version of his team effectiveness model can be seen in Figure 67.

Tichy, Noel, *The Cycle of Leadership*. New York: HarperCollins, 2003.

www.pfdf.org/leaderbooks/tichy

Top–down change

Top–down change is exemplified by leaders and managers who seek to dominate the organization in which they operate by controlling situations and attempting to predict the actions of everyone in that organization. Top–down change is driven by managers, who are essentially responsible for transforming the visions or values of the organization into reality. Typically, top–down change is driven by mechanisms including:

- business planning;
- quality and performance management;
- employee involvement;
- team briefings;
- consultation initiatives.

Total assets turnover ratio

This ratio is a variation on the **fixed assets turnover ratio** and also measures the business's effectiveness in using its assets to generate sales. In this case, the formula is:

$$Total\ assets\ turnover\ ratio = \frac{Sales}{Total\ assets}$$

Suppose that a business has sales of some £3,200,000, with a total assets figure of £2,850,000. Again, the figure for total assets may be calculated as an average of the opening or closing values (used for expanding businesses primarily) or simply as the closing value of the assets at the end of the year. The relevant calculation would therefore be:

$$\frac{3,200,000}{2,850,000} = 1.12\ times$$

The total assets turnover ratio therefore reveals that the business is generating £1.12 in sales for every £1 invested in assets.

A low ratio suggests that the business is having productivity problems. A high ratio may suggest that the business is over-trading on its assets. In other words, the business does not have sufficient assets to support the sales which are being generated. This is often a problem facing new businesses which are expanding. As sales increase, they do not have sufficient cash to invest in additional fixed assets and may also have working capital difficulties. Ultimately, the business may suffer from **liquidity** problems, which means that it may not be able to supply customers, as it does not have sufficient funds to replace the stock.

Temple, Peter, *Magic Numbers: The 33 Key Ratios that Every Investor Should Know*. New York: John Wiley, 2001.

Total quality management (TQM)

The concept of total quality management (TQM) has been stimulated by the need for organizations to conform with regard to quality levels. This need has been brought about in essence by an increased demand by customers and suppliers for higher-quality products, parts and components. The fundamental principle behind total quality management is that the management of quality is addressed at all levels of an organization, from the top to the bottom. Improvements are made on a continuous basis by applying the theories and approaches of management theorists in an attempt to improve quality and decrease organizational costs. The emphasis, primarily on quality, is also very much on people and their involvement, particularly with regard to suppliers and customers. The fundamental principles of TQM are summarized in Table 50.

Bank, J., *The Essence of Total Quality Management*. New York: Prentice Hall, 1999.
Oakland, J. S., *Total Quality Management*. Oxford: Butterworth Heinemann, 1993.

Trait theory

Trait theory takes the view that the personality of individuals consists of a series of broad dispositions, otherwise known as traits. It is these traits that lead to characteristic responses, and individuals can be described according to the ways in which they behave, using adjectives such as dominant, assertive, friendly or outgoing. It is widely accepted that there are five basic factors which determine the personality of an individual:

1 Emotional stability – whether the individual is calm or anxious, secure or insecure, self-satisfied or self-pitying.

Table 50 Principles of total quality management

TQM principle	Description
Committed and effective leaders	A commitment to and a belief in the principles of TQM by those key decision makers at the top of the organizational structure is essential. They have to portray this commitment to the lower levels of management in an effective style of leadership by providing resources to make changes happen.
Planning	It is imperative that all changes are planned effectively, particularly as the TQM approach may be fundamentally different from the approach currently adopted by an organization. All planned changes must be integrated throughout the organization, with cooperation at all levels and functions. With quality, or improved quality, as the key dimension, a longer-term strategy will be adopted throughout the whole of the organization's functions, from new product design through to getting the product to the end-user.
Monitoring	A continuous monitoring system will be put into place so that the process of continuous improvement can be supported and developed. Problem identification and the implementation of solutions will be sought.
Training	Without education and training, employees and management will lack expertise and awareness of quality issues. It will be difficult to implement changes in organizational behaviour unless there is a comprehensive and effective educational scheme which not only seeks to provide the initial information and understanding of techniques, but constantly updates those techniques in order to reinforce understanding. Without this investment, short-term TQM benefits will be difficult to achieve, as will the long-term impact of TQM through conventional measurements, such as increased efficiency and general growth.

T

$\Rightarrow$

Table 50 Principles of total quality management (*continued*)

TQM principle	Description
Teamwork	The development of empowered cooperative teams is an essential pre-requisite of TQM. Under the system teams are encouraged to take the initiative and often given responsibilities which formerly would have been management roles. Without this involvement and empowerment, TQM is almost impossible to implement as it requires both the participation and the commitment of individuals throughout the whole organization.
Evaluation and feedback	It is imperative that individuals within the organization see the fruits of their labour. TQM requires an integral system which provides not only positive feedback but also rewards for achievement. The evaluation and feedback of TQM will invariably involve the measurement of achievement in both internal and external targets, notably through **benchmarking**.
Long-term change	As TQM becomes embedded, and very much a fact of life, in the ways in which employees think and processes are carried out, there is a permanent change to the way in which attitudes, working practices and overall behaviour are approached.

2 Extroversion – whether the individual is sociable, retiring, sober, fun-loving, affectionate or reserved.

3 Openness – whether individuals are practical, imaginative, prefer routine or variety, and whether they conform or are independent-thinking.

4 Agreeableness – whether the individual is ruthless or caring, trusting or suspicious, helpful or uncooperative.

5 Conscientiousness – whether the individual is organized or disorganized, careful or careless, impulsive or disciplined.

By considering these five factors it is also possible to ascertain whether a particular individual is more inclined towards collectivism (sharing the values of the group and subordinating his or her own personal goals) or individualism (in which personal goals are placed above the group goals).

Trait theory is not universally accepted as a means by which to understand personality, and many critics believe that trait theory does not actually predict real behaviour. When coupled with situationism, meaning that personality can change according to the situation, however, there is a much clearer and more applicable set of measures.

Coupling trait and situational variables can assist in understanding personality. It also assists in predicting behaviour. It is certainly clear that traits are sometimes more influential than situations, but in many cases, when the situation and the trait are taken together, it is possible to be much more accurate in predicting exactly how someone will behave in a particular situation.

Transfer pricing

Transfer pricing is a form of internal pricing policy which requires particular parts of a business, or groups of businesses, to ensure that they still meet their profit targets, even when supplying products and services to another business, or division, under common ownership.

Feinschreiber, Robert, *Transfer Pricing Handbook: Transfer Pricing International: A Country-by-Country Guide*. New York: John Wiley, 2002.

T

Uu

Unity of command

Unity of command was originally suggested by **Henri Fayol** as one of his primary principles of management. Fayol suggested that employees should only receive instructions from a single superior. If this principle was undermined then it would bring about violations in authority, and discipline would be jeopardized. Ultimately, Fayol argued, the stability and order of the organization would be threatened.

Many subsequent theorists have disagreed with Fayol; and given the fact that he was writing in the late 1940s, he could not have anticipated the changes in **organizational structure** and in the way in which work is carried out. None the less, he proposed that any form of dual command would lead to uncertainty and hesitation, and ultimately to conflict between managers.

Fayol, Henri, *General and Industrial Management*. London: Pitman, 1967.

Vaill, Peter

Peter Vaill is a management consultant and author who is primarily concerned with **organizational development** and approaches to learning. He contends that, in business, managers and leaders continually struggle to stay up-to-date with new information and skills. Traditional ways of passing this information on to them no longer work. He suggests his own guides to management learning and development, primarily through self-direction, creativity, ownership and continuous learning. In his book *Spirited Leading and Learning*, Vaill addresses what he considers to be the three critical process issues which face businesses, namely:

- the development of effective leadership;
- continuous learning for leaders and their businesses;
- bringing spirit back into work.

Vaill, Peter B, *Managing as a Performing Art: New Ideas for a World of Chaotic Change*. New York: Jossey-Bass Wiley, 1991.

Vaill, Peter B., *Learning as a Way of Being: Keeping Afloat in Permanent White Water*. New York: Jossey-Bass Wiley, 1996.

Vaill, Peter B., *Spirited Leading and Learning: Process Wisdom for a New Age*. New York: Jossey-Bass Wiley, 1998.

www.ccl.org/connected/enews/articles/0803vaill.htm

Value chain

The term 'value chain' was coined by Michael Porter in 1985 to describe the activities of an organization and how they are linked to the maintenance of a competitive position within the market. 'Value chain' can be used to describe activities both within and external to the organization, relating them to its competitive strength. The analysis itself values each activity which adds to the organization's products or services. In other words, it considers the organization's employees, and available funds, as well as machinery and equipment. The supposition is that the ways in which these resources are deployed determine whether the organization is able to produce products and services at a price which customers are prepared to pay. By successfully organizing the resources, the business may be able to achieve a degree of competitive advantage.

As can be seen in Figure 68, Porter identified five main areas, or primary areas, related to the delivery of a product or a service. These were inbound logistics, outbound logistics, operations, marketing and sales, and service.

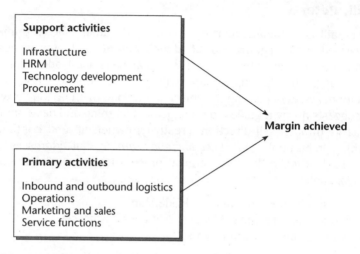

Figure 68   Five areas of the value chain

These activities are supported by procurement, technological development, human resource management and the overall infrastructure of the organization. In his diagram Porter also incorporates a margin, which refers to the profit margin between the costs of the primary and support activities and the price which the customer is willing to pay.

In the majority of industrial sectors, however, the organization's value chain is simply part of a larger structure, which incorporates the supplier's value chain, the distribution channel's value chain and the customers' value chains. The position of the organization can be seen in Figure 69.

This more holistic impression of the overall system suggests that the progress of raw materials, components and products across the entire value chain requires consideration of the other elements' requirements in terms of a profit margin. In other words, depending upon the relative strength of these elements within the value chain, margins can be squeezed or enlarged. Internally, at least, an organization can seek to

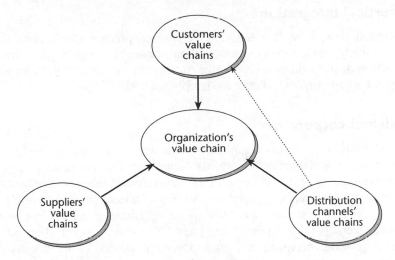

Figure 69 Position of the organization's value chain

improve its margins by adopting tactics such as **just-in-time (JIT)**, whilst not passing any of the associated cost savings on up the value chain, but retaining them as an additional profit margin.

Porter, Michael E., *Competitive Advantage*. London, Free Press, 1985.

Velocity

Velocity has three associated sub-definitions, all of which are related to the movement of currency in the economy:

- *Velocity of circulation* – broadly the number of times a unit of currency is used over a specific period of time. This is calculated by dividing the total amount of money spent, by the amount of money which is in circulation in the economy.
- *Income velocity (of circulation)* – which refers to the number of times a unit of currency is part of an individual's income over a specified period of time. This is calculated by working out the ratio of the gross national product compared with the amount of money which is in circulation in the economy.
- *Transactions velocity (of circulation)* – which refers to the number of times that a unit of currency is used in transactions over a specified period of time. This is calculated by working out the ratio between the money spent (on products and services) and the amount of money which is in circulation in the economy.

Vertical integration

Vertical integration is a business acquisition process which aims to secure adjacent levels of the supply chain. Typically, a manufacturer will seek to acquire either a supplier or a distributor or retailer in order to gain a more firm control over the supply network.

Virtual corporation

In literal terms, a virtual organization does not exist. However, the term is used to describe a flexible organization which does not have a physical presence or central organizational structure and relies on a network of remote employees engaged in a variety of telecommuting and telework activities. It may also refer to an organization which employs outworkers, paid on a piece-rate system. The virtual organization acts as a provider of work, and as a fulfilment service or intermediary between the outworkers and the customer.

Vision

See **mission statement.**

Vroom, Victor

Victor Vroom, together with Edward Lawler and Lyman Porter, put forward his theory to suggest that the relationship between people's behaviour at work and their goals was not as simple as was first imagined. Vroom realized that an employee's performance is based on personality, skills, knowledge, experience and abilities. This being the case, it was apparent that some employees would be more suited to their job role than others and that some would understand instruction more readily than others. The theory proposed that:

- Each individual has a different set of goals.
- People will only try to achieve their goals if they think they have a chance to attain them.
- The value of the goal, in personal terms, affects motivation and behaviour.

Vroom's expectancy theory is one of the most popular motivation theories. It basically depends upon the following three factors:

- *Valence* – this is the depth of the want that the employee feels for either extrinsic rewards (money, promotion, time off, benefits) or intrinsic rewards (satisfaction). Management needs to discover what the employees want by offering a variety of rewards, so they can select something they would value.

- *Expectancy* – everyone has different expectations and different levels of confidence about what they are capable of doing. Even employees who have fulfilled their valence wants, when asked to do something that they feel unable to do, will not be sufficiently motivated to attempt it. Even though there may be a promise of an additional desired reward, an employee who is not motivated, will not fulfil. Management would need to discover the employee's resource, training or additional supervision needs in order to improve his or her opportunity to succeed, and remove the chances of failure.

- *Instrumentality* – this is all centred around the employees' expectations about whether they will get what they want, even if it has been promised them by their employer. Managers should ensure that promises of rewards are fulfilled, and ensure the employees are aware of what relevant rewards are linked to improved performance.

Using Vroom's theory, a business could identify the characteristics of the job that would allow the employee some of the following to encourage motivation:

- self-development opportunities;
- satisfaction opportunities;
- recognition opportunities;
- a degree of independence in deciding how tasks should be handled;
- a varied range of tasks;
- a variety of surroundings;
- opportunity for interaction with others;
- challenging and varied but clearly stated goals, with an indication as to the expected performance.

Vroom, Victor H., *Work and Motivation*. New York: Jossey-Bass Wiley, 1994.

www.mba.yale.edu/framesets/faculty.asp?/faculty/professors/vroom.htm

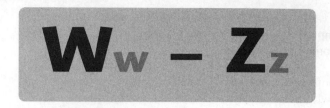

Ww – Zz

Walking the floor

See **management by walking about.**

Waterman, Robert

Robert H. Waterman, Jnr was the co-writer with **Tom Peters** of the seminal text *In Search of Excellence*. It was published in 1982. Peters and Waterman were, at that time, consultants and they examined 43 of the 500 top performing businesses in the US. In Search of Excellence had eight key themes:

- a bias for action – an active approach to decision making.
- being close to the customer – the business should learn from the people it serves;
- autonomy and entrepreneurship – the encouragement of innovation and the development of those with creative ideas;
- productivity through people – recognizing that all managers and employees, regardless of rank, are quality assets.
- hands on, value-driven – management should show its commitment and make a positive contribution.
- stick to the nitty gritty – concentrate on **core competences** and on markets in which the business is successful;
- simple form, lean staff – organizations should not be overly bureaucratic and should strip out managerial levels which do not add value.
- simultaneous loose–tight properties – teams should be given autonomy, but they should be controlled via centralized value systems.

Peters, Tom and Waterman, Robert H., *In Search of Excellence: Lessons from America's Best-run Companies.* London: Profile Books, 2004.

Weber, Max

Max Weber (1864–1920) based his ideas about bureaucracy on his studies of such disparate organizations as the Catholic Church, the

Prussian army and the empire of the Egyptians. He concluded that employees frequently suffer from inequity in most areas of work, from selection to promotion. His key points are summarized in Table 51.

Table 51   Max Weber's views of bureaucracy

Principle of bureaucracy	Description
Division of labour	The workforce is split into specialized areas according to expertise.
Chain of command	There is a pyramid-shaped organizational structure, which defines the hierarchy and the authority of the organization.
Rules and regulations	There are formalized rules governing the running of the organization, which assists the organization in dealing with the potential disruption caused by changes in management.
Impersonality	Management is detached from the workforce to ensure that sentimentality or familiarity do not impede decision making.
Selection and promotion	Selection of employees and their subsequent opportunities for advancement in the organization are strictly governed by their utility as far as the organization is concerned. Friendship plays no part in the advancement, which is usually based on seniority and express achievements.
Documentation	There is a meticulous system of document creation, completion and storage, to chart all activities for the purposes of monitoring and the evaluation of those activities.
Centralization	All decisions are made from the upper strata of the organization, where individuals reside who have seniority and clearly recognizable achievements over a period of time.

Verstehen: Max Weber's HomePage
www.faculty.rsu.edu/~felwell/Theorists/Weber/Whome.htm

Weick, Karl

Karl Weick is concerned with process and information-system theory in the organizational context. He believes that all parts of an organization are equally important and mutually dependent. Weick suggests that the organization is as complex as the information which passes through it. His primary concepts are:

- *Enactment* – how an organization adapts or adjusts itself to the environment. He uses the term 'sense making' to describe managers and employees seeking to discover the limitations of their abilities to deal with situations.
- *Organizational learning* – he believes that organizations do not necessarily learn; they seek to find ways of dealing with different situations, using tried and established methods. The learning process involves interacting with different stimuli.
- *Information processing* – organizations take information from their environment and try to make sense of it. Internal and external communication is the key to 'sense making'.

The organizations will attempt to understand complex information, dealing with it in three stages:

- *enactment* – defining and trying to manage the information.
- *selection* – narrowing it down and deciding what is important and how to action it.
- *retention* – deciding what part of the information needs to be retained for later use.

Weick, Karl E., *Sensemaking in Organizations: Foundations for Organizational Science*. New York: Sage Publications, 1995.
Weick, Karl E., *Making Sense of the Organization*. London: Blackwell Publishers, 2000.

www.pfdf.org/leaderbooks/weick

Wheatley, Margaret

Margaret Wheatley has been a consultant for some 30 years. In 1996 she was the co-author of *A Simpler Way*, which, unlike many other management improvement books, approaches self-organization through a mixture of photographs, poetry and prose. She presented a very different way of organizing, leading and working together.

Wheatley, Margaret and Kellner-Rogers, Myron, *A Simpler Way*. San Francisco, Ca: Berrett-Koehler Publishers, 1999.

www.margaretwheatley.com

Wholly owned subsidiary

A wholly owned subsidiary is a business which is entirely owned, usually by a holding company, or alternatively by another business that owns the majority or all of its stock or share capital. Wholly owned subsidiaries are common in business, particularly when bought by an organization that wishes to expand its overall influence and control in a given market, yet retain the acquired business as a separate legal identity. This may also be for practical and commercial reasons, such as the need to retain brand names and trademarks under their existing names. Wholly owned subsidiaries are also commonly owned by multinational businesses, who seek to acquire foreign businesses and bring them into common ownership under a holding company, in order to facilitate the parent company's entry and operations in an overseas market.

Wildcat

See **problem child.**

Working capital

Working capital is the amount of capital which is employed by a business in its day-to-day trading operations. It is calculated by subtracting the business's current liabilities, such as trade creditors, from its current assets, which would include stock, debtors and cash. Ideally the working capital should be sufficient for the business to be able to pay its immediate debts, otherwise it will struggle to continue its operations, which might indicate that the business needs to reappraise the relationship between its assets and its liabilities.

The working capital turnover ratio is normally calculated as:

Current assets – current liabilities

The turnover, however, compares sales with average working capital and is expressed in the following manner:

$$\frac{Sales}{Average\ working\ capital}$$

Therefore, a business which has current assets to the value of £7m and current liabilities of some £3m could incorporate both working capital calculations in the following manner:

- The working capital would first be worked out by subtracting the current liabilities from the current assets, which gives a total of £4m.

- The sales figure of, say, £30m would then be divided by the balance which represents the working capital, i.e. £4m.
- This is expressed as the number of times the working capital has been turned over; in this instance, 7.5 times.

The lower the turnover, the higher the indication that funds are being inefficiently used. If there is a high turnover, the assumption is that cash difficulties may arise if sales decline.

Rao, P. M. and Pramanik, A. K., *Working Capital Management*. New Delhi: Deep and Deep Publications, 2002.

Numbers

4Cs

See **competitive intelligence.**

4Ps

See **marketing mix.**

5 Forces

See **Five Forces model, PEST analysis** *and* **Porter, Michael.**

5Ss/5Cs

'5Ss' is shorthand for five Japanese words which describe the workplace and individual cleanliness. These are:

- *Seiri* – straighten up your workplace or desk.
- *Seiton* – sort out your equipment.
- *Seiso* – sweep and clean your workplace.
- *Seiketsu* – spotlessly maintain your appearance and character.
- *Shitsuke* – self-discipline to follow rules, procedures, and standards.

The 5Ss are also related to lean manufacturing and workplace organization. The prime benefits of each of the 5Ss are:

- that it can be done;
- that everyone is able to participate;
- that waste is made visible;
- that it has a wide area of impact, in as much as it improves set-up times, quality, safety, morale and productivity.

Applying the 5Ss to lean manufacturing requires an ordered logic and the 5S words represent the 5 steps, as can be seen in Table 52.

There are several interpretations of the 5Cs. Broadly, they refer to service delivery and may be typified as being:

Table 52 Steps in the application of the 5Ss

Step	S	Action
1	Sort	Remove unnecessary machinery, components and other clutter from the workplace.
2	Straighten	Ensure all items required are at their point of use.
3	Sweep	Clean, and eliminate anything which could affect work.
4	Standardize	Establish routines and standards.
5	Self-discipline	Sustain the 5Ss by making them second nature.

- consistency;
- continuity;
- consultation;
- contingency;
- clarity.

There are also 5Cs associated with credit, being:

- character (integrity);
- capacity (sufficient cash flow to cover interest payments);
- capital (net worth);
- collateral (sufficient assets to secure the debt);
- conditions (generally of the borrower and the prevailing state of the economy).

5WH problem solving

The 5WH approach asks five questions in regard to the five elements of any problem (see Figure 70).

The 5WH problem-solving technique begins with establishing the objective, and asks the fundamental question as to why there is a specific problem which needs to be remedied. This done, the five key elements of the problem-solving technique address the following:

- What? (object) – which defines the parameters of the problem.
- Who? (subject) – which further defines the parameters of the problem and establishes who will have responsibility.

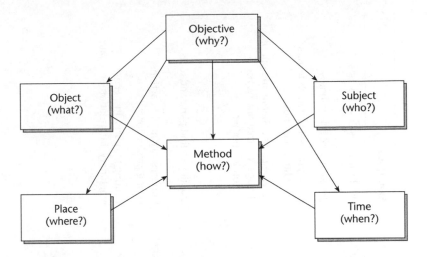

Figure 70   The 5WH questions

- When? (time) – asking if there are any time-related issues relevant to the problem-solving issue and how the progress of the problem-solving exercise will be monitored.
- Where? (place) – establishing precisely where the problem lies within the business.
- How? (method) – explaining the methodologies which will be employed to address the 5WHs.

Hicks, Michael J., *Problem Solving in Business and Management: Hard, Soft and Creative.* London: Thomson Learning, 2004.

7S Framework

See **Seven S Framework.**

7 Wastes

Taiichi Ohno made the original definitions of the seven types of waste, which describe any activities that add to costs, but do not add value. In effect, these are seven types of *muda* and are the targets of the pursuit of waste elimination. The seven wastes, or *muda*, are described more clearly in Table 53.

Table 53 The 7 Wastes

7 Wastes or *muda*	Definition	Causes	Examples
Over-production	Producing more than the immediate demand	Inaccurate forecasting	Producing to sales forecasts
		Long set-up times	Avoidance of set-up times
			Batch processing, which results in additional output
Transportation	Moving products or components when that movement does not add value	Batch production	Moving parts either in and out of storage, or from one work station to another
		Poor storage	
		Functional layouts	
Motion	Movement of employees that does not add value	Disorganized workplace	Inability to find parts and tools
		Poor work station design	Unnecessary motion actions during production
Waiting	Creating idle time due to materials, information, people or equipment not being ready	Lack of priorities and communication	Waiting for parts, inspection, machinery, information or repairs
		Work imbalance	
		Centralized inspection	
		Order delays	

Table 53 The 7 Wastes (*continued*)

7 Wastes or *muda*	Definition	Causes	Examples
Processing	Adding processes to the production which do not add value for the customer	Delays between processing stages Lack of customer understanding	Poor design and paperwork
Inventory	Holding more materials, components or products than are immediately required	Supplier lead times Long set-up times or lead times Paperwork Poor ordering procedures	Raw materials, work in progress, finished goods and consumable supplies
Defects	Allowing work with errors or mistakes to slip through the process	Process failures Batch processing Poor machinery Under-trained staff	Scrap, reworking, defects, corrections and missing parts

Index

Note: page numbers in **bold type** indicate definitions. Most references are to the UK, unless otherwise indicated